RECONCEPTUALISING THE HUMAN: EXPLORING CRITICAL POSTHUMANISM IN SELECT NOVELS OF A. E. VAN VOGT, DON DELILLO AND OLAF STAPLEDON

RECONCEPTUALISING THE HUMAN: EXPLORING CRITICAL POSTHUMANISM IN SELECT NOVELS OF A. E. VAN VOGT, DON DELILLO AND OLAF STAPLEDON

Aishwarya Mishra
Gurudev Meher

BLACK EAGLE BOOKS
Dublin, USA | Bhubaneswar, India

Black Eagle Books
USA address:
7464 Wisdom Lane
Dublin, OH 43016

India address:
E/312, Trident Galaxy, Kalinga Nagar,
Bhubaneswar-751003, Odisha, India

E-mail: info@blackeaglebooks.org
Website: www.blackeaglebooks.org

First International Edition Published by
Black Eagle Books, 2025

RECONCEPTUALISING THE HUMAN: EXPLORING CRITICAL POSTHUMANISM IN SELECT NOVELS OF A. E. VAN VOGT, DON DELILLO AND OLAF STAPLEDON
by **Aishwarya Mishra | Gurudev Meher**

Copyright © Aishwarya Mishra | Gurudev Meher

All rights reserved. No part of this publication may be reproduced, stored in a retrieval system, or transmitted, in any form or by any means, electronic, mechanical, photocopying, recording or otherwise without the prior permission of the publisher.

Cover & Interior Design: Ezy's Publication

ISBN- 978-1-64560-742-7 (Paperback)

Printed in the United States of America

CONTENTS

Preface		07
I.	Introduction	11
II.	Relocating the Contemporary Human: A Paradigm Shift from Humanism to Critical Posthumanism	26
III.	Enhancing the Human: Vulnerable Bodies and Posthuman Vision in A. E. Van Vogt's novels	64
IV.	Intertwining Human Subjectivities: Hybridising the Idea of Man in the novels of Don Delillo	177
V.	Apocalypse of the Human: Human Mutation and the Practice of Critical Posthumanism in the novels of Olaf Stapledon	227
VI.	Conclusion	305
	Bibliography	317

Preface

In an age where humanity grapples with its own evolution—biological, technological, and philosophical—the concept of Critical Posthumanism emerges as a powerful lens through which to reconsider our identity. This book titled, *Reconceptualising the Human: Exploring Critical Posthumanism in Select Novels of A. E. Van Vogt, Don Delillo and Olaf Stapledon*, explores the shifting definitions of what it means to be human, tracing the arc of posthuman thought and its implications for literature, philosophy, and the future of existence.

Since the Renaissance's clarion call, our poetry and prose have exalted humanity's sovereign mind—rational, autonomous, invincible. Yet as the postmodern dawn cracks open, machine and flesh fuse, and Critical Posthumanism erupts like a thunderbolt. Thinkers such as N. Katherine Hayles and Neil Badmington seize on the fantasy of downloading human consciousness into cold circuitry, branding it an overcharged Humanism that clones the old dualist myth of the solitary, sovereign man. Badmington hammers out a framework of Critical Posthumanism designed to punish that very Humanism from within, ripping open its seams by exposing the fractured psyche of man himself.

Once the fixed nucleus of cosmos and culture, man now drifts stunned beneath the neon glare of digital gods. We are no longer islands but nodes converging with ecosystems, biomes, alien forms—in short, with anything not strictly human. For centuries, Western liberal Humanism—celebrating agency, self-reliance, independence—ruled unchallenged. It claimed compassion, tolerance, justice as our birthright—and reserved all others to the margins of reason. But Freud's psychoanalysis, Derrida's Poststructuralism and Foucault's Postmodernist electric scalpel have repeatedly carved at its edges.

Humanism's proud edifice—rooted in individual liberty and the triumphant realization of talent—now trembles under the Critical Posthumanist onslaught. Its anthropocentrism is revealed as a brittle veneer. Across novels by A.E. van Vogt, Don DeLillo and Olaf Stapledon, we see man conceived as an autonomous titan, only to be mauled by the very nonhuman forces he believed he could master. Man's face, once sketched among the stars, now blurs into circuits, genes and algorithms.

At the heart of Critical Posthumanist speculation lies a radical claim: there is no universal, spiritualized 'human essence.' We are organic beings, forged by and submerged in physical processes we once sought to dominate. Technology is not our prosthesis but our bloodstream. Donna Haraway's 1985 "A Cyborg Manifesto" detonates the final taboos by proclaiming the cyborg our emblematic creature—hybrid of flesh, machine and animal, unshackled from traditional ontological boundaries. In her vision, humanity becomes an open system, co-evolving with technologies, sharing an ecosphere with every other life form. We are 'Humanimals,' merged organisms whose bodies and identities are intertwined with software, biotech and genetic code.

In 21st-century fiction, digitalization and globalization shatter the once-united front of Humanism. Haraway's cyborg resonates across narratives that question human ontology under biopolitics, genetic engineering and machine learning. Here, the line between fact and fiction collapses; the proud pillars of instrumentalism, exceptionalism and exclusivism topple. We see instead a human as a porous, hybrid node—constantly fusing, merging, metamorphosing with nonhuman others: cyborgs, interstellar travelers, superhuman intelligences.

Critical Posthumanism does not merely dethrone man from his anthropocentric throne; it redefines him. By deconstructing the self and rewriting the definition of 'human,' it forces us to stare into the abyss of our own becoming—no longer isolated sovereigns, but ever-evolving composites of flesh, metal and code, marching toward futures we can scarcely imagine.

This journey into Critical Posthumanism is not merely an academic pursuit—it is a meditation on the transformation of human existence in an increasingly interconnected, technologically saturated world. By engaging with the thinkers and narratives that shape this discourse, we step into the unknown, where humanity dissolves and reforms in ways we are only beginning to comprehend.

Dr. Gurudev Meher
Associate Professor
Department of English
Ravenshaw University, Cuttack

CHAPTER I

Introduction

The desire to rise above the self has continuously been declared in countless philosophies. It is a notable feature of the ontology of man. In the contemporary period, one witnesses a mixing of the frontiers of humans with other species. This has mainly happened because of our worldwide affiance to technology which has led our way to an age of mechanics. In this age, the subjective identity of man is codified to an extent accrediting alteration and hybrid metamorphosis. Nonetheless, the quasi-human features and substitutes of bionic and machinic types have emerged in the skyline. This in turn leads to a series of humanoids with blurred demarcation.

Following this, one can experience a current irregularity in the instance of concern regarding such likelihood. This in turn is more approaching and genuine to highly technologically flourishing civilization and more distant from underdeveloped societies. Following the enlightenment period, the techno-positivistic attitude has found its place in the integration or replacement of a human with a suprahuman or machine.

The notion of Critical Posthuman rejoices in extensive popularity in the age of Anthropocene. In this age, the ecosystem is dominated by the activities of man. The choice of transforming into a posthuman is due to the mechanical progress that is directly linked to globalization. The world is now experiencing an eruption of expertise in nonhuman and posthuman concerns. The Critical Posthuman compels us to think about the position of man and reevaluate it focusing on ethics and subjectivity. These issues, "also impact on the aims and structures of critical thought and ultimately come to bear on the institutional status of the academic field of the humanities in the contemporary neoliberal university" (Collini 49).

In terms of philosophy, the posthuman is prompted by a combination of anti-humanism and anti-anthropocentrism. Anti-humanism centres on the appraisal of the humanist notion as the universal prototype of man whereas Anti-anthropocentrism reprimands hierarchism and progress in environmental justice.

The Critical Posthuman conveys a critical agreement that focuses no more on "originary humanicity" (Kirby 233). The term Critical Posthumanism points at the advent of a new form of thought, "that is not merely a culmination of the two main strands of thought, posthumanism and post-anthropocentrism, but rather a qualitative leap in a new and more complex direction" (Wolfe 24).

This transference in outlook moves in the direction of Poststructuralism or alternately defined as a deconstruction of man by the Poststructuralist, Michel Foucault in the year 1970. Man is placed at the core of the universe due to his reason and rationality. This faculty of reasoning is envisioned as the generator of a scientific world.

N. Katherine Hayles and Neil Badmington have denounced the "apparently posthumanist aim" of transferring awareness into computers. They argue that "it is symptomatic of a kind of hyper-humanism which replicates the dualist fiction of an immaterial and autonomous human subject described in Descartes' metaphysics" (qtd. in Roden 18).

Neil Badmington suggests that Critical Posthumanism serves as a philosophical remedy to humanism. It strives to discern and deconstruct man from the inside, discovering his internal conflicts and inconsistencies.

The term, humanism, has varied meanings. It talks of those who uphold the nobility of humans in accord with their morality. The French philosopher, Jean-Paul Sartre, in his text, *Existentialism is a Humanism*, states that "existence precedes essence" (Sartre 2–3). This implies that "humans are radically free and self-defining agents whose existence is prior to any concept of what they ought to be" (Sartre 2–3).

This statement is an atheistic remark. He conceives the world as Godless which tends to mean that whatever humans become is due to their actions.

The Renaissance philosopher, Pico della Mirandola, in his book *Oration on the Dignity of Man*, thus presents the self-modelling of man:

> I have placed you at the very centre of the world, so that from that vantage point you may with greater ease glance round about you on all that the world contains. We have made you a creature neither of heaven nor of earth, neither mortal nor immortal, in order that you may, as the free and proud shaper of your own being, fashion yourself in the form you may prefer. (5)

Aristotle in his text, *Nicomachean Ethics*, asserts that human beings possess the faculty of reasoning which cannot be found in any other being. This hints at the fact that rationality permits humans to subdue emotions and develop creative temperaments such as courage and friendship. Humans can only gain access to the metaphysics. He also talks about the nonhuman animals who seek pleasure but showcase no moral values.

Immanuel Kant, in his *Transcendental Humanism* asserts that humans create the world by establishing virtue and meaning in it. Kant thus contends:

> … nothing in nature is intrinsically good. Only beings that are rational and capable autonomous agency can be regarded as ends-in-themselves. Lacking reason, animals can only be means to human ends. The beings whose existence rests not on our will but on nature nevertheless have, if they are beings without reason, only a relative worth as means, and are called things; rational beings, by contrast, are called persons, because their nature already marks them out as ends in themselves, i.e., as something that may not be used merely as means, hence to that extent limits all arbitrary choice (and is an object of respect). (46)

The Critical Posthumanists maintain that Western humanism is founded on a two-fold notion of an analytical, independent subject whose temperament is translucent and the critic, Veronika Hollinger asserts that it is "unmarked by its interactions with the object-world" (273).

Critical Posthuman theorists such as N. Katherine Hayles and Neil Badmington apply the theory of Critical Posthumanism to the latter modernity that contributes to the erosion of the self-validation and self-affirmation subject of man, starting from Rene Descartes to his successors. This erosion is technoscientific in nature. The dualisms maintained by Descartes' between outer mind and inner mind following its mechanism is quite difficult to discern as the computational rebellion reveals that rationality can be executed by the mechanical procedures. This point of view is illustrated by Donna Haraway in her essay, "A Cyborg Manifesto":

> Late twentieth-century machines have made thoroughly ambiguous the difference between natural and artificial, mind and body, self-developing and externally designed, and many other distinctions that used to apply to organisms and machines. Our machines are disturbingly lively, and we ourselves frighteningly inert. (152)

Critical Posthumanism is a reciprocation to the replacement of the dualism of human and nonhuman. It is a composite presupposition of the subject of man which is assumed as sovereign and self-sufficient, "with a view to the deconstruction of anthropocentric thought" (Badmington, *Theorizing Posthumanism* 15).

This sort of deconstruction is composed of substantiation of multitudinous methods in which the novels represent the transcendence of man or distinctness from a machine cut out to encase man from the inhuman or nonhuman other. For Katherine Hayles, the concept of Critical Posthumanism delineates uploaded or transmitted immortality into bodies and the extension of consciousness through cybernetics.

Hayles believes that these phenomena are similar to a space saga and minds can go beyond their bodies by choosing soul engines:

> I was reading Hans Moravec's *Mind Children: The Future of Robot and Human Intelligence*,

enjoying the ingenious variety of his robots, when I happened upon the passage where he argues it will soon be possible to download human consciousness into a computer. To illustrate, he invents a fantasy scenario in which a robot surgeon purees the human brain in a kind of cranial liposuction, reading the information in each molecular layer as it is stripped away and transferring the information into a computer. At the end of the operation, the cranial cavity is empty, and the patient, now inhabiting the metallic body of the computer, wakens to find his consciousness exactly the same as it was before. How, I asked myself, was it possible for someone of Moravec's obvious intelligence to believe that mind could be separated from body? Even assuming such a separation was possible, how could anyone think that consciousness in an entirely different medium would remain unchanged, as if it had no connection with embodiment? Shocked into awareness, I began to notice he was far from alone. (*How We Became Posthuman* 2)

Furthermore, the President of the International Academy of Practical Theology, Elaine Graham, presupposes that "a posthuman successor species should be conceived as the apotheosis of the rational self, free to subjugate a bodily nature conceived as abject and threatening" (Graham 9). The analysis of Badmington, Graham and Hayles asserts that the progression of nonhuman and ethical hankerings can be employed to go beyond the concept of being mortal.

The remarks about deconstruction are implicit in the Critical Posthumanist subject. Hayles declares that "deconstruction is the child of the information age, crediting Derrida with the insight that speech is a cyborg act, never simply present or absent but dependent on operations and contexts that exceed the consciousness or understanding of the speaking subject" (*How We Became Posthuman* 44). Hayles uses the concept of deconstruction to appertain to the philosophical questions regarding textuality and language that Jaques Derrida mentions in his works.

For many centuries, in Western culture, liberal humanism has been popularly contemplated as the determining criteria for man's survival. It embraces a humanist concern distinctive of agency, independence and perspicacity that the nonhumans do not own. This point of view has been freshly challenged. Starting from the psychoanalytical theory of Sigmund Freud, the Poststructuralism by Jaques Derrida and the Postmodernism of Michel Foucault, the frontiers of Critical Posthumanism have been incessantly attacked.

Not long ago, the arrival of the theory of Critical Posthumanism witnessed the expansion of technology and the capacity of neo-liberal and cyber capitalism. These trends have their impact on the relationship of human and nonhuman which later serves as a ground for the comprehension of the 'new human'. Regardless of the dissimilarities relating to the future of mankind, a Critical Posthumanist turn has announced the termination of any existing policies of liberal humanism. It can be witnessed both in culture and literature.

The aim of this book is to acknowledge the aforementioned point of view. Inspecting the contemporary literature, specifically that are produced during the last years of the 20th century and the initial years of the 21st century, this book aims to contend that as the universe is turning towards Posthumanism, humans mingle with nonhumans, giving way to the deconstruction of humanism. This deconstruction occurs due to the blending of humans and nonhumans dripped with the aspects of automation, mass media and brainy machines.

In due course, several analyses of critics have been made on select novels of A.E. Van Vogt, Don Delillo and Olaf Stapledon. Some of them are as follows, In the novel *White Noise*, Donneva Crowell investigates the rhetoric of culture that has a crucial part in the lives of the Americans. This rhetoric imparts an idea of security to the Americans. The feeling of pessimism attached to the idea of ensnaring created by the rhetoric of culture appears to have matured. Delillo accepts that the terror of death is the core of human inspiration and reveals it as, "the highest, most intelligent form of life on earth, the very existence is tinged with irony"(45).

Another Critic, Ross Maffey inspects the altering depiction of technology in both the novels, *White Noise* and *Zero K*. He tracks down the theoretical and philosophical maturing in the novels focusing on the dual themes of mortality and disaster. Both novels express a sense of longing for disaster to be away from the genuine world. In addition, the novel *Zero K* portrays the dullness of life in a sphere that is dominated by technology. It also "offers a refuge from the impending disaster that lies waiting within technology as the creators no longer have control over their creation" ("Changing Channels" 23).

Jay Shelat attends to technology and art singularly, brought out by the present-day caricature of the villain capitalist. This role is played by Ross Lockart in the novel who acts as a straddle between technology and art. The novel depicts the significance of art and its purpose as complementary what one receives for surviving in a chaotic world ("Convergence" 66). Jeffrey Lockhart tussles to comprehend the inspiration behind Artis and Ross' decision to go through the cryonic process of freezing and he chooses art or language particularly to decipher the numerous circumstances he is in and to achieve transcendence.

Brian Chappell puts forward a procedure for reworking the novel *Point Omega*. He analyses the novel as a metafictional gesture in the direction of making the fiction indispensable to the novel. This has been made possible by going through the novel's tripartite formation. He states that "the main narrative of the novel consists of his first-person account of a traumatic experience in the desert of California with Iraq War propagandist Richard Elster. The novel talks in an omniscient third-person mode, of an unnamed man viewing Douglas Gordon's film 24-Hour Psycho at the Museum of Modern Art" ("Death and Metafiction" 45).

The characters in the novel become acquainted with trauma by choosing fiction besides deserting fiction. This confirms Delillo's belief in fiction to deal with the ill effects of the 21st century.

Alan Marshall points out the postmodern concept of sublime abandoning transcendence and approving of immanence. She refers to the proponents of the sublime such as Immanuel Kant, Zizek, Lyotard and Jameson, "in an attempt to shed light on the modality of the merging of the sublime and the ridiculous. This concept of the sublime reflects the decline of metanarratives and the exhaustion of possible experiences as the hallmarks of the postmodern era" ("From this point on" 134).

The Professor of Library Studies, Jules Sturm stresses on the fact that:

> Fatness begins by turning attention to the multiple cultural instances in which fatness has been intrinsically linked with notions such as self-neglect and poor self-management. In Foucauldian terms, one analyses the fat subject as a failed homo economicus, an individual who has failed to be an entrepreneur of himself, being for himself his own capital, being for himself his own producer, being for himself the source of his earnings. From this perspective, one analyses instances of collective hatred towards fat subjects as direct results of the biopolitical triplet of responsibility, rationality, and morality. Morality is the bridge into the field of posthumanism, in which, as one demonstrates, these biopolitical imperatives also apply, reinforced by the field's fascination with prosthetics and enhancement. Where, by biopolitical standards, fat subjects have failed to manage themselves, posthuman subjects find themselves guilty of not responsibly, rationally, and morally manipulating themselves to optimal productivity. Using criticism that disability studies scholars like Sarah S. Jain and Vivian Sobchack have voiced about posthumanism, one can demonstrate the ways in which, within posthumanism, all subjects can be found as lacking when compared to their potential, enhanced posthuman version. (72)

Farid Parvaneh confers a Baudrillardian approach towards Don Delillo's *Point Omega* in the milieu of his definition of the present world being regarded as 'hyperreal' including his two ideas of 'ecstasy and inertia'. According to Baudrillard, the contemporary time is hyperreal. During this instant,

> ... the subjects do not have access to 'real' primarily because they are supplied with the 'simulations' first and then with the 'real' entity and probably never confronted with the 'real' itself through media, advertisements, and virtual world. Thus, the perception they have of incidents, objects, places and even other people is 'hyperreal'; edited, censored, beautified and exaggerated versions of reality; more real than real. *Point Omega* can be examined as Delillo's 'hyperreal' version of Alfred Hitchcock's Psycho since the movie is screened in the course of the novel and despite the similarities between the novel and the movie they end contrastingly. Symbolically 'real' is not found in the novel due to 'Mobius spiralling negativity' which is one of the features of Baudrillard's definition of 'hyperreal' age. Baudrillard believes in the triumph of objects over subjects. While the object's world is perpetually cultivating frenziedly, objects and technologies begin to dominate the stupefied subjects consequently he states when the objects are moving toward their 'ecstasy', the subjects are stricken in 'inertia'. This supremacy of

objects and technologies will be displayed in Point Omega regarding Richard Elster's inert behaviour and reaching the 'omega point' that Teilhard de Chardin envisions for human race is rendered impossible due to Elster's destiny in the framework of Baudrillard's concept of evolution. (67)

In A.E. Van Vogt's *Slan*, Nicholas Osborne Pagan emphasises on human and nonhuman tendencies by creating two orders of aliens, one with tendrils and another without tendrils. The first-order slans have extraordinary telepathic qualities while the second-order slans are limited in their abilities. Further, he compares the two orders of slans with the Jews of the Third Reich (Pagan 51).

The alteration of humanness or the significance of becoming human in a world dominated by the culture of technology can be real. The most celebrated theorist and critic, N. Katherine Hayles believes that humans are already posthuman ahead of the advent of technology. In the present times, when Critical Posthumanism is taken into consideration, Hayles is picked up as an advocate of the theory of Critical Posthumanism. Specifically, post-publication of Hayles' magnum opus *How We Became Posthuman?* in the year 1999 where she states that Critical Posthuman is not the collapse of humanity, as it is claimed by theorists of transhumanism, rather it is the culmination of, "a certain conception of the human" (286).

The genesis of the human that the theory of Critical Posthumanism strives to explode is the singularity of man. Hayles views the theory of Critical Posthumanism as, "emergent rather than given, distributed rather than located solely in consciousness, emerging from and integrated into a chaotic world rather than occupying a position of mastery and control removed from it" (291).

According to Hayles, the Posthuman co-occurs and communicates with others similar to automation or any non-human in a larger network. The self is diffused to a mere narrative and there is a fragmentation of subjectivity. Due to this, the extraordinariness of man or anthropocentrism appears as myth. She adds that the dualistic nature of body and mind allows humans to transcend their body to the arena of virtual reality. This sort of existence imparts immortality to man.

Liberal Humanism has appreciably influenced the contemporary era and is considered to be the source of principles such as individualism and liberty. The principles of liberal humanism are identified by reason, rationality, exceptionalism and free thinking. One of these principles i.e., human exceptionalism is disputed by the theory of Critical Posthumanism.

The intelligence is collectively distributed to varied agents. The automation with which humans communicate is a chunk of their intellect. Hayles puts forth that the "collective heterogeneous quality implies a distributed cognition located in disparate parts that may be in only tenuous communication with one another" (3-4).

Therefore, intelligence and sensibility are not specific to humans but an action that are performed by the human and the nonhuman actors.

This sort of renewed understanding of perception and intellect influences the dialectic of humans as opposed to nonhumans and man's association with the environment. Correspondingly, Hayles suggests that man is no longer the core of the universe. Man has lost dominion over his surroundings. In accord with the view of liberal humanism, self-awareness differentiates man from other beings. But in the case of Critical Posthumanism, self-awareness has been downgraded to an insignificant role in dealing with subjectivity and recognition of man.

As mentioned by Hayles, "The posthuman view considers consciousness, regarded as the seat of human identity, as an epiphenomenon, an evolutionary upstart trying to claim that it is the whole show when in actuality it is only a minor sideshow" (2-3).

Based on the renewed understanding of self-awareness, subjectivity and recognition of man do not possess an intelligible definition. The human is considered a hybrid being not constrained by any biological frontiers. The major differentiation between the idea of liberal humanism and Critical Posthumanism is the biological body and embodiment.

Concerning this, Katherine Hayles states, "In contrast to the body, embodiment is contextual, enmeshed within the specifics of place, time, physiology and culture, which together compose enactment. Embodiment never coincides exactly with 'the body' [...] Embodiment is the specific instantiation generated from the noise of difference" (196).

Critical Posthumanism authorises a vigorous understanding of the strategy in which the world evolves and how humans adapt to the change. Taking into consideration the various innovations in technology namely, virtual reality, Artificial Intelligence, and machine learning among others, humans have arrived at a point where they mingle with the nonhuman other.

This rejects the conventional worldview of the Westerners which talks about God as the sole creator and that humans are endowed with the gift of a soul. The

French philosopher, Rene Descartes' dictum, "I think, therefore I am" (*Discourse on the Method* 73) fits perfectly to the assumption. The interrogation, how is human distinct from other creatures is incessantly asked. The world is under constant change by Artificial Intelligence. Therefore, if a robot or cyborg takes possession of self-awareness and rationality, will it be recognised as a human? If humans have only the soul and the outer body is that of a cyborg, will the being still be called a human? These engrossing questions are frequently interrogated by the Critical Posthuman theorists.

Automation creates new future arenas for humans. My assertion in this book is that the theory of Critical Posthumanism envisages the displacement of humans from the focus of the universe and reclaiming their subjectivity and autonomy. To investigate and contribute to this argument, this book will go through the novels of A.E. Van Vogt, Don Delillo and Olaf Stapledon whose contributions delineate the condition of man in the contemporary period of technology.

A profound analysis of the texts will answer questions such as the way the characters of the texts transform themselves from the principles of liberal humanism to Critical posthumanism, the scheme that talks about the conflict of autonomy and identity during the advancement of technologies. To synchronise with the theoretical framework, it presents a study of the theory of Critical Posthumanism to understand the condition of the Posthuman.

CHAPTER II

Relocating the Contemporary Human: A Paradigm Shift from Humanism to Critical Posthumanism

Taking into account the philosophy of Humanism, one can outline humans as a lifeform who are constantly involved in the process of world-making and the formation of culture. Humanism can be described as an attitude towards life. It is a worldview that elevates the status, power and authority of man. It allocates a special position to human beings who exercise their reason and rationality to view the world from a different perspective. Humanists emphasize cognition, empiricism, autonomy and solicitude. They reject all authoritative and anti-democratic credence. The Virtual Community of Humanists point out:

> Humanism is a philosophy, worldview, or life stance based on naturalism- the conviction that the universe or nature is all that exists or is real [....] Humanists seek to understand the universe by using science

and its methods of critical inquiry - logical reason, empirical evidence and sceptical evaluation of conjectures and conclusions- to obtain reliable knowledge. Humanists affirm that humans have the freedom to give meaning, value, and purpose to their lives through their independent thought, free enquiry and responsible creative activity. Humanists stand for the building of a more humane, just, compassionate and democratic society using pragmatic ethics based on human reason, experience, and reliable knowledge- an ethics that judges the consequences of human actions by the well-being of all life on Earth. (qtd. in Dacey 7)

Humanism begins from the faculty of human experience. Human beings possess the latent powers that enable them to be creative, communicative and speculative. These sensibilities empower them to exercise the extent of freedom of choice and free will. Humans are considered to be loftier due to their intellect, ethics, morals, and position in the world. Self-development and fulfilment are the qualities that make them unique from other creatures.

The 'human nature' in general is first studied by the early Greek thinkers such as Anaximander, Leucippus, Empedocles and Socrates. The first cartographer, Anaximander (611-547 B.C.E.), deduced from some initial observations that the evolution of humans must have begun from an animal. The philosophers Democritus (460-370 B.C.E.) and Leucippus have speculated on the matter that everything in the universe is made up of tiny particles known as 'atoms' that are inseparable and indestructible. These atoms move freely and endlessly to combine to form objects based on natural laws.

The Socratic philosophers have claimed that knowledge of the cosmos can be acquired through keen observation supported by cognition. They have examined what it means to be human. Socrates has studied the human nature in the sphere of ethics. He asserts that Goodness is knowledge, and Ignorance is vice. The supreme virtue can be only acquired through knowledge. One can lead a purposeful life if one rationally evaluates its worth. He puts it as "The unexamined life is not worth living" (qtd in Dacey 12). He also tries to find the premises of morality in rationality rather than any religious underpinnings.

'The Socratic method' or the dialectic is the methodology that Socrates used to explore the truth. It is in the form of a debate or discussion in which a hypothesis is proposed and then it is simultaneously dismembered through multitudes of questions and answers until the truth is disclosed. This technique states that the search for truth or knowledge can only be performed by humans. Humans should let their minds be free so that they can travel wherever the purpose or objective leads. These convictions are conjectured by Greek philosophers like Plato (427-347 B.C.E.) and Aristotle (384-332 B.C.E.). In most of their monumental writings, they have shown the ability of the human mind to gain cognizance and disclosure of truth. Humans can maintain their pre-eminence by wholly developing their scope for reasoning, virtuousness, well-being and citizenship.

Various other ancient philosophies aim to outline the development of humanistic traits. The doctrine of Epicureanism founded and preached by Epicurus (341-270 B.C.E.), has emphasized the idea that happiness is the way to a good life. Epicureanism believes that happiness is analogous to pleasure and savage life- hypersexuality, greed and gluttony.

The Hellenistic Period brought with it a fresh era in Western culture and civilization. The period spans between the demise of the Macedonian ruler, Alexander the Great in 323 B.C.E. and the rise of the first Roman emperor Augustus Caesar in 31 B.C.E. The Romans have reexplored the western civilization and the empire lasted until 500 B.C.E. Besides being erudite designers, counsellors and administrators, the Romans acquired their creative faculty, philosophical geniuses and the concepts of salvation and enlightenment from the Greeks.

The Roman Empire was thrown out by the Visigoths and the Middle Ages started. The Middle Ages lasted for more than a millennium beginning from the Fall of the Western Roman Empire to the fifteenth century. After the Fall of Rome, there was a decline in literature, art and heritage in Europe. The classical and humanist trends were on the edge of disappearing with remains hardly found in any abbey. After the collapse of the Roman Empire, there was none left dominant to hold the shattered pieces of the civilization. The church-state system developed in which the state handled the secular matters while the spiritual matters were controlled by the church authorities. The philosophers tried to acquire the remnants of the classical era and worked to align church preaching with the present-day Aristotelian logic and science. This convention of scholasticism has led to the growth of many institutions that have paved the way for the development of modern varsities.

Then the age of cultural regeneration i.e., the Renaissance began, a period marked by the change in literature, art and renewed fascination towards classical learning that has led to the foundations of present-day science and philosophy. With the repudiation of Aristotelianism and Scholasticism, humanism emerged in its entirety. Initially, the proclivity for humanism can be seen in the curriculum where the humanists are seen to train the scholars with the Greek *paideia* or the *humanities*.

The idea of Humanism originated with the classical philosophers of the East and West. Among the Westerners, one can start with the pre-Socratic philosophy by picking out the Greek Protagoras, whose proclamation "Man is the measure of all things" (qtd. in Burrell 1) is considered the dawn of humanism. Hence, very likely, the scholars assume humanism as a part of Neo-protagoreanism. During the period of Socrates, the Sophists wallowed in casuistry and stimulated scepticism. The Greek philosopher, Socrates attempted to modify this temperament and enhance the wisdom of man's persona with the assertion, 'Know Thyself' (qtd. in Best 1). He emphasised the significance of objective reality that was congenial to the individualistic attitude of Sophists. Along these lines, he planted the seed of wisdom that was directly linked to man.

Socrates' disciple, Plato made a point of reference to rationality in his moral teaching. Even, Aristotle reviewed reason and rationality as placed on the highest pedestal and contributing to the magnificence of man. He prefers to assume man as a simple human and not as any supernatural being. In the early literature of Greece that is contributed by Homer, man is presented as scuffling against the supernatural force known as destiny. Another philosopher named Sophocles glorifies man in his words: "Numberless are the world's wonders, but none
More wonderful than man" (11).

The early Greek thinkers thus opine that,

...to understand his own morphology as well as that of the universe is man's highest function, and leads to the state of well-being which is virtue. This is the apogee of humanism – which, for the Greek, was an attitude and habit of mind rather than a philosophical system or cult. (qtd. in Baker 63)

After the devastation of the Greco-Roman empire, Europe was overshadowed by medievalism. Man is initially regarded as a transgressor and the only way out is to have faith in Jesus to be relieved from the sins. The clergy of the church and the monks of the monastery preached asceticism to common men.

The European Renaissance has laid out the pavement for classical thought in humanism. This started in the backdrop of a political scenario. In 1453 when Constantinople was attacked by Turkey, the scholars who resided in Constantinople had to run away to Italy with their massive literary endeavours. They occupied the city of Florence and displayed their Greek literature and classics to the world. They communicated with the Italian scholars who helped in exhuming the native Latin literature.

The Greek classical literature is imbued with the spirit of humanism. Therefore, political growth is significant in the escalation of attraction towards the Greece and Roman classical literature and the ensuing proliferation of the spirit of humanism.

Exerting themselves from the cocoon of Biblical faith, international scholars globally exhibited an unprejudiced attitude towards 'new' knowledge. Most importantly, the controlling component in ancient culture is aesthetic. Its impact engulfed religion as well. By all accounts, in the fifteenth century, the liberal nature which nurtured as a result of inquisitiveness allowed man to be human which is similar to being humane. Therefore, the classical writings are named 'Humanities' and the ones who research these writings are 'Humanists' contrary to the previous nomenclature named scholastics. The attributes and peculiarities of man such as reason, justness, and nobleness are glorified in the Greek classics.

The classical literature of Greece is imbued with the romanticisation of man. This concept is unhackneyed for the Christians of mainland Europe. Literature is aligned to Christianity which preaches the idealisation of the ways of God. Initially, man was not apotheosized. The Christianity of the Middle Ages sermonised asceticism as worthwhile. However, the literature written in ancient times taught about the present world and presented that humans lived in complete harmony with the celestial beings in antiquity.

There are many narrations of the contact and proximity of God and man namely the tales of Mahabharata. In Greek stories, Leda, a beautiful maid could entice the principal deity Zeus who later takes the form of a swan to generate affection for the maid. For passion for physical recreation and games, there are many colosseums constructed in the distant past. All in all, these activities unfolded new vistas for the man that made him recognise himself in contemporary times and inside the limits calibrated by birth and demise.

During the times when the Renaissance heralded in the European continent and narrations of integrity and accomplishments of man spread their wings, the pious Christians were bound to amend their stance and assume Reformation. The advent of Christian humanism is an outcome of a settlement. Furthermore, the church's clergy is seen to desert the passion for heathen literary texts and hankered to create literary works based on classics. Hence, it is discerned that the spirit of man is regarded as supreme. Bhim S. Dahiya, a critic writes,

> Among the various themes that became popular during the Renaissance owing to the impact of humanism were the ideals of liberty and love, the ideals of perfect courtier, gentleman, citizen, or magistrate, as also the centrality of man in the universe and his responsibility to set up an ideal society informed by the humanistic values. (31)

The ascription of the characteristics of man to God named anthropomorphism has an immense impact on humanism. Critics opine that in John Milton's chef d'oeuvre, *Paradise Lost*, he is seen by the side of Satan rather than God. Milton's another work, *Tenure of Kings and Magistrates* proclaims, "All men were naturally born free" (3). Attributes such as reasoning, liberalism, criticism, rationality and the change of awareness from paradise to earth enchant a contemporary man. In this manner, the emphasis of classicism on Renaissance humanism has elaborated and glorified the notion of an ideal man.

As stated by Aristotle, the purpose of literature is to create ideal men and citizens. He has drawn the attention of the readers towards the ethical and didactic nature of literature written during the Renaissance. In his *Poetics*, *Ethics* and *Politics*, he contends:

> Believing that emotions and imagination were the best channels for moving people to love and acquire public and private virtues, the Renaissance writers practised in their writings the idea of delightful teaching. Thus, to teach and delight remained the

cornerstone of the Renaissance classicism or the Renaissance aestheticism. (qtd. in Dahiya 29)

The ethical teachings are secular and not religious. There is varied literature on biography that is produced for the sole aim of exposing the moral characteristics of the personalities. Renaissance's influence on religion can be a point of reference here. As the devout European Christians regard the classical literature of Rome and Greece as heretical. Yet, the hostility between the period of the Renaissance and the church is perceived to be momentary. Even as Legouis and Cazamian claims, "A rebellion against the spiritual authority was first incited by the Reformation, which was soon afterwards the enemy of this ally, the Renaissance" (212).

The Italian Renaissance also incorporated the rationalistic rebellion of man against the ideals of Christianity. This in turn has resulted in the questioning of the dogmas and the practice of selling pardons by the priests. The priests remain petrified at the essence of sensuality that was exhibited in the literature of that time. They developed a sense of fear that rationality would hamper religious beliefs. Then, before long, Plato's idea of poetry came into existence. Essentially, the stoics had faith in the ideologies of Christianity. While the Epicureans supported the humanist ideals as they were mostly sceptic and believed in liberalism.

The moralists such as Seneca and Cicero pleaded with the clergy. The qualities such as fair play, wisdom and fortitude were showered. The magnificent narrations and poetry that were written attracted the reading group in the church. This transformation became irresistible for the moralists.

The Reformation movement got a stimulus from the authority of King Henry VIII. These developments brought to light the ideology of Christian humanism. As explained by Merriam-Webster's Third New International Dictionary, Christian humanism is, "a philosophy advocating the self-fulfillment of man within the framework of Christian principles" (99). It is apparent that human-centred belief is mainly an outcome of the Renaissance. Thus, it can be constituted under the categorisation of Renaissance Humanism.

During the eighteenth century, much emphasis was given to the creation of a gentleman from man, defined as one who speaks the aristocratic language, behaves courteously in public, and keeps himself upgraded with societal trends. Essentially, these characteristics signify a person belonging to a high-born society.

Other great writers namely, Matthew Arnold, Auguste Comte and Thomas Paine have worked for humanism. Matthew Arnold, the English critic is more attentive towards culture. His terrible experience is the ultimate downfall of culture with "sweetness and light" (Arnold 1) by "the ignorant armies of anarchy and darkness" (Arnold 5).

Auguste Comte plays with the notion of religion in humanity. He desires a religion that is surrounded by the principles of humanism with a scope for doctrines and rituals. He also, "takes altruism and action for the sake of all humanity as its guiding principle" (qtd. in Wernick 256).

However, George Eliot rejects this idea and advocates ethical religion. Friedrich Nietzsche, the German philosopher, expends the conviction of Superman which serves as an answer to the question cropping up after the 'death of God'. Nietzsche regards Superman as the supreme or absolute man by way of constant will to strength, can rise beyond hopelessness to attain ultimate freedom.

In the twentieth century, the age-old faith was abandoned. There were numerous interrogations about the idea of man, who starting from the Enlightenment age was regarded as an intelligent and rational being. The atomic bombardment in Hiroshima and Nagasaki, the world wars, the Holocaust and the resulting brutality and annihilation appeared to be a massive shock. The description of the savagery was displayed in documentaries and films. This aroused terror and the ultimate modification of the idea of man in the minds of people. The nature and rational faculty of man were on the verge of reanalysis.

There is another way to comprehend the situation:

> But for all the Wagnerian and gothic primitivism in which the Third Reich chose to project its public personality, there was no escaping the recognition that the systematic purging of Jews, homosexuals and other racial impurities was the result not of some inexplicable descent into irrational, atavistic barbarity but of supremely modern rationality. The cool framing of objectives, the logical planning of complex systems, the orderly deployment of technology and resources: all these testify to a piece of demographic engineering as measured in its symmetry, as eloquent in its appalling fashion of individual genius and collective enterprise as the Parthenon itself. (qtd. in Davies 26)

Karl Marx, the twentieth-century political theorist opines that the epitome of 'Universal man' is absolutely rhetoric, "The heady rhetoric of 'Universal Man' that accompanied the revolutions of the eighteenth and nineteenth centuries tended to give way, once its ideological work was done, to the promotion of a rather narrower and more pragmatic set of class interests" (qtd. in Davies 51). The notion of humanism is rejected as an opinionative camouflage for the domineering perplexities of contemporary society, the deprecation of a large number of humans for whom it endeavours to speak. The followers of Marxism are disinterested in the ratiocination of the Enlightenment. Karl Marx thus writes:

> Communism is the positive supersession of private property as human self-estrangement, and hence the true appropriation of the human essence through and for man; it is the complete restoration of man to himself as a social, i.e. human, being. […] This communism, as fully developed naturalism, equals humanism, and as fully developed humanism equals naturalism, it is the genuine resolution of the conflict between man and nature, and between man and man, the true resolution of the conflict between existence and being. (qtd. in Johnson 348)

Scientific or naturalistic humanism was quite popular during the twentieth century. It denounces all kinds of mysticism and views man as an entirely natural being whose good health and prosperity are dependent upon his endeavours, independent of any abstract aid. This field of vision can also be found in existential philosophy. And, the trailblazer of existential humanism is Jean-Paul Sartre. Scientific humanism also repudiates any idea of immortality and focuses on the present life. It refuses the presence of any divine being and religion in its entirety. A well-known scientific humanist, Corliss Lamont states:

> Humanism is the viewpoint that man has but one life to lead and should make the most of it in terms of creative work and happiness that human happiness is its own justification and requires no sanction or support from supernatural sources; that in the form of heavenly gods or immortal heaves, does not exist; and those human beings, using their own intelligence and cooperating with one another, can build an enduring citadel of peace and beauty upon this earth. (21)

Julian Huxley, an evolutionary biologist has pioneered the concept of Evolutionary Humanism which is contingent on scientific humanism. His well-known text, *The Humanist Frame* assists the secular and logical faculties of contemporary culture. It is fundamentally focused on shrewd discernment and elucidation of Charles Darwin's thesis on evolution. It puts forth the idea that all species have emerged through the procedure of evolution and man is an essential and unique part of it. Man is distinctive because he is aware of the whole radius of evolution and he is at the helm of continuing this process further with the assistance of tools such as science and rationality.

Religious humanists continue to believe that humans have personal and communal needs which can be fulfilled functionally by religion. Here the word 'functional' signifies the role that it has in an individual's life be it personally or collectively. Religion serves the desires of people who share a similar philosophical perspective. The person might adopt any form of doctrine, paganism or mysticism either not being connected to any religion or even if attached then doesn't opt for religion to derive ethical values.

The centrality of humans in the philosophy of humanism carries a humane ethicality. Religious humanists think that non-religious humanism is indifferently cerebral and repudiates the psychological faculty that allows humans to become genuinely humane. Furthermore, religious humanism serves two functions:

> To serve personal needs, Religious Humanism offers a basis for moral values, an inspiring set of ideals, methods for dealing with life's harsher realities, a rationale for living life joyously, and an overall sense of purpose. To serve social needs, Humanist religious communities (such as Ethical Culture societies and many Unitarian-Universalist churches) offer a sense of belonging, an institutional setting for the moral education of children, special holidays shared with likeminded people, a unique ceremonial life, the performance of ideologically consistent rites of passage (weddings, child welcomings, coming-of-age celebrations, funerals, and so forth), an opportunity for affirmation of one's philosophy of life, and a historical context for one's ideas. (Edwords 09)

The codes of belief may vary and be restored by new ones, but the motive of religion for people is consistent. The individuals do not feel that anyone has to decide between yielding to their desires in terms of conventional beliefs against not implementing them. The people who recognise the conventional religion as outlandish, seek solace in unconventional religion. While this kind of expansion was occurring in Europe, in America, a literary critic, Irving

Babbit propounds the term 'New Humanism' due to which there was a complete non-acceptance of the high degrees of religion and science.

It centres on rationality and free will in imaginative, intellectual and moral trials. It lays down discretionary power for a rationalist and illuminated self. It is essential to cite that in modern humanism, an argument has been incensed on the grounds of philosophy or creed that acts as the milieu for modern humanism. The individuals who give credence to philosophy are regarded as Secular Humanists while the ones who regard religion as true are known as Religious Humanists. Nevertheless, both kinds of humanists have similar worldviews and fundamentals. Both have signed the well-known Humanist Manifestos I and II. And, it is just the difference in the viewpoint of their practices in religion or philosophy that separates them.

Western culture has been appraised since the 1970s and even the philosophy of humanism has been debated. A different criterion regarding man is taken into consideration. Man is identified as an output of sociocultural constraints and not as an individual focused on self. This adjudicates a new interpretation of language:

> Humanist ideology depends upon a fundamental assumption about the primacy of the autonomous and unified individual. For humanism, 'man is at the centre of meaning and action; the world is oriented around the individual. Each individual is different, each possesses a unique subjectivity; yet also, paradoxically, each shares a common human nature. The combination of unique individuality and common human essence cohere around the idea of a sovereign self,

whose essential core of being transcends the outward signs of environmental and social conditioning. Post-structuralism has sought to disrupt this man-centred view of the world, arguing that the subject, and that sense of unique subjectivity itself, is constructed in language and discourse; and rather than being fixed and unified, the subject is split, unstable or augmented. (Rice and Waugh 119)

The association of ethnic minorities and feminists have instituted humanism as a tool for present power structures in society. Postcolonial critics regard humanism as a controversial concept. They have traced the genesis of the concept and have identified the imperfections. In consonance with their opinions, it was initially a didactic venture known as *studia humanitatis* based on a curriculum corresponding to medieval scholasticism such as natural science, astronomy, law, theology and medicine.

The disagreement between scholasticism and the philosophy of humanism delineates the disaccord between the science of nature and man. The humanists the ethical grounds and preferred the fundamentals of non-scholarly fields. Although they assert to be the prototype of human civilisation, they have debarred the medical professionals and technicians as their profession is regarded as ordinary as compared to the field of liberal arts.

The interference of feminism in humanities affects the standard and global presumption of knowledge structure based on gender. Postcolonialism castigates the cultural dominance of European wisdom to bring into the picture the structural value and activity of non-European society. The experiment is to showcase the ostracism created by the orthodox knowledge structure that puts on the nomenclature of humanism and even to retrieve the deprecated knowledge belittled earlier. Postcolonialism views that the study of humanities is debauched by an obligation to assert a fraudulent generality. So, the rift between conventional and new humanism may be based on structural grounds of knowledge systems.

The philosophy of Humanism has encouraged the creation of united and autonomous states. This discovery is similar to Karl Marx and Fredrich Engels as they debate that the dominating class is forced to display its desires as common desires of all societal members, in the best possible manner of totality as the only logical and universally justifiable ones. It may be stated that humanism has emerged in the times when these confirmed interests are in constraint or want for assertion.

Nonetheless, Micheal Foucault, the structuralist critic has warned against the inversion of the current ranking of knowledge that will furthermore result in another ranking. Giles Deleuze and Felix Guattari, the French philosophers have proposed that the marginalised knowledge must abandon the idea of becoming 'major' or in other terms 'canonical', rather they should aspire to emerge as non-canonical or minor. Presently, "Although the precise implications of this project remain unclear, we might say that all 'minor' knowledge need to retain the memory of their subjugation and deterritorialisation and, therefore, of their creative affinity with other fields of 'non-culture" (Gandhi 53). It is comprehensible that the principal admonition of New or Modern Humanists is the absence of full representation carried out by the school of Old Humanism.

The Postcolonial critics have noted the untenability

of the concerns of the theory. Few critics opine that their policies have damaging upshots on society. Gayatri Spivak, a subaltern literary theorist, declares that "the recent concessions to marginality studies within the first world metropolitan academy inadvertently serve to identify, confirm and thereby exclude certain cultural formations as chronically marginal" (Gandhi 16).

Spivak alerts that the term 'third-world' in Postcolonial theory may sustain genuine communal and political subjugations which depend on differences between the 'periphery' and the 'centre'. Apart from this, the anti-postcolonial denigrators highlight the separation of the deconstructive situation of postcolonial practitioners and the socio-economic plight of people whose survival lies on the metropolitan borders.

This has been disliked by the critics such as Aijaz Ahmad and Arif Dirlik. The only thing that matters is that the role of humanism is to outshine the human and deals chiefly with the interests of man. As man lies at the centre of all creation. And if any action proves to be destructive to man, then it shall be deemed to be rejected.

In this regard, the widely known Humanist Manifesto has emerged every so often. It defines the meaning of the term Humanism and acts as a part of the worldwide Humanist movement. The distinct features of this movement are the politico-economic facets of the day-to-day life of man. It is an amalgamation of the three manifestos contriving a perspective based on Humanism. The first one is the original one published in the year 1933 mentioned as Humanist Manifesto I, the second is the Humanist Manifesto II published in the year 1973 and the third is Humanist Manifesto III titled 'Humanism and Its Aspirations' published in the year 2003. The signatories of these manifestos are both secular and religious humanists. The central idea of all manifestos is the expansion of the philosophy and creed which deserts the faith in divinity or deity. All three manifestos deviate from each other in terms of tonality, form and aim. The Humanist Manifesto coauthored by Raymond Braggand and Roy Wood Sellars is produced with about thirty signatories inclusive of the popular American psychologist, John Dewey. It introduces the idea of a new religion and talks of humanism as a movement based on religious lines. It shall be utilised to go above and put back prior religions that are primarily focused on mysticism.

This record figures a series of fifteen strains of beliefs. Firstly, religious humanists look at the universe as self-existent and uncreated. Secondly, the philosophy of humanism signifies that man is an integral part of the natural world and is an outcome of an unending process. Thirdly, humanism adopts an organic outlook on life. In this context, the humanists deduce that the age-old mind and body dualism must be abandoned. Fourthly, the philosophy of humanism predicts that man's civilisation, as evident in historical and anthropological facts, is the effect of a steady growth because of his interconnection with the cosmos and heritage.

The human who emerged from a specific culture is to a large extent influenced by it. This philosophy also claims that the essence of the macrocosm represented by advanced science rejects the belief in any mystical phenomena. It does not repudiate the prospect of undiscovered realities. Rather, it justifies that the manner to ascertain the survival and utility of reality is possible by way of an intellectual investigation and analysis of their interconnection with the needs of man.

Fifthly, Religion should design its aspirations and schemes concerning an inquisitive spirit. Religious Humanism contemplates the accomplishment of man's identity to be ultimate for man's existence. It also forages for its blossoming and complete attainment in the present times. This serves as a clarification for the social enthusiasm of the humanists, instead of the old demeanour associated with worship and devotion. The religious humanist expresses his religious disposition powerfully to encourage social welfare. This will at a time demoralise affectionate and imaginary desires and count up for life's contentment.

Unquestionably, the religious establishments, their rituals, ecclesiastical practices and social activities ought to be reformed as soon as possible to function efficaciously in the modern era. The humanists are strongly satisfied by the idea that the subsisting predatory and profit-oriented society might be insufficient and a revolutionary modification in techniques and motifs must be initiated.

An interactive and considerate economic system ought to be ingrained so that the impartial dispensation of life's means can be possible. The objective of humanism is the emergence of an untied and ubiquitous society in which individuals willingly conspire for a common welfare. The Humanists seek a shared existence in the cooperative world. The philosophy of Humanism asserts to confirm life and not reject it. It shall seek the newfangled possibilities and not escape from them. It must try to create a sustainable life for everyone. And basing on these subjects the humanists maintained their credence.

The reason to use 'A Humanist Manifesto' instead of 'The' is intended because of the upcoming Manifestos to come after it. The designing of the ideologies in these written statements is a continual process. In many sections of society, the writing up of private Manifestos is highly motivated.

The Manifesto that comes after the first Manifesto is documented by Edwin H. Wilson and Paul Kurtz. It endeavours to upgrade the Manifestos that are before this. It starts with the declaration that the overindulgence of Nazism and the second world war has proved the first Manifesto to be optimistic in nature. It designates an unsentimental and pragmatic attitude in the seventeen-point declaration, which is described to a larger degree than the versions prior to this.

Nonetheless, the first Manifesto continues to exist with the aspiration that poverty and war will entirely be antiquated. Many schemes in the record, for instance, resistance to racism, armaments for mass extermination and bracing human rights are justly undisputed. Its authorization for control of birth rate and divorce shall be legalised. Technology shall be considered as a means to enhance life and this applies to the contemporary Western civilisation. Moreover, its suggestion for an international system of court has been executed. It also reinforces the liberty of abortion. But it rejects the idea of the supernatural.

The emphasis of the second Manifesto lies on an economically unbiased attitude while departing from commiseration with a libertarian socialistic frame of mind. The document was at the beginning issued with a few attestants but gradually it became popular and acquired numerous votaries.

One of the writers of AHA, Gloria Steinem presents that the AHA or American Humanists Association database motivates the browsers to write their name. In the end, it is mentioned that the attestants "do not necessarily endorse every detail" of the official paper. (73) The few popular lines from the Manifesto published in the year 1973 are, "No deity will save us; we must save ourselves," (31) and "We are responsible for what we are and for what we will be" (29). The two ideas may confer hardships for the believers in Christianity, Islam and Judaism or anyone who believes in yielding to an omnipotent God is the sole leap of faith. Focusing on the part that secondary schools should play to accomplish the objectives elucidated in the Second Humanist manifesto, John Dunphy writes, "The battle for humankind's future must be waged and won in the public school classroom by teachers who correctly perceive their role as the proselytizers of a new faith: a religion of humanity that recognizes and respects the spark of what theologians call divinity in every human being." and "Utilizing a classroom instead of a pulpit to convey humanist values in whatever subject they teach, regardless of the educational level – preschool day care or large state university" (*The Humanist* 13).

The Third Humanist Manifesto entitled 'Humanism and Its Aspirations' was issued by the American Humanist Association (AHA) in the year 2003. It is jotted down by the members of the committee accommodating six ideologies taken from the previous Manifesto. As mentioned in this the wisdom of the universe is procured through continuous inspection, scrutiny and logical investigation. Humans include an intrinsic and unique creation of nature and the outcome of a desultory developmental mutation.

The principles are obtained from man's wants and desires as appraised by the enterprise. The ultimate attainment of life is possible in the involvement of man in the fulfilment of humane ideologies. Additionally, it views that man is sociable by his nature. He extracts sense when he is acquainted with other individuals and toils for the betterment of society. This Humanist Manifesto has been signed by twenty-one Nobel Laureates.

There are other documents apart from the authoritative Humanist Manifestos. There has been The Council for Secular Humanism formed by Paul Kurtz in the year 1980. This organisation is more critical concerning the purpose of Humanism. This manifesto is sanctioned as 'A Secular Humanist Declaration'. The key points include free investigation, severance of the church from the state, liberty, morality established on rationality, ethical teachings, scepticism and evolution. The torchbearers of this movement comprise, Felix Adler, F.C.S Schiller, Thomas Paine, Albert Einstein, Charles Francis Potter, Bertrand Russell, Auguste Comte, William James, John Dewey, Julian Huxley, Thomas Mann and Roywood Sellars.

It shall not be out of order if one refers to Humanism in the Indian context. The historic spiritual customs as pronounced in the *sastras* contain numerous meanings. Firstly, it shall be split into two categories, the atheistic and the theistic. The philosophy of humanism can be found in both of these categories. The Vedas distinctively look at man which is *Manurbhava* or Be human. Man is depicted as an archetype of logical thinking in the Upanishads.

The non-dualistic credo of the philosophical school of Uttar Mimanasa Darshan rejects any primary differentiation between the soul and the deity which is allocated to man (Atman and Brahman). Man can liberate himself from any kind of *Maya* or the earthly filthiness of *Kama, Lobha, Moha* and *Krodha*. It must be noted that as the Renaissance humanism encourages man to become a superior being by imitating the qualities of a gentleman in terms of mental and bodily sense. While, on the other hand, the Indian context of philosophy desires man to transform into a higher personality by spiritual means to have infinite access to happiness known as *Ananda*.

In the pre-Buddhist era, the philosophy of Carvaka was similar to Western Epicureanism. The believers in this philosophy suggested the plausibility of sensorial insight. The reasoning focused on cognitive calculation is repudiated. The universe consists of the four components such as the Earth, Air, Water and Fire. Apart from all this, the presence of hell and heaven is merely superficial. The supporters do not have faith in any divine presence or transcendental faculty known as God. The Soul and the Body are regarded as one. And, lastly, death ends the existence of humans. The Sanskrit sloka, *Yaavet jeevet sukham jeevet, rin kritvam ghrit pivet* denotes that while one is alive or present on earth, one must feast, drink, make merry and lend to swallow butter milk or ghee.

The classical Western Humanist thoughts opine that there is a multitudinous resemblance between Indian mythology and Greek mythology. The deities and humans interact among themselves and they unite during any contestation with any demonic forces. In the Greek context, Venus is the daughter of the chief deity Zeus and mother Leda, the earthling while in the Indian context, Karna is the son of the Sun God and mother Kunti, the earthling. Other narrations can be detailed as in the times of the Trojan War, the Sun was ordered by Joshua to remain motionless so can he can emerge victorious in the war but Phaeton, the son of the God of Sun steered a winged carriage in the sky that brought about his death. The same incident is evident in the Indian mythology of Ramayana.

The philosophies of Buddhism and Jainism signify atheism as they denounce the idea of God. They believe in the concept of Dharma as majestic. Again, the patrons of the Bhakti movement gospelize the unchallenged loyalty to a divine being who is regarded as the supreme liberator of man. The abdication of the caste system in their terms aligns with their thought on humanism.

Preachers such as Guru Nanak, Namdev, Kabir, and Chaitanya emerged in a new civilisation when divinity was supported by ritualism. This version of humanism is consolidated as Spiritualistic Humanism. And, the preachers opine that the good will of humans lies in the enhancement of spirit. Referring to the humanism by Guru Nanak, one of the critics named Wazir Singh states:

> In the flowering of spiritual life, aesthetic development of man was placed even higher than rational development. Higher still was ethical development which prompted man to engage in a cooperative quest for an ideal community united in spirit and feeling. The goal he envisaged was the perpetuation of 'peak moments' of the experience of harmony with the core of reality. (177)

This concept bears a resemblance to the philosophy of Vedantism of perceiving spiritualism in man's soul. And the idea of humanism in India is under the purview of spirituality. The eminent figures of modern India such as Mahatma Gandhi, Swami Vivekananda, and Rabindranath Tagore teach the idea of humanism. Vivekananda has reconceptualised the Bhagavad Gita to the emphasis on action in the contemporary world. He has assembled youth to constitute an organisation to become spiritually efficient. In his myriad compositions, he has confirmed the oneness of humankind. One of them can be clearly stated:

> When a man has reached the highest, when he sees neither man nor woman, neither sect

nor creed, nor colour, nor birth, nor any of these differentiations, but goes beyond and finds that divinity which is the real man behind every human being – then alone he has reached the universal brotherhood, and that man alone is a Vedantist. (Vivekananda 392)

In *The Religion of Man*, Rabindranath Tagore criticizes the communal biases against women and the marginalised. A critic named Kunjo Singh remarks, "In all his novels […] Tagore emphasizes the importance of man above all types of orthodoxy, narrow-minded sectarianism, religion, parochialism and violence" (Singh 143).

Another critic Harish Raizada claims that "his unswerving faith in the joy of life, freedom of the individual, respect for human personality, man's obedience to his conscience and his enjoyment of life through love and sacrifice – the universal virtues which stands for humanism in life" (78).

It cannot be ignored that Tagore is an artist that lured him to be nearer to the aestheticism in humanist philosophy. A critic, Srinivasa Iyengar opines, "He tirelessly pursued the ideal of Beauty, and Beauty was to him also Love, Truth, Goodness and Power. In poem or play or story or novel, in reminiscence or exegesis or exhortation or prophecy, Tagore is essentially of a piece and the total impact of his life and work is indeed that of a modern Leonardo da Vinci, or a multiple power and personality" (112).

Other notable Bengali writers such as Tarashankar Banerjee and Saratchandra Chatterjee were on this track. Tagore even refused to accept Western nationalism as it views man as a political creature. The exclusivism of Western nationalism is evident when it regards the inhabitants of other countries as lower in status which is based on the thoughts of Adolf Hitler. Mahatma Gandhi indicates that when one is in the service of mankind, he or she serves God in a way. As Gandhi led a simple way of life like that of a common man, thousands of people recognised themselves with Gandhi. In this regard, V.S. Narwane writes: "Gandhi's humanism had a moral-social bias, while Tagore's was coloured by his aesthetic-mystical experience; but both were firm believers in the worth and dignity of the human individual. They were both partial to the theistic rather than the pantheistic or absolute traditions in Indian philosophy" (113).

Both Tagore and Gandhi have adopted the essence of Universal Humanism as cherished in the message of Vedantic philosophy *Vasudhaiva kutumbukam* which implies that the world is united as a family. Among the modern thinkers, M.N. Roy is focused on Radical Humanism alternately termed New Humanism. He discards both state ownership and democracy. He is convinced by the necessary logical and ethical character of man and man's ability to come up with an unchained and equitable social stratum. His magnification of man and emphasis on the attainment of economic, social and political liberty concerning man secured for him a good deal of followers.

Another philosopher, Dr. Sarvepalli Radhakrishnan has elucidated the texts of Indian philosophy for the Westerners. His attempt lies in Spiritual Humanism in the Indian context. In the year 1997, the organisation, Indian Humanist Union based in New Delhi issued a few points. It states that the basis of Humanism lies in the promotion of the human code of conduct and the construction of a considerate society. This society will be built along the lines of sensitivity and ability of man rather than associating it with abstract faculty such as rationality and free investigation.

This statement underpins certain inferences to the point of view on Humanism. Some of them are human morality does not require any outward sanction and is linked to the intuitive faculty that is inherent to man. Both man's nature and the natural world are defined by meanness and selflessness, human code of conduct only appropriates the latter. The philosophy of Humanism is convinced by the fact that there lies a close connection between both of the central values, man's self-independence and fellow feeling and the essence of free investigation is closely associated with enhancing human values.

The objective spirit of untethered examination includes the embracing of improbabilities in place of convictions, inflexibilities or points of view. It will ultimately bring about modesty, forbearance and sympathy that will in the end cause the promotion of mores and create an utterly humane community. It is found that religious beliefs appear to be futile in matching the requirements of humans and at last, are inclined to invalidate compassionate attitudes.

Consequently, Humanism is convinced by the liberty of an individual inclusive of the right to self-reliance and fulfilment of an individual's talents. A humane society features a compassionate attitude, tolerance, unitedness, equality and justice. It should be seen not only in the temperament of man but also in the natural world. Lastly, it must be concluded that the philosophy of Humanism centres on man. It underscores the integrity of man and acknowledges him as the measure of everything. In every type of humanism, the only thing that remains similar is the belief in man's potential.

While the broader term, Humanism focuses on

man's prospects, the concept of Posthuman reconsiders humans by its association with the nonhuman. On the other hand, Critical Posthumanism is a theoretical perspective delineating a more compounded and analytic correspondence between the human and the inhuman or subhuman. Classified in the genre of Speculative Fiction, Critical Posthumanism postulates that humans live in a condition beyond being human. The prefix 'Post' in Posthumanism asserts the emergence of a new era and hints at the inception of a living being who is radically transformed by intermingling with the 'non-human other'. It addresses the question of what connotes being human in an epoch where there is a species-wise blurring of boundaries of the body and identity-morphing that has dynamically grounded the man-machine interconnection. The mechanics of cloning, Artificial Intelligence, machine learning, stem-cell engineering, subfreezing of human corpses and Xenotransplantation i.e., grafting of organs and tissues between various categories of species have effectuated the initiation of a new organism. There are various strands of Posthumanism based on the vision of how humans are perceived. One of them is Critical Posthumanism. The word 'Critical' in Critical Posthumanism signifies a more complex alliance between humans and the non-human. Critical Posthumanism contributes to the regeneration of humanistic values in the face of technological interventions.

It presents the conception of humans as an open system that allows its fusion with technologies and other life forms. Human is identified as co-evolving, co-existing, sharing ecosphere and life processes with other forms of life. Furthermore, technological intercession in the human body does not act as a mere prosthesis but is inherent to it. This brings into a picture what can be called a new organism known as the 'Humanimal'. The 'Humanimal' is a hybridisation of humans with the biological features of a non-human or an animal that more or less makes them harmoniously segmented and co-dependent.

Critical Posthumanism appraises the transhumanistic and humanistic focus on normative rationality. It rejects the exclusivism of 'animal', 'human' and 'machine'. Rather, it discerns human subjectivity as a conglomeration of animals and machines. It offers a more comprehensive understanding of life and a substantive ethical reaction to non-human beings in an epoch of the intermingling of numerous forms of species. It locates the human body in a domain that is embedded with vegetation, animals and machines. It favours co-existence, mutualism, concurrence and responses with diverse species on earth rather than autarchy, self-sufficiency and segregation of humans. Human experience, sapience and logical reasoning are shaped by the sensoria of other biotic creatures that later make them autopoietic i.e., renewing, maintaining and creating one's parts.

Varela contends that every human order is an "autopoietic, autonomously functioning, languaging, living system" (2). "What we understand as uniquely human, therefore, is the consequence of hybridization and exchange of material and immaterial- data, such as in the genetic code [...] different elements" (qtd. in Nayar 20-21).

In the recent date, Critical Posthumanism has been a crucial subject for inquiry. Sherryl Vint, professor of media and cultural studies enumerates the critical approach along the side of biopolitics and bioenergy as "terms of critical currency for the late twentieth and early twenty-first centuries" ("Animal Studies" 444).

In general, the main principle of Critical Posthumanist speculation entails that the quintessence of humans lacks universality. Humans are physical beings immersed in and sculpted by physical processes and applications that prevent the likelihood of a ubiquitous or spiritualistic human temperament. The origination of human is modelled on the apprehension of the living world and technology employed to overpower or overcome all the natural forces and objects. Donna Haraway's "A Cyborg Manifesto" published in the year 1985 is a significant work in which Haraway asserts that the cyborg ought to be considered as a crucial creature of the late twenties. The cyborg is competent enough to transcend the ontological precincts that have conventionally influenced and delimited the Western discourse. Haraway argues that the frontiers setting apart the human, the non-human animal and the machine are not well-constructed and have been altogether effaced subsequently by the instantaneous technological expansion of the late twenties.

Regarding this, she rather proposes a somewhat ontological flexibility in which the non-human animal expresses its standpoint from the angle of moral uniformity with humans and the machine infiltrates the biological being, the former now compelled to acknowledge its numerous technological and organic incarnations as elemental to its being. Haraway declares that the cyborg, "a hybrid of machine and organism, a creature of social reality as well as a creature of fiction" ("A Cyborg Manifesto" 7).

Certainly, the cyborg excludes the combination of the biological and the machinic: this conglomeration suggests unity, whereas Haraway accurately argues to escape from the demand for unities, as these can be altered into the desire "to be autonomous, to be powerful, to be God" ("A Cyborg Manifesto" 35). As stated by Ira Livingston and Judith Halberstam, the purpose of posthumanist speculation is "not to replace a stuck mind-body [sic] dualism with a heterogeneous monism, but to insist on the sameness of every assemblage"—that is, on the partiality of identities which can never be comfortably resolved into either unity or duality (8). Instead of the totalising narratives, the notion of shifting and fragmented identity holds great significance, "without clear boundary, frayed, insubstantial" (Haraway, "A Cyborg Manifesto" 35). The cyborg as suggested by Donna Haraway is a specimen of a being that is neither wholly organic nor entirely machinic. It holds the contrasting elements in tension in a way without empowering one to settle with another and in the process proposes, "a way out of the maze of dualisms in which we have explained our bodies and our tools to ourselves" (Haraway, "A Cyborg Manifesto" 39).

Donna Haraway's "A Cyborg Manifesto" encloses a sort of law-breaking and deconstructive vigour that has unmistakably smeared a definite strand of cultural theory in contemporary times, focusing on the features of the human, encapsulated under the title of Posthumanism. In *Theorizing Posthumanism*, Neil Badmington describes the features of the classical replica of the human being. He puts forward an analysis of how human nature has influenced the Western discourse now and then starting from the era of Rene Descartes:

> There is an absolute difference between the human and the inhuman: only the former has the capacity for rational thought. Reason belongs solely to the human and, as such, serves to unite the human race. 'We' may have different types of bodies, but because reason is a property of the mind (which, for

Descartes, is distinguishable from the body), deep down 'we' are all the same. (4)

It is often declared that Classical humanism is fascinated by a sort of ubiquitous and fundamental human spirit focussed on the idea of reason and rationality, supposed to be immanent in all genuine human subject matter, who are in a way presumed to be intrinsically similar (a notion evident in recent cultural discourses concerning our presumed arrival at 'post-race' and 'post-gender' societies). (Badmington, *Theorizing Posthumansim* 4). The problem with such a belief is the technique by which it shimmers over the required possibility of this discernment of man's nature, modifying explicitly the European set of principles or beliefs into all that Tony Davies describes, "the myth of essential and universal Man: essential, because humanity—human-ness—is the inseparable and central essence, the defining quality, of human beings; universal, because that essential humanity is shared by all human beings, of whatever time or place" (24). As a consequence, it strikes out the crucial distinctions between various types of people, deducing that whatever is accurate for a few European citizenry will ultimately apply to all.

Critical Posthumanism strives to decentralise the representation of humans by highlighting the subservience of the seemingly discreet, ubiquitous and independent human subject interminably to external forces and occurrences. Neil Badmington applies the expression retroactively to a broad range of traditional and modern-day thinkers whose writings hold up a somewhat anthropological decentralising feature of the theoretical framework of Posthumanism. Michel Foucault in his well-known work, *The Order of Things*, maintains that humans are the "invention of recent date, being framed by Western cultures and emerging in conjunction with the human sciences apparently evolved to investigate it during the beginnings of nineteenth century" (400). Michel Foucault undermines the idea of a comprehensive and sovereign human being by disclosing its historical and communal inception- including any "change in the fundamental arrangements of knowledge, he is also of the opinion that, 'man would be erased, like a face drawn in sand at the edge of the sea" (422). For Neil Badmington, the aforementioned idea displays a radical Posthumanist dialect. He posits that this is also evident in the works of the contemporaries of Michel Foucault such as Franz Fanon, Louis Althusser and Jean Baudrillard, and additionally the geniuses namely, Sigmund Freud and Karl Marx. Therefore, Neil Badmington's description of Posthumanism embraces not only the writings of the writers namely, Donna Haraway whose emphatic predictions have been to distress the stated frontiers between the human, non-human animal and machine, but of all the writers who have implicitly championed as a critique of the traditional or classical European subject of the human.

Similarly, Badmington comprehensively studies the concept of Posthumanism. According to him, any onslaught on the classical humanistic representation of the self-governing, rational content consists of equivalent fragments "certainty, security, and mastery", ought to be conceived as Posthumanism (*Theorizing Posthumanism* 16). This type of inclusive point of view is not uncustomary. Cary Wolfe, an American academician and a pioneer of Posthumanism describes the theory as "nam[ing] a historical moment in which the decentering of the human by its imbrication in technical, medical, informatic, and economic networks is increasingly impossible to ignore" (15). For both Wolfe and Badmington the posthumanist activities are focused on questioning the "ideals of human perfectibility, rationality and agency that work together to widely elaborate the humanism of the Western world starting from the Enlightenment age" (Wolfe, *What is Posthumanism?* 13). By promoting such attributes to the position of general human standards, Cary Wolfe contends that humanism has unreservedly eliminated those who never reveal themselves from all-inclusive ethical ruminations, a factor that accounts for the entirety starting from agribusiness to bondage.

This has also impersonated the range to which the subject of the human is equivalently determined by its organic and machinic personifications, elements which undoubtedly configure the course of actions in which humans and the society interconnect with the physical non-anthropoid sphere around them. Traditional humanism has emphasized a finite perception of the human as a single, independent and well-organised subject matter- the Cartesian and the abstract man utters 'I', as Jacques Derrida states, at the core of every narrative of politics, ethics, metaphysics, language and many more (qtd. in Allender 11). The broader framework of Critical Posthumanism stresses confronting these boundaries by recognising the organic and machinic origins of humans. Wolfe states that this approach should not be considered negatively. Critical Posthumanism never proposes a misanthropic non-acceptance of man either as vulnerable to the superficial biological or mechanical agencies, i.e., being an anti-humanist or as a fiction text. Moreover, it is about embracing an egalitarian cognizance of subjectiveness that has scope for other beings customarily perceived as being of political or moral value. A comprehensive awareness of Critical Posthumanism as stated by Neil Badmington and Cary Wolfe in actuality presents a well-established and enormously felt need for a long time by varied thinkers to inquire about Western narratives of the rationality of man and his universality.

Cary Wolfe observes that Critical Posthumanism 'comes both before and after humanism'—it emphasises "the embodiment and embeddedness of the human being in not just its biological but also its technological world". (*What is Posthumanism?* 15). The idea that is central to Critical Posthumanist speculation is to deconstruct the partition between human and non-human or creatures other than humans transposing the insistence on, as Rosi Braidotti envisages it, *bios*—the sphere of human life— to '*zoe*', 'the dynamic, self-organizing structure of life itself' that includes both the human and non-human (*The Posthuman* 60). Simultaneously, it is definite from existent facts concerning environmental destruction, changes in the climate pattern and disappearance of landscape structure and others, that the ecosphere encompasses commonly different varieties of biotic creatures. This identification elaborates the expression 'natural world' to embrace several types of inorganic occurrences, stemming from landscapes, water bodies to weather systems. Harold Fromm, an Ecocritic states that one cannot eliminate the dependency of a living being on the mundane, since "steps taken to preserve the environment', and with it such physical phenomena as 'clean air', also work to preserve the essential grounds for 'biological existence' itself" (37).

Certainly, such a lump of nonbiological tendencies offers a substantiation of Donna Haraway's model of the cyborg. Subsequently, Bruno Latour maintains that the phenomena for instance the ozone hole, deforestation and global warming are extremely problematic to conceptualise as per any traditional scheme. He questions, "Where are we to put these hybrids? Are they human? Humans because they are our work. Are they natural? Natural because they are not our doing. Are they local or global? Both" (50).

Anyhow, the basic contingency of biological species inclusive of the material essence of humanity is determined for an extensive study of Critical Posthumanism where man is perceived to be hanging on both the material and natural world that is subject to threat by the human-centric approach of traditional humanism.

Pramod K. Nayar suggests that "the human must be understood as a material as much as an intellectual entity, enmeshed in localised processes of becoming, but a becoming-with other life forms—that is, as an embedded and systemic component of a mutually constitutive material environment" (*Posthumanism* 47).

The replica of a man living in organic fusion with the material surrounding prevents the probability of an abstract and ubiquitous human. Robert Pepperell, a Professor of multidisciplinary subjects, posits, "In the posthuman schema it is a mistake to separate the thing that thinks and the thing that is thought about—in other words, to separate mind from matter" (33).

An important concept that emerged during the 1980s or the second phase of cybernetics is 'autopoiesis'. This concept has been propounded by neurophysiologists of Chile namely Francisco Varela and Humberto Maturana to present a report on the material arrangement of organisms in a way delineating their interrelation with their surroundings. (qtd. in Hayles 149).

Precisely, the term autopoiesis signifies self-creation.

It distinguishes the biological species as a self-creating structure, away from the surroundings encircling them and reactive to impetuses or commotion from the surroundings. Such stimuli of the environment activate the nerve system of the organisms who in turn expound the stimuli based on the hierarchy that incorporates their material being. It is to be noted that each organism responds differently depending on the habitual activities of their being. Cary Wolfe states that the concept of autopoiesis "forces us to rethink our taken-for-granted modes of human experience [...] by recontextualizing them in terms of the entire sensorium of other living beings and their own autopoietic ways of bringing forth a world" (*What is Posthumanism?* 25).

As Cary Wolfe observes, humanity is "fundamentally a prosthetic creature that has coevolved with various forms of technicity and materiality, forms that are radically not-human and yet have made the human what it is" (*What is Posthumanism?* 25).

Conclusively, human is not merely a creation of nature but an equally important technological being who is alternatively known as "Homo Faber" as named by Tom Shippey. ("Literary Gatekeepers and the Fabril Tradition" 42).

The conglomeration of humans with a technical prosthesis configures an essential feature in the Critical Posthumanist narration of Human epistemology and ontology.

CHAPTER III

Enhancing the Human: Vulnerable Bodies and Posthuman Vision in A. E. Van Vogt's Novels

Critical Posthumanism entails the termination of the humanist conviction of man in its entirety and comes up with an advanced alteration to the fore. The term 'critical' has a dual meaning. At the outset, it takes under its purview the receptiveness towards the revolutionary essence of technocultural modification and focuses on a particular progression of thought that is critically betrothed to humanism. This in turn has evolved a long way off from the tradition of humanism itself. Thus, the focus is to reconsider accepted forms of the critique of antihumanism so that they can adapt to the present altered state and revolutionise them when possible.

The origins can be traced back to the French philosopher, Jean-Francois Lyotard's *A Postmodern Fable* which unearths the explication of 'Human'. The opening line of the essay, "What a Human and his/her Brain – or rather the Brain and its Human – would resemble at the moment when they leave the planet forever, before its destruction; that, the story does not tell" (Lyotard 12). Here, Lyotard engages in an incorporeal narration. He questions whether there will be any Homo Sapiens when the world ends or the solar system perishes.

And, if they still exist, they shall entirely mutate themselves reconstructively and technologically as a means to remain alive during the detonation of the Sun. He further interrogates if there will be a continuation of the tale after the apocalypse as few species might have disappeared from the inferno to narrate the tale. Thus, there shall be room for the process of posthumanisation to occur with an aim to empower man to deal with the situations and lead the quasi-humans to go on ensuing intergalactic journeys.

In his book, *The Postmodern Condition*, Lyotard conveys the improbability of the active system, brain or human in addition to its eventuality:

> The Human, or his/her brain, is a highly unlikely material (that is, energetic) formation. This formation is necessarily transitory since it is dependent on the conditions of terrestrial life, which are not eternal. The formation called Human or Brain will have been nothing more than an episode in the conflict between differentiation and entropy. The pursuit of greater complexity asks not for the perfecting of the Human, but its mutation or its defeat for the benefit of a better performing system. Humans are very mistaken in their presuming to be the motors of development and in confusing development

with the progress of consciousness and civilization. (Lyotard 20)

The critical posthumanism visions itself as being part of a high-level technological growth. It settles in the deconstructiveness of humans and technology which is a medium to attain this. The Professor of Rice University, Cary Wolfe, "opposes the fantasies of disembodiment and autonomy, inherited from humanism itself" (Wolfe 15). He divulges how humanism envisages that to nurture as a human is equivalent to something superior and considerable than any mechanical and animal form. But he states that "the decentring of the human…is increasingly impossible to ignore, a historical development that points towards the necessity of new theoretical paradigms" (Wolfe 16).

Wolfe endeavors to display his thoughts to enlighten the readers in this manner:

> The perspective I attempt to formulate here [...] actually enables us to describe the human and its characteristic modes of communication, interaction, meaning, social significations, and affective investments with greater specificity once we have removed meaning from the ontologically closed domain of the consciousness, reason, reflection, and so on. It forces us to rethink our taken-for-granted modes of human experience, including the normal perceptual modes and affective states of Homo Sapiens itself, by recontextualizing them in terms of the entire sensorium of other living beings and their own autopoietic ways of "bringing forth a world" [...] ways that are, since we ourselves are human animals, part of the

evolutionary history and behavioural and psychological repertoire of the human itself. (Wolfe 25)

Focusing on the specificity of this matter, in her work, *How We Became Posthuman*, N. Katherine Hales, sets down how in an age of the advancement of technology humans have started to define themselves in a radically different manner. Hayles desires to visualise re-embodiment to "put back into the picture the flesh that continues to be erased in contemporary discussions about cybernetic subjects" (Hayles 5).

Timothy Morton, a Professor of ecology, proposes that the discoveries made by Charles Darwin on the process of evolution have varied implications in a way making it an abstract process. For instance, the horse a person rides is an abstract activity of simply an ephemeral articulation of cells in changeability. In his essay, "Tensions in the Mesh", he clearly chronicles,

> There is indeed something humiliating about this reversal of immediacy into abstraction, in the same way Copernicus and Galileo brought humans down to Earth. [...] Evolution strikes another great nail into the coffin of common sense. It is worth pausing briefly to let this stunning conclusion sink in. We cannot see, touch, or smell evolution. It evades our perception. (20)

He further explains, "All of this is profoundly antiteleological. ...The lack of teleology is humiliating— literally, it brings us down to Earth, which must be good news for ecology" (*The Ecological Thought* 22). He provides a perception of the cosmos by taking an example of the mesh which "does away with boundaries between living and non-living forms" and focuses on the unification of all forms. He notes, "Humans maintain the human-animal boundary by erecting rigid walls made of quasi-humans, humanoids, ambiguous nonhumans, or inhumans" (*The Ecological Thought* 88)

Pieter Vermeulen, an author of contemporary literature, recognises the focus on technologization and enunciates the bountiful possibilities that critical posthumanism offers especially on sensing away from anthropocentrism (124).

Similarly, In *Philosophical Posthumanism*, Francesca Ferrando, the posthuman philosopher, embraces the idea that critical posthumanism is all-inclusive and "rooted in an extensive critical account of what it means to be human" (191). She also asks, "What does it mean to be posthuman in our existence" (243)?

Karen Barad, another practitioner of Posthumanism, "marks the practice of accounting for the boundary-making practices by which the 'human' and its others are differentially delineated and defined" (136). She chronicles that posthumanism "does not presume that man is the measure of all things. It is not held captive to the distance scale of the human but rather is attentive to the practice by which scale is produced [...] and eschews [...] the body as the natural and fixed dividing line between interiority and exteriority" (136).

This subject matter can be found in A.E. Van Vogt's *Slan*. In this novel, a nine-year-old lad, Jommy Cross resides with his mother, Patricia Cross in a serene countryside. They have come to the middle of the centropolis which is surrounded by large parks, buildings and skyscrapers. The authoritarian of the whole planet, the ruthless Kier Gray, lives in the main building of the government which is located at the centropolis. Long ago, this region was owned by the Slans who governed the area for a short period. The Slans are the scion of humans, variants having tendrils on the top of their head that help them study the minds of human beings. The humans believe that the Slans are living even now regardless of all the preventive measures. They are captured and the internal parts of their body are examined. They possess a different category of physique with tendrils on their head that allow them to read the thoughts of everyone around them. Patricia asks, "They're working fast. Can you catch their thoughts, Jommy" (Vogt, *Slan* 9)? They can read the minds of people from distances and untwine faraway reverberations into articular impressions.

They are the mysterious race of mutated humans who are skilled with magical powers. They are hiding themselves from the human race that fears and despises them and strives to wipe out them in its entirety. The entire novel is set in an unidentified location in the future time, where the involvement of automation has considerably come to the fore.

The presently accessible technologies are involved in reinstating former functionaries of the human such as visual, hearing and reflex performance of limbs. It also empowers man with new capabilities that he has experienced formerly. Kevin Warwick, the foremost human having a microchip placed inside his body and as a result regarded as a cyborg claims,

> I was born human. This was merely due to the hand of fate acting at a particular place and time. But while fate made me human, it also gave me the power to do something about it. The ability to change myself, to

upgrade my human form with the aid of technology. To link my body directly with silicon. To become a cyborg - part human, part machine. This is the extraordinary story of my adventure as the first human entering into a Cyber World; a world which will, most likely, become the next evolutionary step of humankind. (*Cyborg* 71)

At the beginning of the novel, Jommy Cross's mother is shot by an agent of the secret police at one corner of Capital Avenue. He is left alone to seek a way to survive. As he grows up to his adulthood, he is unaware of any other Slan who can assist him. Providentially, Jommy Cross being a Slan is more powerful and quick-witted than any man of the same age. He spends his childhood in hiding from the world. When he blossoms into adulthood, he initiates his quest for the technology that is devised and concealed by his father. This technology can rescue the Slans from being slaughtered in their entirety.

In the year 2006, Kevin Warwick set up FIDIS or the 'Future of Identity in the Information Society' established at the University of Reading. This organization is intent on ethicbots which hints at the ethical facets of robots and cyborgs. There was a conference on "Android and Eve" held in the year 2009 at the Institute of Molecular Biotechnology where his specific statement, "Human beings are destined to be a subspecies" (2). This expression implies that humans and machines are going to merge in the near future. Here, Warwick focuses on the dynamic and advancing side of man. Furthermore, he is not summoning for desertion of the body of man to achieve immortality through virtual reality. Rather, he is engaged in the unification of the human body with the machinic forms in connection with the creation of a new kind of being such as the cyborg.

Jommy's mother is more skillful than him. She can traverse spaces and untwine faraway reverberations into comprehensible caricatures. As they enter the centropolis, the secret police attempt to capture them and Jommy tries to keep pace with his mother. The thoughts of his mother pierce his brain, "There are some ahead of us now, Jommy, and others coming across the street. You'll have to go, darling. Don't forget what I've told you. You live for one thing only- to make it possible for slans to live normal lives" (Vogt, *Slan* 9). The slans can live peacefully only if their opponent, the autocrat, Kier Gray is killed.

Jommy is abducted by the agents of the secret police. His mind encounters a series of reflections of people who contact and inform the police about a boy being seized by occupants in a car. He can read the minds of the men who are seated inside the car. A heavy-built man named, John Petty, the leader of the secret police of Kier Gray, makes an effort to guard his contemplations. Despite that, he can read the undercurrent of his thoughts that states about killing a slan girl named Kathleen Layton so that the authoritarian, Kier Gray can be enfeebled. Sam Enders, the chauffeur and guard to John Petty requests the chief to go on a search for the Slan named, Jommy Cross. As Jommy tries to flee before the car stops, he is hit by the rear end of the car. He attempts to run past an old lady and secrets himself near an empty space. Enders makes an effort to shoot the boy but misses his aim. John Petty warns, "Enders, do you realize that we left Capital and Main ten minutes ago? That boy- There he is! Shoot him, you fool" (Vogt, *Slan* 11)! John Petty orders the headquarters to border the district with police and soldiers at Fifty-seventh Street to capture the little shrimp. "We've got to surround the district at Fifty-seventh

Street. Concentrate every police car and get the soldiers out to" (Vogt, *Slan* 11).

The whole world around him becomes blurred and lusterless. Jommy stumbles through the dark storehouse. The street has become deserted. He fails to peruse the indistinct thoughts that are crept forward from the gloomy buildings. He hauls himself down and the night becomes darker as he contends across the pavement. Many people are behind him as they are enticed by the news of getting rewarded with ten thousand dollars, who could get hold of the slan. He is terrified of being thwacked by the mob with brooms and sticks. He vigorously makes his way towards a space that unfolds to the earth. Although it is annoying for him, he adjusts himself inside a hole. The police force searches for him in every nook and cranny. While he does his utmost to get out of the stringent site, he is banged by the thought of the presence of a person. He is grasped by an old woman and utters with shrillness, "Granny'll take care of you, she will. Granny's smart" (Vogt, *Slan* 14). The old woman tries to control her thoughts as she knows that slans are efficient in reading the minds of other people.

She believes that "because slans can read thoughts, she kept mind very still, thinking only of cooking" (Vogt, *Slan* 14). The rapacious old lady hits his head with a stick and he is dragged towards a tottering old cart. Then, he is spirited away by the avaricious old dame.

The institutor of the Society for Psychical Research, Frederick Myers, has devised the expression, 'Telepathy'. He suggests that the connection of one mind with the other is feasible in the absence of any intervention of the body. This operation can travel over large regions and can connect to other beings to sense them regardless of any material contact. He puts forth that, "all cases of impressions received at a distance without the operation of the recognized sense organs" (147). It is generally the assimilation of the notion of intuition. Consequently, it is apparent that the idea of Telepathy allows one to comprehend the mind of other humans with the help of mental linkages bereft of the use of any indicator or language (147).

While in the palace of Kier Gray, Kathleen Layton is captivated, when she views the sprawling city from a distance. The conurbation seems colourless and dead in the twilight. The buildings and effusive water of the river appear unilluminated in that sunless sphere. A slan named, Davy Dinsmore stands beside her but she is disinterested in him. As, it has been a long time since she has used the slan way of reading the minds of people, having mental correspondence regarding human contemplations, human aspirations and human hatred. "Entering that brain in its present state would sicken her outlook for a month" (Vogt, *Slan* 17). Dinsmore says that Kier Gray wants Kathleen to be killed on her eleventh birthday. "Mr. Kier Gray had to promise the cabinet that he'd have you killed on your eleventh birthday. And don't think they won't do it, either. They killed a slan woman in the street the other day" (Vogt, *Slan* 17). Three years ago, Kathleen was bullied by Davy Dinsmore in the presence of his mother but the all-powerful, Kier Gray made an appearance and declared that "Kathleen Layton is a property of the State, and in due course, the State will dispose of her" (Vogt, *Slan* 17). This implies that she will be killed in the meantime.

Robert Jastrow in his book 'Post-Human Intelligence' expresses that Posthumanism is unrelated not to the augmentation of humans rather it is transcending humans with the help of informatics. His article begins with a survey on the uniqueness of man's intellect that has a resemblance with a few commentaries stated in the writings based on transhumanism. He describes that the Australopithecus have differentiated themselves from the primates due to their larger size of the brain, "and that our own ancestor, Homo, with whom Australopithecus co-existed for a while and who saw the size of its brain increase even more – which might explain why our ancestor species survived our cousin's" (12). "The correlation between the size of the brain and the survival and development of the species worked, until then, in favour of the humans, but Jastrow argues that the species is on the verge of being surpassed. Since the size of our brain has not grown significantly in the past hundred thousand years, we may have reached the end of our evolution (16), and the so-called "posthuman intelligence" will in fact be achieved by computers. The computers available in the 1970s have not measured up to the human brain yet; they surely work faster, but do not have much memory capacity and cannot form connections similarly to the brain. Nevertheless, Jastrow contemplates future computer development, based on the speed of previous development (from the 1950s onwards) and concludes that the memory and reasoning capacities of artificial intelligence might eventually exceed ours, by far (18). Jastrow mentions several studies, but only one of them is shared by scholarship of the posthuman; by way of conclusion, Jastrow indeed quotes "the leader in artificial intelligence research" (18).

In the novel, Kathleen returns from her reverie and goes to her private room. She wakes up anxiously from her sleep. Her slan tendrils heave distinctly from her hair and oscillate gently with the wave of air. The tendrils appear like thin filaments of brightened gold shimmering dully in the twilight against the black hair that covers her plain and youthful appearance. The intimidating musings that trickle from the palace percolate through those delicate antennas. Kathleen wakes up from her sleep, quivering. "There remained only a dim confusion of mind pictures that washed in a never-ending stream from the countless rooms of the vast palace" (Vogt, *Slan* 18). The reflection of thought remains in her mind for a short duration. The thought is about the execution of Kathleen Layton. And, this rumination is possible on the part of the chief of secret police and anti-slan, Mr. Kier Gray or any of his henchmen. Kier Gray brutally hates her. This contemplation trembles her brain and her life is at stake. "...the memory of its horrors had not dimmed. Yet the reality was worse than the memory. Grimly, with an almost mature persistence, she held herself in that storm of mind vibration, fighting to isolate each individual pattern in turn" (Vogt, *Slan* 19).

Thoughts hover over Kathleen's mind, driven by a sense of insistence. An indubitable kaleidoscope is carved that is significant of multitudinous intrigues, misadventures and nightmares of people with psychological insinuations. The deadliness of the thought is so controlling that it rowels Kathleen to hopelessness. At the present moment, she is aware that the man who is going to assassinate her has been trying to evade her for a long time. "His thoughts were so carefully diffused, deliberately flashing to a thousand different subjects, seeming simply overtones to the confusion of mind noises all around" (Vogt, *Slan* 19). The assassin enters her bed chamber as she lies on her bed. She lays still with the slightest motion and her life is at the mercy of this man. She interprets the thoughts of the brutal creature. His thoughts to murder her flashed before he could disseminate them. She comes to know his purpose as he pushes himself up the carpeted flooring and bends over her. She tosses the blankets over the killer and moves out of the bed. She scampers and utters, "Do you actually believe that you can catch a slan in the darkness" (Vogt, *Slan* 21)? The murderer follows the voice and she slips through a paneled door to the luxurious office room of the omnipotent, Mr Kier Gray. Gray was seated at a desk and was occupied in writing a letter near the desk lamp. "As he wrote, she was able to follow the surface of his thoughts" (Vogt, *Slan* 21).

Kathleen screams that a man John Petty, the chief of secret police, is trying to kill her. Overhearing this possibility, Kier Gray responds with utter astonishment, "John Petty's bid for supreme power. I almost feel sorry for the man, he is so blind to his own shortcomings. No chief of secret police has ever held the confidence of a people. I am worshipped and feared; he is only feared. And he thinks that all-important" (Vogt, *Slan* 22). His intention of murdering Kier Gray before a certain date will diminish the standing of Kier Gray in the council. John Petty tries to dishonour Gray with the council by circulating the notion that Gray wants to keep Kathleen alive so that he can replace Gray politically.

Kathleen overtly makes a rejoinder, "He's a fool to go against you, that's what I think. And I'll help you all I can. I can help, with reading minds and things" (Vogt, *Slan* 22). Kier Gray replies with contempt that they (human beings) are at times weird to the Slans. They are filled with hatred that resulted in a war between humans and slans long ago. He adds that the Intelligence Quotient of an adult slan is two to three hundred times higher than that of a normal human. Kier Gray orders Kathleen to stay in his office chamber and read the minds of John Petty and other council members who are going to arrive at the moment for an investigation regarding the attempt to kill Kathleen before the notified date.

Kathleen sits in between the group of council members. The men observe her with detestation. They want her to be killed. John Petty protests the presence of Kathleen in the meeting as her childish appearance might fill anyone with mercy. John Petty utters that, "Because she's a slan, and by heaven, I won't have a slan sitting in the same room with me" (Vogt, *Slan* 24)! She tries to decipher his mind but it appears to be unclear and his face is expressionless. "She caught the faintest overtone of irony, and realized that John Petty understood the situation perfectly. This was his bid for power; and his whole body and brain were alert and deadly with the tremendousness of the knowledge" (Vogt, *Slan* 24).

Kier Gray retorts that Kathleen is present here not for trial but to give proof regarding John Petty's attempt to murder her. To this, Kathleen examines the mind of John Petty and concludes that his mind is calm and alert. Petty retaliates, "And, once and for all, I think we should settle right now the juridical problem of whether a slan's word can be taken as evidence of any kind" (Vogt, *Slan* 25). Kier Gray angrily responds that John Petty is trying to make this offer in order to win and replace the political standing of Kier Gray.

The stillness in the room makes Kathleen curious. For a little while, the ponderings of the occupants in the room had become obscure. It appeared as if a blockade had been created between their mind and hers, "for their brains worked on deep, deep inside them, exploring, gauging chances, analyzing the situation, tensing against a suddenly realized, deadly danger" (Vogt, *Slan* 26). Kathleen acts according to Kier Gray's thoughts as he commands her to move to the seat that is present in the corner of the oak-panelled room so that she shall be invisible to the members present in the chamber. At the present moment, Kathleen can't show her telepathic abilities as the minds of men are controlled and their whole attention focuses on what should be said and done.

Sandor Ferenczi, the psychoanalyst from Hungary, elucidates that tenseness nourishes the fecundity of conveying telepathic information while the calm mind enhances its potential to acquire messages. Apart from this, the recipient answers in an insensate way to the transmission of thoughts and actualizes those heedless outcomes that are closer to the unconscious system of the transmitter. His ideas focus on the significance of psychical or brainy research to the field of psychoanalytic theory and the relevance of psychoanalysis in psychical or brainy research. His ideas on telepathy merge with the practice of psychoanalysis through the belief 'dialogue of the unconscious' that can be generated between two nearer beings, where, "the unconscious of two people completely understand themselves and each other, without the remotest conception of this on the part of the consciousness of either" (109).

Kier Gray responds with a vague countenance, it gives the impression that this is not merely an altercation for power between Petty and Gray but it has something more to it. One who possesses the supreme power epitomizes both order and a sense of stability and the one who nevertheless wants it, when he accomplishes it, tries to secure his position. He establishes order on those who are in opposition to him. "This means executions, exiles, confiscations, imprisonment, torture" (Vogt, *Slan* 26).

According to Kier Gray, Petty cannot diminish

himself to a subordinate position. Analogous to Napoleon and Stalin, he remains an all-time danger. Therefore, he is attempting to make him a disciplined person. "But a would-be leader can simply be disciplined and put back on his job. And that is my plan for John Petty" (Vogt, *Slan* 26). With regards to this, John Petty yells, he has no such intention of splitting into two groups when the situation of failure in slanizing the human babies is awful. The attempt of the slans "to slanize the human race, with its resultant horrible failures, is the greatest problem that has confronted a government" (Vogt, *Slan* 27). John Petty adds at that moment that Kier Gray should resign from his position and this is supported by other council members.

Kier Gray angrily reiterates that there is hardly any scientist who can match the abilities of the super scientists owned by the slans. Peter Cross, a slan was imprudently assassinated three years ago by the cop who seized him but was influenced by the psychology of the mob as they are petrified at the thought of their infants being slanized. Kier Gray adds that there can be a possibility that the discoveries of human scientists will be taken over by the slans or the slans can endeavour to gain control of the world:

> What incentive is there for a human being to spend a lifetime in research when in his mind is the deadening knowledge that all the discoveries he can hope to make have long since been perfected by the slans? That they're waiting out there somewhere in secret caves, or written out on paper, ready for the day when the slans make their next attempt to take over the world (Vogt, *Slan* 28)?

Kier Gray with dark passion stated further, "Our

science is a joke, our education a mass of lies. And every year the wreck of human aspirations and human hopes piles higher around us. Every year there's greater dislocation, more poverty, more misery. Nothing is left to us but hatred, and hatred isn't enough. We've either got to terminate the slans or make terms with them and end this madness" (Vogt, *Slan* 28).

Kathleen perceives that Gray's mind is filled with peace and tranquillity. He restates that Kathleen should be kept alive as a subject for examination. By executing her, Gray's political reputation might be at stake and this is the thing that John Petty wants so that he can replace Kier Gray politically. "She will be kept alive as a study subject. I, personally, am determined to make the best of her continued presence by observing the development of a slan to maturity. I have already made a tremendous body of notes on the subject" (Vogt, *Slan* 29).

Kathleen discerns the brains of the occupants in the room which makes her mind weak as she becomes aware of the truth. She believes that the men support the leader rather their minds are filled with apprehension as Kier Gray is going to leave his seat and now, they have better sport with the young, burgeoning group. One of the three sitting there who is in unquestioning support of Gray, Mardue says, he cannot declare herself as the dictator as he has been elected by the council and now, he can be expelled if the council wishes so. "we have a perfect right to elect someone in your place. Someone, perhaps, who will be more successful in organizing the extermination of the slans" (Vogt, *Slan* 30).

To take control of the situation, Kier Gray commanded that all the eleven officers present in the room would have to confront the firing. With the tremendous firing of the bullets, all the officers one after another wriggle on the ground. Jem Lorry, a man with a dark and crooked face utters that he needs Kier Gray to be an authoritarian to the people. "We need you, your terrific reputation, your brains, and we're willing to help make you a god to the people- in other words, to help consolidate your position and make it unassailable" (Vogt, *Slan* 32).

Jommy Cross wakes up in a dark little dilapidated room. He is chained to the odious bed in his ankle. When he rises from the bed, he sees a tall and cadaverous woman. The woman vocalizes that Jommy has recovered from fever and now they can have an intense conversation. Jommy has a glimpse of her thin, oval head with the brain of the woman. "Every twisted line in that wrecked face had its counterpart in the twisted brain. A whole world of lechery dwelt within the confines of that shrewd mind" (Vogt, *Slan* 34). Seeing his demeanor, the old lady retorts that Granny was once a popular beauty. And, she has saved Jommy's life.

Sigmund Freud in his *Dreams and the Occult* admits the presence of telepathy in the transmission of thoughts by which the expert and the patient appear to respond to the occurrences in the other being's life. He exclusively puts forth that a physical phenomenon occurs between the two minds that later takes the form of a psychical phenomenon.

Jommy explores the mind of the woman and tries to discover her actual name. There is a sequence of images of an imbecilic stage-struck young lady, with the dissipation of glamour, debased to a lower level, knocked down by misadventures and a panorama of offence photographed in her brain. He tries to extract himself from the obscenity of Granny's brain. The old lady asks whether slan can read minds. Jommy answers that he can see what she is thinking at the present moment. But, when slans are unwell they sleep for a long time. The reason why he is awake is because he thinks that his life is at risk. "...forced me awake because it thought I was in danger. We slans have a lot of protections like that. But now I've got to go back to sleep and get well" (Vogt, *Slan* 35).

Burning with curiosity, the old lady wants to know whether slans create monsters out of humans. Jommy answers with rage, "It's one of those horrible lies those human beings talk about us to make us seem inhuman, to make everybody hate us, kill us" (Vogt, *Slan* 35). He narrates his childhood days when his father and mother met on the street and discovered that they were slans. They never put anyone in danger. The humans cornered and shot him dead. He could have retaliated but he failed to do so. He owned the strongest weapon anyone has come across. "...so terrible he wouldn't even carry it with him for fear he might use it" (Vogt, *Slan* 36). Jommy concluded with this as he cannot disclose the secret of the weapon.

To keep Jommy awake, the lady went on interrogating, "What is a slan? What makes you different? Where did slans come from in the first place? They were made, weren't they-like machines" (Vogt, *Slan* 36)? Jommy answered in the negative. The old woman pressed on the matter that Granny wanted the slan to make money for her. "Life's too hard for old Granny- too hard. If you won't help Granny, she'll have to go on doing other things" (Vogt, *Slan* 37). He agreed to stay with them and help Granny acquire the riches of the world as this "would make an ideal retreat for a slan boy who had to wait at least six years before he could visit the hiding-place of his father's secrets; who had to grow up before he could hope to carry out the great things that had to be done" (Vogt, *Slan* 37).

Jommy passes through a garden where a tower had

been constructed by the slans, "only to have it fall to the victors after the war of disaster" (Vogt, *Slan* 38). He had resided near the city for the last nine years but had never come across the glorious accomplishment of his clan that is presently captivated by Kier Gray and his crew. He recollects his mother's words, "Human beings will never know all the secrets of that building. There are mysteries there, forgotten rooms and passages, hidden wonders that even the slans no longer know about, except in a vague way. Kier Gray doesn't realize it, but all the weapons and machines the human beings have searched for so desperately are buried right in that building" (Vogt, *Slan* 39). Jommy's thoughts are disturbed by Granny's voice who declares angrily that this palace is not for the slans and further commands him to follow her.

As he moves in that rickety old card accompanied by Granny and the old lady, thoughts hammer his brain. He enters the jewellery store and makes an effort to take away the pendant that is labelled with fifty-five dollars. But he could detect the exasperation and hostility in the brain of the marketer seeing a kid enter the store. As he walks through the store, he stumbles into a retreating man. He is filled with surprise when he realizes that the strong-built man is an adult slan. He rapidly treads on the heels of the man and struggles to penetrate through the man's mind but fails incessantly. It is shocking for him to comprehend that the stranger is a slan "who couldn't read minds, yet guarded his own brain from being read" (Vogt, *Slan* 41). Jommy runs after the slan stranger as he leads his way to the Air Center.

The inclination to land up at the stars has thrust the astronomers to review the evolution of cosmic energies. It initially started by seeing through bare eyes and later optical telescopes have been used by scientists to keep track of the interstellar. The mechanism of orbits and the movement of stars are observed by scientists using satellite mechanics. Space voyaging has become possible with Voyager I and II. Astronomers are travelling to outer space to gain information regarding the exoplanets and stars. These technologies are quite common in this novel.

The region of the Air Center is governed by the whole aircraft manufacturing around the globe. He stops near the door of the Air Center as the stranger slan disappears from the place. This is the region from where the slans work and govern the greatest transport in the cosmos. The place is occupied by thousands of slans. As he moves forward, he encounters two bareheaded and tendrilless slans. "His gaze searched almost frantically for the golden strands of tendril that should have been there. Tendrilless slans! So that was it! That explained they couldn't read minds" (Vogt, *Slan* 42).

There are two varieties of slans, one with golden-colored tendrils and the other, with no tendrils. The slans possessing tendrils on their head have many psychic abilities. They can spot and telepathically commune with other slans. At the same time, they can also read the mind of humans. But the tendrilless slans lack any psychic ability. They can hide their thought process from the slans possessing tendrils. The first category of Slans can be assassinated to near extermination. Both types of slans have enormous intelligence.

When the two tendrilless slans try to capture Jommy, he runs to a door in the corridor and shuts it from the other side. After saving his life from the second type of slans, he tries to read their thoughts. One of them whispered, "If the snakes find out we control Airways" (Vogt, *Slan* 44). Jommy ran with all his might. It was dark outside and a torpedo-shaped spaceship plunged into the sky. It gleamed for a moment and was lost in the space. In utter astonishment, Jommy remarked, "Had these tendrilless slans realized the dream of the ages- to operate flights to the planets? If so, how had they kept it secret from human beings? And what were the true slans doing" (Vogt, *Slan* 45)? The only thing that is important for him at the moment is to reach Granny's cottage.

Granny vanishes for several days to pay a visit to her pleasurable retreats. Jommy takes care of her by preparing meals for her. He obtains his education which is not quite easy on his part. Many residents near Granny's house dislike her for her antagonistic attitude and sharp tongue. A neighbor named Mrs Hardy's husband lost all her money in a bet. She has travelled to Asia and Europe and gained much information regarding the Slan wars. A cynic and lonely man who was once a History professor named Darrett talked over the Slan war. "I tell you a hundred thousand slans practically took over the world. It was a beautiful job of planning carried out with utmost boldness" (Vogt, *Slan* 49). Darrett adds:

> The world was confused and bewildered. Everywhere human babies were being subjected to the tremendous campaign of the slans to make more slans. Civilization began to break down. There was an immense increase in insanity. Suicide, murder, crime- the graph of chaos rose to new heights. And, one morning, without knowing quite how it was done, the human race woke up to discover that overnight the enemy had taken control. Working from within, the

slans had managed to take over innumerable key organizations. When you learn to understand the rigidity of institutional structures in our society, you'll realize how helpless human beings were at first. (Vogt, *Slan* 50)

Not only Darrett, Jommy follows the minds of other men in the streets. He lays himself in hiding and telepathically follows the lectures of learned men. He reads all the sciences like Mathematics, Physics, and Astronomy but these are not enough for him to suffice his mental faculty. From nine years to his fifteenth birthday, he procures every single thing that is necessary to become an adult slan.

During those six years, he keeps an eye on the tendrilless slans at a distance. The spaceships vault over the sky regularly and at midnight shark-shaped monsters tumble down from space over the same building. All those years space traffic ceased only two times, one for a month and the period when Mars orbited the Sun. He refrains from keeping any kind of contact with the Air Center. As time passes by, his admiration for the strength of the tendrilless slans develops. He abandons himself to the different kinds of physical activity till his fifteenth birthday when he delves into the catacombs and becomes the authoritarian of his father's inventions. "This was the day- long ago it had been planted in his mind, hypnotically set by his father. It did seem important, however, that he slip out of the house without the old woman's hearing him" (Vogt, *Slan* 51).

The night is quite still without any movement. He listlessly moves towards the entrance of the catacombs that has been his aim from the outset. He directs himself to a side street when he overhears a man's voice roaring raucously, "Final warning- get off the street! Get out of sight. The mysterious airship of the slans is now approaching the city at terrific speed. It is believed the ship is heading toward the palace. Interference has been set up on all radio waves, to prevent any of the slan lies from being broadcast. Get off the streets! Here comes the ship" (Vogt, *Slan* 52)!

Jommy is amazed when he visualizes a silver spark in the airspace. There was a jarring of guns in the avenue. "...a long, winged torpedo of glittering metal hurtled by straight above" (Vogt, *Slan* 53). The spaceship seemed like a sparkling point as it headed to the palace. Jommy was filled with bewilderment, "A winged ship! Scores of nights during these past six years he had watched the spaceships soar up from the building in the tendrilless slan Air Center. Wingless rocket ships, and something more. Something that made great metal machines lighter than air. The rocket part seemed to be used only for propulsion. The weightlessness, the way they were flung up as if by centrifugal force, must be antigravity! And here was a winged ship, with all that implied; jet engines, rigid confinement to Earth's atmosphere, ordinariness. If this was the best the true slans could do, then" (Vogt, *Slan* 53).

He passes many locked doors to find the lock of the steel-barred door leading the way to the catacombs. He opened one of the doors and dived down the steps. Soon, an alarm bell rang that was made up of photoelectric cells for protection against slans and other intruders. Yet, none of the guards did appear for an investigation. "On and on it clanged, and still there was no clamor of approaching minds, not the faintest wisp of thought" (Vogt, *Slan* 53).

Jommy moves speedily although he is unaware of his way. A picture is hypnotized into his mind by his father in the past so that he can act following the promptings of the subconscious mind. A keen mental remark commands him to move to the right. He lays hold of the narrow fork and comes back to the place where he can hide himself. At the hiding place, he finds a metal box and takes it out with his trembling fingers. He struggles to imagine his father hiding before the slab to conceal the secret for the future so that his son can find. "This thing might be a cosmic moment in the history of slans, this moment when the work of a dead father was passed on to a fifteen-year-old boy who had waited so many thousands of minutes and hours and days for this second to come" (Vogt, *Slan* 54). At that moment, Jommy could sense thoughts of people nearing him. The vibrations are like, "It's probably someone who ran down when the slan ship came, trying to get away from expected bombs" (Vogt, *Slan* 54). Jommy desperately investigates the metal box for its opening. His hypnotic subconscious mind commands him to get all the contents and places the vacant box back in the pit.

Inside the box, there is a metal rod placed on top of the papers. It measures two inches in the middle and narrow at its ends. There is a button at the end of the bulb. It glimmers so efficiently with its own light that there is enough light for him to read the paper underneath. A note is written on the paper, "This is the weapon. Use it only in case of absolute necessity" (Vogt, *Slan* 55).

Jommy had become so engaged in his work that he couldn't know the guards had already arrived. In the past six years, this is for the first time when he faces the real danger of being a slan. To save himself, he presses the button without any hesitation. If any of the guards fired a bullet, it would be lost "in the roar of white flame that flashed with inconceivable violence from the mouth of the tube of force. One moment they were alive, rough-built, looming shapes, threatening him; the net, they were gone, snuffed out by that burst of virulent fire" (Vogt, *Slan* 55). Jommy trembles with fear at his course of action of taking the life of three humans. As he recovers from this bolt out of the blue, he finds that the passageway is entirely vacant. "Not a bone, not a piece of flesh or clothing remained to show that there had ever been living beings in the vicinity" (Vogt, *Slan* 56). Jommy is not filled with remorse as he knows these men killed his parents and due to the miserable lies, that they kept on circulating, led to the homicide of countless other slans. He recollects a night when his father had stated, that the slans can be the strongest but the difficulty is "what to do with human beings remains a barrier to occupation of the world. Until that problem is settled with justice and psychological sanity, the use of force would be a black crime" (Vogt, *Slan* 56). This implies that a slan can never use force against a human.

Jommy attempts to get out of the place. He slides the gun and papers into his coat pockets and places the metal box back where it was kept before. Clasping the weapon, he moves forward cautiously. As he goes to the busy street, there is a long-standing crowd. It is uncertain whether the slan ship had arrived or not. From the palace, Kier Gray repeatedly passes statements:

> The extraordinary appearance of the slan ship has not altered the respective positions of slans and human beings in the slightest degree. We control the situation absolutely. Human beings outnumber slans probably millions to one; and, under such circumstances, they will never dare come out in an open, organized campaign against us. So be easy in your hearts. (Vogt, *Slan* 57)

Jommy patiently waits there for some additional

information regarding the slans. At last, he walks down the pavement and reaches Granny's cottage.

Davy Dinsmore forages Kathleen Layton for courtship. As he tries to kiss her, he is heckled by Jem Lorry, the most powerful commissioner in Kier Gray's cabinet. Jem Lorry wants to make Kathleen his paramour. But, she protests, "I don't like human beings. I don't like you" (Vogt, *Slan* 63). She added that Kier Gray is her defender. A voice came from Jem Lorry's broadcast radio:

> General warning! An unidentified aircraft was seen a few minutes ago, crossing the Rocky Mountains, headed eastward. Pursuing machines were rapidly outdistanced, and the ship seemed to be taking a straight-line course toward Centropolis. People are ordered to go home immediately, as the ship- believed now to be of slan origin- will be here in one hour, according to present indications. The streets are needed for military purposes. Go home! (Vogt, *Slan* 63)

After the speaker signs off, Jem Lorry acknowledges that a single ship cannot transport major munitions, lest it has a bunch of factories supporting it. The old-fashioned atomic bomb cannot perhaps be constructed in a cavern. This is also not used by slans in a slan-human war. After an hour of conversation between Jem Lorry and Kathleen, a silver spaceship tilts towards the palace. As it comes nearer, a metallic capsule falls from it on the pavement to the garden. It lay shimmering like a precious stone under the sun. Then the spaceship sparkles in the sky and then vanishes within seconds. Thenceforth, Kathleen fabricates that she is in a secret mental alliance with the captain of the slan's space ship and she can unquestionably interpret the messages that are present in the capsule dropped by the spaceship so that she can refrain the councillors from handing her to Jem Lorry.

She fails to read their minds as she enters the room where the councillors are seated. Kier Gray's voice fills the room, "that not only this organized million exist, but there is, in addition, a vast total of unorganized men and women slans, estimated at ten million more. What about that, Petty" (Vogt, *Slan* 65)?

John Petty, the chief of the secret police answers:
> Undoubtedly there are some unorganized slans. We catch about a hundred a month all over the world, who have apparently never been part of any organization. In vast areas of the more primitive parts of the Earth, the people cannot be roused to antipathy to slans; in fact, they accept them as human beings. And there are no doubt large colonies in some of these remote places, particularly in Asia, Africa, South America and Australia. (Vogt, *Slan* 65)

Nowadays, only a few colonies exist and they have practised self-defence to a great extent. If these plans withdraw to the outskirts of the Earth they vanquish themselves as they are disconnected from books and intellectual minds that will lead to their better development. He adds, "The danger is not from these remote slans but from those living in the big cities, where they are enabled to contact the greatest human minds and have, in spite of our precautions, some access to books. Obviously, this airship we saw today was built by slans who are living dangerously in the civilized centers" (Vogt, *Slan* 66).

Kier Gray agrees with the statement given by John

Petty. He further states that, the letter contained in the metallic capsule talks about the million slans who want to end the rift that has subsisted between slans and humans. They condemn their goal of ruling the world that defines the first slans, elucidating the idea that "ambition as due to a false conception of superiority, unleavened by the later experience that convinced them that they are not superior but merely different" (Vogt, *Slan* 66). They also hold Samuel Lann, the human biological scientist responsible for this. Samuel Lann is the first creator of Slans. They have also got their names from Samuel Lann: S. Lann: Slan. In addition to this, he has stimulated the notion in his creation that they will rule the world soon. They also claim that their philosophers have concluded that these slans are unscientific beings and they haven't produced any exquisite inventions in physical science. Kier Gray continues with the last page of the letter that affirms that Slans cannot overpower the military capability of humans. "Whatever improvements we may make on existing machinery and weapons will not decisively affect the outcome of a war, should such a disaster ever take place again" (Vogt, *Slan* 67). The letter ends with a negotiation of a peace treaty so that the slans "must hereafter have the legal right to life, liberty and the pursuit of happiness" (Vogt, *Slan* 67). After reading the letter, Kier Gray declares that there is no question of compromise and that all slans in the entire globe should be assassinated.

Due to the behavioral, phylogenetic and biological intersections between the human and the nonhuman, the groups together have an extraordinary significance. This feature is obvious in the entire novel. Furthermore, Kathleen is appalled to hear these words from Kier Gray. Within no time, Jem Lorry is on Kier Gray's feet asking for forgiveness. He insists, "I am left no alternative but to state- with qualifications, however- that I am in favor of accepting this offer. My main qualification is this- the slans must agree to be assimilated into the human race. To that end, slans cannot marry each other, but must always marry human beings" (Vogt, *Slan* 68). Kier Gray concedes the idea and clarifies the plan of action, firstly, to get associated with humans they should initially be identified. The slans must be caught and kept as captives. Secondly, they must be forced to settle on an island at the outset. Once they have gathered, they will be bordered by planes and battleships and slaughtered. Thirdly, they must be strained to carry out fingerprinting and their photographs must be taken to inform the police headquarters in the interim.

Finally, Kier Gray mutters, the slan-human mating requires testing. Multitudinous case studies of slan-human attempts to procreate babies are within easy reach in the library under the title 'Abnormal Marriages'. The men and slans appear similar to a certain extent. The slans are more muscular due to the quickening of the process of electro-explosions that activate the muscle. The two hearts can operate independently of the other with easy pumps. The tendrils that telepathically send and receive information are practised by humans everywhere. He continues, "What Samuel Lann did with his mutation machine to his wife, who bore him the first three slan babies- one body and two girls- over six hundred years ago, has not added anything new to the human body, but changed or mutated what already existed" (Vogt, *Slan* 73). For his experiment, Samuel Lann brings up the babies of the three creatures- monkey, slan and human under extreme scientific constraints. The baby monkey develops learning abilities faster than the slan and human baby.

The human baby and slan baby try to communicate faster than the monkey baby. The slan baby develops telepathy soon. The quickness of the brain is seen in slan babies but human baby excels in education. This faculty of telepathy i.e., reading the minds of people is advantageous to a slan baby. It gives him an insight into the psychology and easy ingress to education. But, in case of a human baby, it fails to have a hold over eyes and ears. This makes the slan a distinguishing figure.

Scores of men come near Granny's cottage with submachine guns for an encounter as a human who is found sheltering a slan must be hanged to death. He carries the old woman to the roof of the building. He becomes extremely tired. They enter the building and run to its centre to take control of the airship. He takes out the atomic gun from his pocket. Both Jommy and Granny mount the airship. He sees dozens of tendrilless slans sitting inside the ship. The ship leaves the building and then the city.

An adult tendrilless slan named Joanna Hillory fires a bullet from the doorway that hits the instrument board. She rigidly stands there as she sees his gun aiming at her. Despite her anger, she is filled with beauty. Her sight reminds him of his mother which compels him to leave her alive. She is married to an engineer on Mars and is now impregnated by him. She is assigned the duty of space travel as this would put minimum pressure on her body. She utters, "So you swallowed all that about my being a poor little bride, with a baby coming and an anxious husband waiting! A full-grown snake wouldn't have been so credulous. As it is, the young snake I'm looking at will die for his incredible stupidity" (Vogt, *Slan* 84).

Jommy's mind becomes blank at the realization of his defeat by this witty lady. The lady starts interrogating

Jommy's age, which he answered as fifteen. She gestures that Jommy is at a phase of mental development. And, as long as he answers her questions, she will not use her electric gun. Without wasting any time, Jommy says what if he doesn't speak the truth. The lady smiles and restates, "Truth is implicit in the cleverest lies. We tendrilless slans, lacking the ability to read minds, have been forced by necessity to develop psychology to the utmost limits" (Vogt, *Slan* 86).

Johanna Hillory adds as a further remark that the slans with tendrils "wouldn't betray us because they wouldn't want our greatest invention, the spaceships" (Vogt, *Slan* 86). She continues to speak with her charming voice that the tendrilless slans have traversed the Venus, the Mars and the Moon but they have never come across any slan or spaceship. Although the slans are alert by reading minds, they do not possess antigravity screens for the creation of a rocketship and they are deprived of space travel.

She also talks about the slan war that the tendrilless slans have been living in for four hundred years. They hide themselves in remote areas so that they cannot be discovered by anyone. They developed friendly relations with the true slans against their mutual opponent- the human beings. No sooner their solitary civilization is demolished by slans with tendrils. The tendrilless slans attempt to make peace with the true slans but it is nonetheless fruitless. Eventually, they realize that they are safe in the extremely threatening, human-dominated cities as the true slans with revealing tendrils did not dare to intervene. As a result, a single inhabitation of the true slans is not found anywhere.

The tendrilless slans consider the true slans superior because of their ability to read minds. As a consequence of this, Johanna cannot allow Jommy Cross to escape from being killed. She belabours, "Your youth has saved you for ten minutes, but now that I know your story, I can see no purpose in keeping you alive" (Vogt, *Slan* 89). In the control room of the spaceship, Jommy Cross assures Johanna that the true slans will never act against the tendrilless slans. Jommy Cross, being the son of Peter Cross, is most important than any other slan. As a further remark, he adds, "The day that I find the true slans, the war against your people will end forever. You have said that my escape would be disaster for the tendrilless slans, rather, it will be their greatest victory" (Vogt, *Slan* 99).

Jommy unfastens Johanna and adjusts the antigravity plates for a safe landing. Then, the rocketship lands on the ground and the city lights are visible during dawn. The woman asks Jommy about how he feels about death at the moment. He answers:

> The nervous system of a slan is an almost impregnable fortress. It cannot really be touched by insanity or 'nerves' or fear. When we kill, it is because of policy arrived at through logic. When death approaches our personal lives, we accept the situation, fight to the last in the hope of an unpredictable factor turning up to save us, and finally, reluctantly, give up the ghost, conscious that we have not lived in vain. (Vogt, *Slan* 100)

Following his reply, Johanna proclaims that she believes his story and it is for the first time that she has met a slan who is very idealistic. She begs him not to betray them with slaughter and destruction. She also utters not to test their patience as "it is suspicion, not tolerance, that rules us. But now, good bye" (Vogt, *Slan* 101).

After bidding adieu, Mrs. Hillory leaves the place and the ship accelerates towards the periphery of the city. In Granny's laboratory which is located near the farm, Jommy studies his father's projects and discoveries. He equips himself with the required skills to command the illimitable energy that he possesses for both slans and humans. He tracks down the fact that his father's innovation ensues from two facts. The origin of power can be scaled down to minute kernels of matter and the outcome may not be a semblance of heat. It can be transmogrified to motion, vibration, radiation and electricity as well.

He indulges in building weapons and other equipment. He converts a mountain into a fortress, bearing in mind that this would be insufficient against any attack. Countless days pass as he loiters around the cities in search of true slans but he cannot find only the tendrilless slans. In the newspapers, there are only articles on the tendrilless slans.

Kathleen Layton eagerly waits for the council meeting so that she can have easy access to Kier Gray's study room. While examining the papers on his study table, she gets trapped. Subsequently, Kier Gray and John Petty enter the room. They interrogate her presence in Kier Gray's chamber. The chief of the secret police, John Petty, recapitulates that Kathleen is going to turn twenty-one and by all means she is going to become an adult. He asks Gray, "Is she to live on here until she eventually dies of old age a hundred and fifty or some such fantastic term of years of from now" (Vogt, *Slan* 110)?

John Petty states further that Kathleen is a threat to the state and therefore he wants her to be out of this place to which Kier Gray agrees. He orders Kathleen, "gather your clothes and possessions and prepare yourself for departure in twenty-four hours" (Vogt, *Slan* 111).

As Jommy Cross travels to the far south, he can see policemen searching for a true slan girl. He becomes hopeful of the presence of a true slan and purposefully moves in the direction of the thought that flickers in his mind, "Attention, slans! This is a Porgrave thought-broad-casting machine. Please turn up the side road half a mile ahead. A further message will be given later" (Vogt, *Slan* 114).

He becomes excited after realizing the fact that slans might be present somewhere near him. He crosses the pathway that leads him to another message, "This is a Porgrave broadcaster. It directs you, a true slan, to the little farm ahead, which provides entrance to an underground city of factories, gardens and residences. Welcome. This is a Porgrave" (Vogt, *Slan* 115).

Jommy's car crosses the small ridges on the side and arrives at a long stretch of garden covered by weeds. There is an archaic and dilapidated two-storey farmhouse with an outhouse and garage beside it. From the broken doors, a lady with a gray dress comes out whom Jommy identifies as a slan. The slan named Kathleen is astonished and stands there dumbfounded glancing at Jommy. Within no time she frees her mind and lets her thoughts reach him, "We musn't stay here. I've been here too long already. You probably saw in my mind about the police, so the best thing we can do is to drive away immediately" (Vogt, *Slan* 116).

Jommy gets a spark of thought from her mind referring to the machines that are present in the cave city. He assures her that he owns few weapons that are incomparable to the capacity of the humans such as the car in which he has arrived at the farmhouse. He states that this car is made up of ten-point steel and is "a very special means of escape. It can go practically anywhere. I hope there is room for it in the cave" (Vogt, *Slan* 116).

After hearing his response, Kathleen inquired about ten-point steel. With regards to this, Jommy Cross retorts that everything is based on his father's discovery of the "first law of atomic energy- concentration as opposed to the old method of diffusion" (Vogt, *Slan* 117). He points to the fact that "all metals are held together by atomic tensions" which adds to the robustness of the metal" (Vogt, *Slan* 117). In the matter of steel, he renames it as the theoretical potential one-point. When steel was invented, its capacity was about two thousand points and gradually with new procedures its capacity increased to one thousand points.

He thus states further:

> Tendrilless slans have made five-hundred-point steel, but even that incredibly hard stuff cannot compare with the product of my application of atomic strain, which changes the very structure of the atoms and produces the almost perfect ten-point steel. An eighth of an inch of ten-point can stop the most powerful explosive known to human beings and tendrilless slans! (Vogt, *Slan* 117)

He concludes by saying that although an atomic bomb can destroy a huge ship, it cannot even infiltrate the ten-point steel.

As they enter the cave, they see various inoperable machines, saws, and tools lying there. They discuss the secret entrances that lead to this city. Kathleen voices out that, "there are only two entrances given on the list in Kier Gray's desk- and I've located no others" (Vogt, *Slan* 118). Jommy rejoices that this cave is safe for them as the police are searching for the slan.

Jommy looks at Kathleen's dead body in dismay. With a single press of the button, he would have blown

John Petty, the murderer of Kathleen to nothingness but he refrains from doing so. Scores of men with machine guns enter the cave from the secret passageway. He races his car with immense speed as the police organization tries to capture him.

As the human and the non-humans share a significant relationship, the mixing of both species results in relatively huge brains, grasping hands and dynamically unique features. It is noticeable that another novel of A.E. Van Vogt namely, *Supermind*, inculcates these subjects. Steve Hanardy, a sentient human has both humanistic and animalistic demeanour with narrow eyes and a fleshy physiognomy. As a human being, he can think and behave rationally. He is born on one of the moons of Jupiter known as Europa. He blooms as a delirious worker and spacehand on both the merchant and passenger ships that hastens huge quantities of debris from the moons to liveable meteorites of Jupiter. Currently, this region has become an ever-expanding trade zone, adhering to this Hanardy has owned a freighter. He makes the initial trips to a meteorite that Professor Ungarn, a scientist inhabits with his female child named Patricia.

The Posthuman is grouped under the heading which is extracted from progression in automation and technology. These have incessantly fuelled the propagation and rebuilding of man. Taking into consideration such evolution, numerous interrogations have come up regarding the description of humans. Although formerly, the human in the biological sense was considered entirely an outcome of carbon procedures. But presently, human is the result of some procedure based on silicon or bionics. The sector of Information Technology has remodelled the characteristics of human relations as they function closer to the tempo of light.

A philosopher named Serres views the body and humankind as in a constant transformation due to the significant growth in technology that cannot be left unrecognised.

Donna Haraway is focused on puncturing the unscholarly confirmation to the notable oppositions, that contain political inferences in association with biology: male and female, human and animal, fiction and reality, animal and machine, nature and culture, mind and body, science and society. Haraway is popular for imparting a renewed sense of life to a 'cyborg', a being uniting both non-organic, cybernetic and organic characteristics. According to Haraway, the present system consisting of social, political, cultural and economic is succoured by the narrations made by science or constructs designed for self and the cosmos. It also takes under its purview the political stories depicting the inequalities that prevail in the world. The word 'cyborg' is derived from science as Haraway puts it all humans are cyborgs incorporating both organism and machine.

In the novel, Jeel, the Dreegh goes to the control room of the spaceship where a woman named Merla is found lying on the cot. He bents and whispers in her ears that they are decelerating the spaceship. Despite hearing this, she didn't move a bit. Her refined nostrils widen with every single breath. He raised her arm but she lay there like a scrap of spiritless wood. She remains taut and lifeless. He peers into one of her eyes which appear like a darkened eyeless azure. In the calmness of the speeding ship, he contemplates that if he resuscitates her, she will acquire more power to strike him. He injects a drug into her forearm and murmurs through her ears that they have neared a star cluster where they can find blood and life.

After a few minutes, the woman regains her senses.

She miserably stands and asks if there is any galactic on this planet. He answers with a sense of diabolic euphoria, "There are no Galactics out here. But there is an observer. I've been catching the secret ultra signals for the last two hours and warning all ships to stay clear because the system isn't ready for any kind of contact with Galactic planets" (Vogt, *Supermind* 4). Thereafter, he goes near the control board and adjusts the automatics. He mumbles that the signals are supposed to be turning to their highest potential. The lights of the room are dimmed and an image takes shape on the adjacent wall that exhibits a sparkle of light beam amid the starlit sky. The voice plays out from the screen, "This star system contains one inhabited planet, the third from the Sun, called Earth by its dominant race. It was colonized by Galactics about seven thousand years ago in the usual manner. It is now in the third degree of development, having attained a limited form of space travel little more than a hundred years ago" (Vogt, *Supermind* 5).

The man speaks indistinctly that this is a golden opportunity to call upon the Dreegh tribe on the planet Earth so that they can escape from preserving vessels of blood and the 'battery of life' for the sake of attaining immortality. He moves in the direction of the communicator and adjusts the controls to normalise the motion, space and time of the ship. Finally, the ship batters the aerosphere of the third planet. The metals of the ship remain intact and the atmospheric pressure thickens as they farther with each passing mile. Then the woman decelerates the ship in the murkiness of a little alley. They see a series of city lights flashing from a distance. They walk to the residential avenue in the neighbourhood.

They rest behind a concrete and feel a lack of energy. He retorts, "If you hadn't stolen most of my carefully saved 'life', we wouldn't be in this desperate position. You well know that it's more important that I remain at full power" (Vogt, *Supermind* 5). Merla agrees and says that they both require "a change of blood and a new charge of life" (Vogt, *Supermind* 5). They discuss that their ship has been spotted by the tracers of the Galactic observer. It's unimportant where the machine is buried as the tracers can discover the accurate location of it.

A few minutes later a married couple advanced past them. The woman whispers, "It's a man and a woman. They're 'life,' Jeel, life" (Vogt, *Supermind* 6)! In the smokefall, they pounce on the couple draw blood out of them and leave the bodies in the lonely space so that the matter can be discovered by the newsagents. This will in turn help them to find out the hidden base of the Galactic Observer. He adds, "We must find that base, discover its strength, and destroy it, if necessary, when the tribe comes" (Vogt, *Supermind* 6). After that, they go on to traverse the city to find a building where they can bury their ship.

William Leigh, the reporter of the Planetarian News Service sees the dead couple lying alongside each other on the dead body carrier. With anxiousness, he bents forward near the neck of the lady that exhibits the slits and utters, "This is where the blood was drained" (Vogt, *Supermind* 8). The reporter mentions that the murders have taken place the day before. And now, "the woman's body, electrically warmed for embalming, feels eerily lifelike to his touch. It is only after a long moment that he notices her lips are badly, almost brutally, bruised" (Vogt, *Supermind* 8). Leigh gazes towards the direction of the man and he has similar cuts near his neck and lips.

After the proceedings of the electric embalming, the static electricity of neither of the bodies shows resistance.

On further interrogation one of them says, "This static force is actually a form of life force, which usually trickles out of a corpse over a period of a month. We know of no way to hasten the process, but the bruises on the lips show distinct burns, which are suggestive" (Vogt, *Supermind* 8).

Leigh declares that Professor Ungarn has convinced the government to establish 'Ms brand of mechanical psychology' in every school to put an end to all types of unsocial activities. (Vogt, *Supermind* 8). The attendant announces, "We've radioed Professor Ungarn and, by great good fortune, we caught him on his way to Earth from his meteor retreat near Jupiter. He'll be landing shortly after dark, a few hours from now" (Vogt, *Supermind* 9). The dead bodies are wheeled out of the room.

The editor of the local newspaper voices, "Husband and wife, ordinary young couple, taking an evening walk. Some devil hauls up alongside of them, drains their blood into a tank, their life energy onto a wire or something" (Vogt, *Supermind* 9). Leigh recollects that during the afternoon he had an interview in the college for a paper.

The newspapers have Professor Ungarn's title imprinted with gold on the headline of every page containing the information regarding his discovery of the ship eighteen light years ago and his knowledge of the whereabouts of the ship at this time. Leigh asks the little man three questions, The first one is how he gets to know about Leigh. The second question that he asks is how Professor Ungarn put down his ideas on the paper two days back when he was coming up to this place in a few hours. And thirdly, how he is aware of the particulars of the murder beforehand. The man answers that an adolescent boy named Patrick passed this information and the sheets of paper to him.

He goes to the magnificent suite of the Private Three at the Hotel Constantine and examines it for the murder that has taken place. He hears the voice of a woman disguised as a male from behind who informs him that the spaceship is concealed underneath the building.

She hands him a revolver that has a trigger but no bullets. She asked him to follow her inside the tunnel located in the bathroom of the apartment. He visualises that "there was a hole in the floor at her feet. The square of floor that was the tunnel-covering lay back neatly, pinned to position by a complicated-looking hinge" (Vogt, *Supermind* 13). The tunnel leads to the spaceship concealed under the apartment Constantine. A glimpse of the shining metal is visible from the other side of the ship. As they enter the control room of the spaceship, Leigh sees the control board with mini lights flickering on a metallic wall. The silence breaks with a man's voice saying, "Merla, what would you say is the psychology behind this young lady's action" (Vogt, *Supermind* 14)? At once pointing at them he says, "You have of course noticed that she is a young lady, and not a boy" (Vogt, *Supermind* 14). Then the lady named Merla responds, "She was brought to this star system shortly after she was born, Jeel. She has none of the normal characteristics of a Klugg, but she is a Galactic, though definitely not the Galactic Observer" (Vogt, *Supermind* 14).

Concentrated on the task of seeking pathways for communication in the inaccessible universe, Serres's endeavour on humanity in contemporary times is didactic in approach. Two gaps are to be linked. Firstly, the society and the individual must be taken into consideration. Secondly, the kind of life led between the first and third world. Before this, humanity was ascribed with specific features through social sciences, archaeology and biology that made the task easy to designate the meaning and position of humans. While in the contemporary world with modifications in science and quality of life, man holds less similarity with the human being existing aeons ago. The past life was subsumed under an everlasting predicament and lasted for a short period due to poverty and disease. In today's world, with the advancement in science and technology, man can choose the best way to survive. This idea is explored in Michel Serres's book *Hominescence* published in the year 2001. It deals with the appearance of a new human and opening up possibilities for an advanced body of which man is the sole creator.

Merla enunciates that he is the first Dreegh she has ever met. And that, she has been ordered by the Galactic Observer to advise him to leave the place at dawn. She further adds, "Earth is on the verge of being given fourth-degree rating; and, as you probably know, in emergencies fourths are given Galactic knowledge. That emergency we will consider to have arrived tomorrow at dawn" (Vogt, *Supermind* 15).

Jeel believes that the lady is a Klugg or "the higher Lennel type" (Vogt, *Supermind* 16) and he won't let her leave the place as "She has blood, and more than normal life" (Vogt, *Supermind* 15).

At dusk when everyone was heading towards home, Leigh gazes at his offsider who seems boyish in the dark scenario. The girl orders him not to disclose the matter that he became aware of sometime before as none will be convinced by this. Leigh briskly says that the mechanical psychologist will examine each word. Subsequently, he is blindfolded by the girl. Leigh commands the girl and other kluggs to stay away from the young married. Several minutes later he sees a spaceship that seems like a car. It heaves from the ground high up to the sky and "he had a swift glimpse of white rubber wheels folding out of sight. Streamlined, almost cigar-shaped now, the spaceship that had been a car darted at a steep angle into the sky. Swiftly, it was gone" (Vogt, *Supermind* 19). Later, he connects his wrist radio to a wall socket and asks Jim to get in touch with the Research Alpha team to discuss the matter associated with the Vampire story.

The optimum detector instrument has its restraints. As Jeel positions it, the version that belongs to the Dreeghs indicates William Leigh. He attempts to send a spy ray in the direction of the pointer but it recuperates in the same direction.

The report on Hammond's desk presents a biodata of William Leigh who is appointed as reporter in the Planetarian service. He is born twenty-eight years ago to a teacher, Coster Leesoff and a farmer, Jan Leesoff in the locale of North America. His name is legally changed to Leigh at the age of seven. He remains a below-average student till graduation. But after that, he begins his career in Journalism with International News Survey Syndicate. While working as a news reporter he is extremely injured in the Indian independence riots. He recovers from the ailment and is later examined for overstimulation of his body and mind. Previously, his I.Q. was tested as 123 but now he is "so much more dynamic and intelligent—that he now has an I.Q. of at least 135 or 140" (Vogt, *Supermind* 20).

He has experimented on the Vampires hailing from space and Professor Ungarn and his daughter, Patricia Ungarn as extraterrestrial beings. A confidential psychological machine will be sent to his bedroom to scrutinise his mind while he is asleep.

Sigmund Freud suggests that when man comes

in contact with the alien there is an upshot of uncanny. The idea of uncanny detains strangeness, surprise and bewilderment. For a critic, the idea of 'uncanny' is a sign of an integrated danger and abnormalities emanating from both the psychical and physical deformity of a being which is known to humans. Freud posits that one can accumulate all the features of persons, feelings and experiences that induce the emotion of uncanny. The feeling of uncanny is scary as it is familiar to the minds of man. The alien creates the feeling of ambivalence with uncommon features displaying few known vestiges of man in his speech, actions, personality and appearance. In the words of Michael Beechler:

> The alien, in other words, always positions itself somewhere between pure familiarity and pure otherness, between the speech of the same and the speech of the other. Taking its place on the border between identity and difference, it marks that border, articulating it while at the same time disarticulating and confusing the distinctions the border stands for. (*Border Patrols* 32)

The balls of the machine make a buzzing sound and whirls in the air. He is carried away with the psycho-gas when it reaches his nasal passage. The faint sound of a voice comes from a distance. While the machine whizzes through the air, the soothing gas lulls him to the abyss of sleepiness. As he wakes up from the hypnotic sleep, he hears the voice of Merla, the Dreegh saying, "The girl did a very good job of erasing your subconscious memories. There's only one possible clue to her identity and—" (Vogt, *Supermind* 23). She presses him to provide her with information about Professor Ungarn. To this Leigh answers that he is a scientist who has "invented this system of mechanical hypnosis, and he was called in when the dead bodies were found because the killings seemed to have been done by perverts" (Vogt, *Supermind* 24).

It is a firmly set reality that technology and machines are linked to the field of Science Fiction. A slice of futuristic, innovational technology is contemplated as part of Science Fiction. Technology has a pivotal role in the defamiliarization of the matter in the process of making the known appear to be unknown. Technology such as a spaceship or time machine furnishes the personification of dissimilarity and other. In the words of Michelangelo Buonarotti:

> For human beings, the experience is too much like a dream. Your mind/brain will enact meaning on what happens, as it does on the images that pass through your consciousness in sleep. It is impossible for a human being to take action in the visited world without falling into a psychotic episode. The dream becomes a nightmare, in which the traveller is trapped. I have found no way out of this impasse, and because of the way we construe our consciousness-the mind in the 103 machine-I am not hopeful that a way can be found. We humans may travel only as ghosts, shadows, spectators. (qtd. in Jones 275)

Pointing the metallic weapon at him, Merla commands him to get out of bed and switch on the voice recorder to record what is important for the case. He operates the instrument and utters, "Give me all the dope you've got on Professor Garrett Ungarn" (Vogt, *Supermind* 25). The machine directs him to sign the form.

Leigh inscribes the form while he sees his signature getting dissolved inside the machine. Consequently, Merla asks Jeel who was standing near the bathroom door, that she should read aloud the paper to her or carry the machine with her. Behind the bathroom door, other rooms finally lead to the control room of the airship belonging to the Dreeghs.

The control room's view is similar to that of the Constantine's. Leigh is captured and imprisoned by the Dreeghs. He reiterates that he in no way will assist them in destroying the Observer. The girl warns him that if he doesn't act accordingly then they will kill his mother and add her life blood to their reserves. Leigh is horrified at this conjecture. Then, the airship is lifted into the night sky.

By all accounts, there is no restriction in using the concept of space and time in the genre of science fiction accommodating the subject of space travel, time machines and going past of time. The American Science Fiction writer, Donald A. Wollheim suggests:

> Modern science fiction is delineated by the far boundaries of time and space and galactic civilization is the turning point of this universe building. Galactic civilization implies going to the Mars, and other planets. It also implies colonizing where colonizing is worlds and intellectual kinship. It implies mankind covering the space between the stars. It also implies a civilization taking from each other what is desirable, or what is best for each. It implies an end to boundaries and the acceptance of infinite future and infinite progress outward in the universe. (31)

Hammond gazes at Helen Wendell and turns the viewplate

down as the scene disappears. He says, "... so that is the notorious Dreegh vampire. Life has its moments, doesn't it" (Vogt, *Supermind* 30)? Helen calmly replies that she has experiences with them throughout her life. Doubtfully, she asks Hammond, "Do you think they suspected that we were using the mechanical psychologist as an intermediary for observing them" (Vogt, *Supermind* 29)? He ascends from the couch and enunciates, "Don't forget, we're watching a police operation which one of the Great Ones initiated all of three earth years ago. Do you realize that we may actually have the tremendous experience of being privy to an entire operation by one of these super-beings? This could be the educational opportunity of our lifetime" (Vogt, *Supermind* 30).

Hammond inquiries about the three persons of Research Alpha; Vince Strather, Barabara Ellington and Dr. Gloge, who are supposed to assist him in his endeavour. At the Tokyo facility, Dr. Gloge is embroiled in the Omega project i.e., he is testing the stimulation of Asian Chameleon in its natural living conditions. While the other two are allocated to the British facility.

Europa, one of the moons of Jupiter surrenders a part of the sky to the large mass of the planet Jupiter. The engines transmute the magnetic waves for repulsion and work evenly as the combination of the pull of gravity and counter-pull gives way to the distance. They cover long distances with time. Leigh's space tracker Hanardy declares that the planet Jupiter is behind them. The spaceships are seen hovering beside them that grow outwardly faint and disappear in a blink. It takes two and a half months to travel from Earth to Europa. And, his psychograph report by the mechanical psychologist states the spotting of Ungarn as the Observer.

Leigh observes keenly as Ungarn's meteorite routes his path to one corner. Then, the metallic door of the airship slides open and Hanardy comes out of the control room. Leigh is attacked by Ungarn's army. A few moments later, Patricia Ungarn complains to Hanardy about bringing William Leigh with him. She yells, "You conceited fool! That's William Leigh. He's a hypnotized spy of those devils who are attacking us. Bring him immediately to my apartment. He must be killed at once" (Vogt, *Supermind* 33). He decides to search for the compound automobile airship to elope from Ungarn's meteorite through the Dreegh lines and reach the Earth.

The concept of Extraterrestrial life in the field of science fiction is prevalent both in the past and contemporary times. Issac Asimov, one of the pioneers of science fiction, is ahead of his time when it comes to imagination and prognostication. He has portrayed extraterrestrial species as a major part of this field. He is firmly convinced by the fact that there exist two varieties of aliens in the celestial spaces. One type of alien is the humans who have left the planet, Earth and moved to the Galaxy to build a Galactic Empire of their own. The other type of alien is the mysterious being alienated from Earth devoid of any humanoid attributes.

The doors in the meteorite are locked and "opened to a slight pressure on a tiny, half-hidden push button that had seemed an integral part of the design of the latch" (Vogt, *Supermind* 34). The room is occupied with large machines that seem like an ultramodern astronomical observatory. As another door opens towards the hallway, Patricia enters ordering them to move to level 4 as Professor Ungarn searches for Hanardy to do machine work due to the malfunctioning of energy screens.

When Leigh wakes up from sleep, he is startled to

see the sunlit yard behind the French windowpane. The girl sitting beside him says that he is hypnotised by the Dreeghs in his hotel room and the illusion he is facing is due to the hypnotism of the Dreeghs.

After regaining his senses, he realises how "the Dreeghs had come to his hotel apartment and ruthlessly forced him to their will, the way the 'blackness' room had affected him, and how the girl had spared his life" (Vogt, *Supermind* 39). He feels queer as if his mind fights with some mysterious object or idea. Later, he comprehends that it is another brain. He places his hands on his forehead.

The girl who is gazing at him asks how he is doing. He recollects that he was previously similarly questioned by her. He fastens the hands of the girl with a spring from the wardrobe. He becomes cognizant of the fact that the Vampires are trying to take control of the meteorite. Leigh walks through the empty hallway and heads in the direction of the fourth level where Professor Ungarn and Hanardy are working ceaselessly to replace the energy defence screen.

The room is filled with energy. Born as Kluggs, Professor Ungarn and Patricia are regarded as ignoramuses in the Galactics. Based on the standards of the planet Earth, there are various I.Q. levels such as:

> ...the I.Q. of human morons wavered between seventy-five and ninety, of Kluggs possibly between two hundred and twenty-five, and, say, two hundred and forty-three". Leigh chained the Professor and darkened the room. He sneaked into Patricia's bed chamber and mounted on the tiny spaceship and slipped away. Within no

> time, "the magnetic force rays caught his tiny craft, and drew it remorselessly toward the hundred-and-fifty-foot, cigar-shaped machine that flashed out of the darkness. (Vogt, *Supermind* 41)

Issac Asimov points out that extraterrestrial living signifies the anthropoid notion. In his work *Pebble in the Sky*, he elucidates the usual occurrence that is required to create an animate being. He also presents a few anecdotes that are entirely logical and scientific:

> You see, proteins, as I probably needn't tell you, are immensely complicated groupings of amino acids and certain other specialized compounds, arranged in intricate three-dimensional patterns that are as unstable as sunbeams on a cloudy day… But this marvellous chemical, this protein, must be first built up out of inorganic matter before life can exist. (39)

He catches sight of another spaceship owned by the Dreeghs, Jeel and Merla. Leigh overhears Jeel saying, "Merla, this is the most astoundingly successful case of hypnotism in our existence. He's done everything. Even the tiniest thoughts we put into his mind have been carried out to the letter. And the proof is, the screens are going down. With the control of this station, we can hold out even after the Galactic warships arrive, and fill our tankers and our energy reservoirs for as long as a hundred years" (Vogt, *Supermind* 41).

Leigh is chained to Chesterfield by Jeel. He feels unusually conscious as if his mind has been extracted. A strongly built Dreegh woman comes and tries to converse with him. He is quite surprised to see that the woman is already dead but artificially stimulated to live. The lady acknowledges that it is onerous for the Dreeghs to remain alive and all this happened in the course of an interstellar brawl aeons ago.

With a grim expression on her face, she pronounces that they are seized in the gravitational pull of the Sun that is later renamed as the Dreegh Sun. They are defiled by the beams of the Dreegh Sun that are intensely life-threatening to humans. The antidote to this is a series of transfusions of blood and the life force of humans. For a short period, they are accepting donations from the government but later it is planned to have them annihilated in entirety. Since then, the Dreeghs have been struggling for their existence. Leigh has found the Dreegh woman tensed and cold.

She presses him to kiss her and says that she would allow him to live for many days on one condition, "you won't have any more morals about the matter than I. But you must let your whole-body yield" (Vogt, *Supermind* 43). She was attempting to get his life force by kissing her but he got hers. She posited that no humans could perform such an act similar to this. She annoyingly says, "every time I was able, during the four times we stayed on Earth, I sneaked out. I caught men on the street. I don't know exactly how many because I dissolved their bodies after I was through with them. But there were dozens. And he's got all the energy I collected, enough for scores of years" (Vogt, *Supermind* 43).

Subsequently, Leigh emerges with a renewed vigour introducing himself as "the great galactic" (Vogt, *Supermind* 44). He smiles peculiarly and says that it has been a quintessential experiment on an intentional splitting of personality. Back then, the time manipulators attempted to destroy the Dreeghs. But, the Dreeghs ran away in the grandness of the galaxy. On this account, William Leigh, the great galactic has travelled to Earth to create the personality of William Leigh, the reporter. Owing to this, he had to abandon the unique faculties of his brain and an equal amount of life energy. So, to resuscitate himself, he repeated the scene with Ungarn's daughter so as "to appear directly as another conscious mind in order to convince Leigh that he must yield. The rest, of course, was a matter of gaining additional life energy after boarding your ship, which—he bowed slightly at the muscularly congealed body of the woman—which she supplied me" (Vogt, *Supermind* 44).

Leigh tries to harmonise with both of his personalities. He says to himself, "You have accepted the fact that you were playing a role; and now you have recognized our oneness, and are giving up the role. The proof of this recognition on your part is that you have yielded control of our—body" (Vogt, *Supermind* 45).

Asimov posits that the scientific matter is ineluctable in the context of extraterrestrial life. With the application of Merger's theory, he has envisaged the probabilities in the process of evolution and inter-marriage between two planets due to the similarity that they possess in having the genes of humanoid. He also claims that man is on the edge of scientific advancement. With the utmost prediction of futuristic life, Asimov presents the alien beings luminously and utilises them in his works to recount his perspective on futuristic occurrences such as galactic transportation and colonization of planets that may occur for humans soon:

> Orthodox archaeology insisted on the evolution of Human types independently on various planets and used such atypical cultures, as that on Rigel, as examples of race differences that had not yet been ironed out through intermarriage. Arvardan destroyed

such concepts effectively by showing that Rigellian robot culture was but a natural outgrowth of the economic and social forces of the times and of the region. (*Pebble in the Sky* 34)

Hanardy lies prostrate on the floor tied to a rope. He tries to unfasten the rope and thinks that the Professor and his daughter might be in search of him. He makes an effort to stand on his feet. Beside the echo of the dynamos, the corridor appears to be filled with silence. Due to the vibration, he feels as if he has landed on a planet. It is difficult on his part to discern that he is on a meteorite. By dint of the unnatural gravity, he feels attenuated than on the planet Earth.

He goes to Patricia's apartment to untie her who is lying chained to a wire below the chair. He advances towards her and blames himself for bringing Leigh to the meteorite. Patricia forces Hanardy to relate to her about his escapade from the clutches of William Leigh. Hanardy says that he is at first tied with a rope. Then, he assembles the Dreeghs from the airship and flees. Hanardy decides to unknot Professor Ungarn.

Hanardy traverses to the deepest part of the meteorite where the dynamos are placed and has Professor Ungarn unfastened. The Professor is elated to see himself free. He looks at the screen and exclaims that it is still in good condition. He had preserved the meteorite from the attack of the Dreeghs in such a manner that it is quite easy to discern that he is the uncontested Galactic observer of the vast solar system, "which includes at its top echelon the Great Galactic—who had been William Leigh—and at the bottom, Professor Ungarn and his lovely daughter" (Vogt, *Supermind* 51).

He figures out that the Professor is a saviour. His coach is present here to forbid any communication between the Earth and the galaxy. The planet Earth is below the level of development to inculcate awareness that a huge galactic civilization exists. The spaceships of the lower organisation that are allocated to the galactic union are withdrawn from the area near the solar system whenever they try to become closer. Adventitiously, the Dreeghs saunter into this prohibited region in search of blood and life energy. But in reality, this is a trap for the Dreeghs in which many of them are seized. The Professor starts to toil on the broken segment of the screen drive that emanates energy from it.

Hanardy walks into his cabin and conjures up an image of himself on the metallic wall of his cabin. He identifies himself as a "man who had downgraded himself as a human being, seeking escape in a lonely space job from the need to compete as an individual" (Vogt, *Supermind* 53). He contemplates that the screens are down and a Dreegh is coming near the airlock on a space boat to the outmost part of the meteorite. He believes that the Dreegh would knock down the meteorite in its entirety if he felt convenient.

Ruminating over the matter, Hanardy moves quickly out of his spaceship and goes inside the meteorite. While passing through the way that leads to the airlock, he meets the Professor and Patricia near the corridor. They inform him that Patricia's fiancé, Thadled Madro, the klugg has arrived whom he mistook as a Dreegh. Madro inquiries about the number of Dreeghs who have boarded the ship. To this, Hanardy answers as nine.

Madro states that "it is evident that we must re-assess our entire situation; and I might even guess that we Kluggs could through the chance perceptive stimulation of this man achieve so great a knowledge of the universe that, here and now, we might be able to take the next step of development for our kind" (Vogt, *Supermind* 55). Hearing this Hanardy decides to put out his gun at Madro before he guards himself. The Professor and Madro walk towards the power control room while Patricia is seated on the chair. Ungarn says that the control screen is working in the right manner and they should plan their tasks before the last of the Dreegh's ship attacks them.

Madro pronounces that he cares little about being a Klugg. The Professor amends him by saying that they belong to the lowest level in the hierarchy of the galactic civilization. They toil for days on the other planets. Madro says that the other creatures do not differ from them in intelligence but in their levels of energy. Hanardy says that William Leigh gets the energy from a dark room.

In a few minutes, all of them go down the elevators escorted by Hanardy and stop near a door containing tools inside the cubicle. Hanardy locates the metallic wall inside the cupboard from which William Leigh acquires the energy. The Professor and his daughter examine the metallic wall with a portable instrument. At the outset, Madro has the least interest in what has been occurring over there. He grabs Hanardy and takes him to the corner of the room for a private talk. He is helpless for he is rigorously attacked by the Dreegh. Hanardy says that he hails from the lowest level of the galactic civilization. In his teenage years, he consumes drugs but it doesn't suit his body. He adds that the Dreeghs are sick of the blood and life energy. They can get rid of this and lead a normal life.

The Dreegh, Madro says that he has been commanded by the great galactic to neutralise Hanardy. He focuses a metallic instrument on Hanardy's head that dazzles him. Madro instructs him to locate all the places in the meteorite where the arms and armaments are present. Four of them go to the main quarters. Patricia asks Madro if Hanardy is under his spell. To this Hanardy answers, "I gave Steve a special type of energy charge that will nullify for the time being what was done to him" (Vogt, *Supermind* 60). The Professor asks curtly if Madro can conquer William Leigh by putting a spell on Hanardy. As Hanardy is not his actual enemy whom Leigh has placed in the meteorite to work on his behalf. The Professor utters:

> I suspect that you analyzed Steve has a memory of mental contact with a supreme, perhaps even an ultimate, intelligence. Now, these earth people when awake are in that particular, perennially confused state that makes them unacceptable for galactic citizenship. So that the very best way to defend yourself from Steve's memory is to keep him awake. I therefore deduce that the energy charge you fired at him was designed to maintain in continuous stimulation the waking center in the brain stem. But that is only a temporary defense. In four or five days, exhaustion in Hanardy will reach an extreme state, and something in the body will have to give. What will you have then that you don't have now? (Vogt, *Supermind* 61)

The Dreegh reiterates that when his fellow mates arrive, Patricia and Hanardy will accompany him to Europa. So, he declares that none of them will be assassinated until the task is over. The Professor, his daughter and Hanardy follow Madro to the Spaceport to examine Hanardy's temperament. On their way, Madro neutralises all the mechanical instruments and the sources of energy are also locked. The meteorite screens are nullified and the tools that are used to operate are smashed up.

The mini space boats are also demolished to break off any possibilities of running away. The weapons and power controls present in Hanardy's space freighter are also dismantled. The Dreegh commands Hanardy to remain in the freighter while he orders the Professor and his daughter to accompany him. They silently go outside and the brainiest man of the entire solar system is locked inside the freighter.

Days pass as Hanardy rests on the berth. He indulges himself in going through the repair manuals of the freighter. He feels depressed as time goes by. After four days, Patricia enters through the airlock and asks Hanardy to join her in action. They go to the power control room where the engine is placed.

The Professor says that Patricia wants to inform him regarding his intelligence. Hanardy says that he has intelligence above the average level and that "he belonged in the 55th percentile of the human race, intelligence-wise, and that his I.Q. had been tested at 104" (Vogt, *Supermind* 64). Then the Professor adds, "On the Klugg I.Q. scale you would probably rate higher than 104. We take into account more factors. Your mechanical ability and spatial relations skill would not be tested correctly by any human I.Q. test that I have examined" (Vogt, *Supermind* 64). He continues by saying that he desires to prepare Hanardy to use his I.Q.

Hanardy says that he might be killed by Madro in the next moment but Patricia rectifies him by saying that "above a certain point of I.Q. mind actually is over matter. A being above that intelligence level cannot be killed. Not by bullets, nor by any circumstance involving matter" (Vogt, *Supermind* 64). In the process of manoeuvring, the Dreegh is attempting to get the information of the great galactic out of him. But he doesn't dare to kill Hanardy as his high memory would pose a danger to the Dreegh.

Patricia mentions that he should train his efficient memory and there is less time for this work. He sees that there are various kinds of instruments in the room that would assist him in training his mind. He overhears the conversation between the Professor and his daughter regarding the measurement of human intelligence. He realises that the IQ tests are established on a curve with an average factor of 100. The tests unfold an unpredictability of what comprises the factors of intelligence and whether the person being examined will able to find solutions to brain puzzles. He also concludes that arithmetic skills and information regarding world geography and climatic conditions are also vital for the tests.

Being a Klugg, the Professor observes that they are theoretical persons mainly focused on the primary abilities of the mind. He also discusses the Lennels, a race who have a higher position than the Kluggs, work on certainty which makes them equal to the Dreeghs. Regarding the I.Q. curve that comprises, humans, Kluggs, Lennels and Dreeghs. The average I.Q. levels are 100, 220, 380 and 450.

For the management of movement, the Dreeghs possess an open channel consisting of mathematical, musical or artistic faculty that are reckoned as trials in an individual to a greater extent than his I.Q. allows him. The I.Q. curve of a Great Galactic is only made up of open channels. It is quite popular that "the open channel curve began at about 80. And, though no one among the lesser races had ever seen anything higher than 3,000—the limits of the space phenomenon—it was believed that the Great Galactic I.Q. curve ascended by types to about 10,000. An example of an 800 open channel is Pat. She can deceive. She can get away with a sleight of hand, a feint, a diversion" (Vogt, *Supermind* 66).

Madro, the Dreegh is seen standing behind the Professor who is gazing at the power control board. Hanardy visualises the viewplate that is alighted showcasing the great expanse of space. It seems as if the starlit heaven is around them. They see a light blinking on the other side and exclaim that the other eight Dreeghs are nearing their meteorite. Despairingly, the Professor says to Hanardy that Patricia has plans to use him against Madro before the arrival of the Dreeghs.

Patricia enquires about how many more times the Dreegh spaceship will reach the meteorite. The Professor estimates it as not more than two hours. Hanardy tries to harm Patricia but the Professor stops him by pacifying him. Patricia hands over a metal bar to Hanardy and commands him to murder Madro, the Dreegh before his companions reach the meteorite.

Patricia stands near the door and orders Hanardy to kill Madro when she indicates him. But, Hanardy decides to escape on his freighter by stealing the key appliances from Madro and fix the control board to break free from the place. For this, he should follow the indications of Patricia. Facing his back Patricia utters, "You're a weapon, Steve. I have to figure out how to fire that weapon and escape. Basically, that's all we need to do! Get away from the Dreeghs and hide. Understand" (Vogt, *Supermind* 70)? Hanardy acknowledges the words of Patricia and now he is aware of what he is required to do.

Patricia is doubtful of the strengths of Hanardy

so she decides to initially converse with the Dreegh to know what type of weapon Hanardy is. She interrogates Madro regarding the nature of the intelligence of the Great Galactics. He answers, "The Great Galactic is a sport! Just a member of some lesser race who was released by a chance stimulus so that he temporarily became a super-being" (Vogt, *Supermind* 71). He adds that this stimulus is attainable when there is an accumulation of the required amount of energy.

He thus explains that:

> ...the lucky individual, in his super-state, realized the whole situation. When the energy had been transformed by his own body and used up as far as he himself was concerned, he stored the transformed life-energy where it could eventually be used by someone else. The next person would be able to utilize the energy in its converted form. Having gone through the energy, each recipient in turn sank back to some lower state. (Vogt, Supermind 71)

Similarly, the reporter of Earth, William Leigh, has transformed into the Great Galactic in this space and presently, he has lost his special abilities. But, at the moment there is none to take his place. The difficulty with Hanardy is he requires life energy in large amounts to utilise his memory of intelligence in its entirety. Madro says that he wants to put Hanardy into a state of sleepiness so that he won't be able to use his last potential. Madro takes out a weapon from his pocket and points it at Hanardy's face till he is immersed in a state of sleepiness.

Hanardy has within no time fallen asleep as he is weaker than other humans. In normal humans, there is a lapse of time between wakefulness and sleepiness. For humans who are dull the lapse of time is less than normal. But, For Hanardy who is the dullest one, there is no time lapse between both of these. So, he falls asleep earlier than others. Below the level of consciousness, there occurs a significant time gap. During this, the atomic particles present inside the body perform varied actions. The molecules move in the direction of matter. The thought that exists in Hanardy's mind creates "exact spots of space, saw and identified the other-ness of the Dreeghs in the approaching Dreegh ship, estimated their other-whereness, computed the mathematics of change. It was simple in the virtual emptiness of space, difficult where matter was dense" (Vogt, *Supermind* 74).

The spaceship of the Dreeghs contains eight of them having changed their position from one spot in the space to another. Hanardy feels in the bedroom twistedly and the metal bar is under him. Patricia goes near him to get the metal bar. But his body weight fails her to get it at last she realises that Madro has made him fall in this manner. Patricia is astonished seeing the prognosis of Madro. He also possesses a weapon that Patricia is in search of. She thinks that her father might be visualising the entire incident through his viewpoint. She talks to her father through the intercom and asks for suggestions on how to murder the Dreegh.

Through the viewplate, the Professor sees that the Dreegh ship has already arrived at the place. He leaves the control room and runs to his daughter. The Professor spots Hanardy having been raised onto a powered trolley that is brought from the Dreegh's spaceship. The machine has two bulging translucent cups with a suction mechanism. The right arm of Hanardy is injected with a needle and the cups are filled with a bluish-red liquid.

This process is repeated several times by the Dreeghs. The needle is injected into Madro's right arm and the blood is transfused into his body. Madro awakes from his bed and is greeted by the other Dreeghs. He seems livelier and stronger after the transfusion of life blood. In a flash, Patricia is dragged towards Madro and he scrapes her lips and a blue flame emanates from it.

Madro says, "The existence of such brother-and-sister energy flows, Pat—which you have now experienced—and the Dreegh ability to use them make it likely that we could become the most powerful beings in the galaxy on a continuing basis. If we can defeat Hanardy. We only took about ten percent from you. We don't want you damaged—yet" (Vogt, *Supermind* 76). Another Dreegh named Rilke says that they want to visit Europa to know why the Great Galactic chose Hanardy for the execution of the plan.

All of them board the super spaceship of the Dreegh to fly to the moon named Europa. They carry with them the freighter of Hanardy for landing. They reach Spaceport which is the main city of the moon and go down to Hanardy's spaceship anchorage. Hanardy is in the fourth sleeping stage in which it is outrightly impossible to awaken him. This is the somnambulistic stage in which a person can move in his sleep. Madro points a light at his face from the bar with a delta-wave bandwidth of C-10-13B and a few seconds later Hanardy stirs on his bed. He doesn't take a glimpse at anyone present in the room as he is in the somnambulistic stage. He dresses himself in fine clothes and leaves the place.

He unlatches the airlock and moves towards the gangplank. Madro indicates Patricia to go after Hanardy. Everyone follows Hanardy to the door numbered 517. A middle-aged lady greets Hanardy but she is hypnotised by Madro's mechanical beam of the bar. One after another all the thirteen companions of Hanardy brush their lips with the persons whom Hanardy leads their way and each time the blue fire enthrals them. All the companions are drained in succession. Later, they plan to assassinate Hanardy but Patricia tries to save him.

The principal city of Europa known as the Spaceport reminds one of the naval refilling station of the South Pacific having its own military force. The armed forces work in the restoration and maintenance of airships. Furthermore, the Spaceport resembles an excavation where aircrafts bring the ore of the meteorites and other raw materials that are made free of debris and later transported to Earth.

A peculiar group of thirteen people known as space bums inhabit the Spaceport. The group is incessantly searched by military personnel who report that they are nearing death due to loss of energy. It is also examined that the other inhabitants of the Spaceport are suffering from the same kind of illness.

Hanardy realises that Patricia is about to die due to lack of energy. To save her, he has to gather energy from someplace. For a short term, his somnambulism state is disturbed and restored with the dream state preceded by the state of wakefulness. This leads to a splitting of his personality. The part that is in the state of wakefulness makes him discern that he has arrived at the location. There are in total 193 locations for energy sources. Out of which, thirteen are extremely fluctuating. He extricates the thirteen locations and makes the payment for the existing 180 locations. Seven-tenths of the energy in 180 locations flows to him.

After the transfer of energy, the cosmos dilates and

appears dark. In the darkness, there are the nine Dreeghs. He also sees a red band in a silver strand that resembles his life-blood. He says "that this was the blood the Dreeghs had taken from him when they first arrived at the Ungarn meteorite" (Vogt, *Supermind* 82). He comprehends that the Great Galactic perceive him as a catalyst whose life-blood will cure the Dreeghs of their illness.

Faraway there is a streak of light that resembles the spaceship of Dreegh is visible to Hanardy. It is a thousand light years away from Hanardy. He resumes the flow of particles that result in the passage of time and the nine Dreeghs find them in their airship. They surprisingly see the configuration of stars and ascertain that they will never be able to approach the solar system of Earth.

Patricia gains consciousness and finds herself in a room of the Professor's meteorite. She sighs with relief and inquires about Hanardy. Lying on the ground, Hanardy is trying to remember the incidents before the advent of Madro and the other Dreeghs. The Great Galactic, William Leigh articulates, "Steve, there are billions of open channels in the universe. Awareness of the genius in them is the next step up for intelligence. Because you've had some feedback, if you take that to heart you might even get the girl" (Vogt, *Supermind* 83). With this Steve Hanardy completes the second level of I.Q. rehabilitation of ten thousand and has arrived at the last stage of I.Q. rehabilitation.

Barbara Ellington has been chosen by Dr Henry Gloge, head of the Department of Biology at the Institute of Research Alpha for the stimulation of Point Omega. He plans to visit her bedroom while she is out of place and install instruments that might help him later. He heads for the steno pool to check if she has been transshipped to another place.

Dr. Gloge searches for the girl and finds her near a water cooler in the hallway. He injects the needle jet gun on her shoulder. The gun contains Omega serum in gaseous form. And, when he injects it into her shoulder, there is a threadlike mist at the end of the needle. Barbara then arrives at the office of John Hammond, private secretary to the President, Alex Sloan, of the Institute of Research Alpha. His office is regarded as the principal library complex on Earth.

Barbara enters the chamber of Hammond that is titled 'Scientific Liaison and Investigation'. There are several papers on the table of Helen Wendell, the secretary to Hammond. She hears her voice being heard from the chamber of Hammond. She sees a note from Dr. Gloge on the table for a meeting to discuss the developments in the Omega project. This project is related to the speeding up of the process of evolution in animals. The result is many laboratory animals have died while the test is conducted on them. After reading the note, Barbara leaves for her chamber. She feels unusually drowsy and weak than ever.

Dr. Gloge hides himself behind the shipping crates. He watches Vincent Strather, the admirer of Barbara approaching the storeroom to return the raw materials. Dr. Gloge thinks that Strather might become an advantage to him at the further levels of the experiment. He releases a needle from the jet gun that hits his shoulder and he screams in pain. John Hammond asks Dr. Gloge to meet him in his office to discuss the Omega project. He orders the Doctor to amplify the reports of the project by adding more details to it.

Dr. Gloge's focus is restricted to the lower types of animals. After being asked by Hammond, Gloge says that the laboratory animals effortlessly endured the first type of injection. The survival of the animals drops at the second dose of the injection. But in the third dose, three animals have to date survived. The three animals who survived the third injection belong to the species of Cryptobranchus. In short, Dr. Gloge explains his observations to Hammond in two stances that there is a wide scope for evolution in all forms of life. The Omega serum has restored one of the growths and further stimulations cannot be altered. The second stance is when this experiment is done on active mammals like monkeys, the result appears to be tremendous.

Dr. Gloge presents a second aspect that focuses on:

> ...brain areas which controlled the inhibition of simple reflexes often seemed to be the source of new neural growth and of sensory extension. The serum apparently intensified these effort points, increasing their operational flexibility. What went wrong was that all too often such one-sided inhibitory amplification ended in nonsurvival. However, in Cryptobranchus, the roof of the mouth developed small functional gills. The hide thickened into segmented, horny armor. Short, grooved fangs were acquired, and connected to glands that produced a mild hematoxic venom. The eyes disappeared, but areas in the skin developed sight-level sensitivity to light. (Vogt, *Supermind* 91)

Gloge has planned to operate the initial four injections on Barbara and Vince to record the result of the experimentation of Omega serum. He is filled with fear contemplating his future course as the result of the stimulation of Point Omega in humans. If the result becomes unsuccessful then it would cause the death of two human beings. As his first injection is all set, he heads towards the residence of Barbara Ellington. The Doctor parks his truck and listens to the audio recorder that has been secretly placed in his room of Barbara since last week. He carefully listens to the breath and heartbeat of Barbara which is fast and slow in rhythm. For several minutes, he keenly observes her bodily movements. He is sure that the Point Omega Stimulation would be successful in humans.

Then he proceeds to the apartment of Strather to carefully examine him. His outward form is quite unsatisfactory in comparison to Barbara. His eyes and face are reddened because of the debilitating gas that he let off in the apartment. He seems tensed with a discolouration of the skin texture. With the administering of the first dose, he appears to be dull while Barbara is full of heightened spirits. Although both have survived the first injection, the Doctor decides to leave the place and administer the second injection after a little while.

Barbara goes to the chamber of Hammond contemplating that he might notice any change in her. She feels something unusual and hurries to the washroom. She recollects the time she visited the chamber of Hammond. And that, as she sits on the chair, she witnesses a flow of energy. She feels that an area of the brain responds in the same manner each time she recollects the moment. She battles with the pressure of energy that reaches her circulating through the chair. By now she is aware that "it was a nerve center that reacted to hypnotic suggestion, and so when Hammond said suddenly, "Close your eyes, Barbara!" she complied at once" (Vogt, *Supermind* 98). She follows every command of Hammond.

He asks her to raise her right hand so that he can inject a needle over it. He takes her under several tests. He orders her to answer the questions. When Helen Wendell enters, Hammond says, "All the time I talked to Barbara, the life-range indicator showed eight-four, above the hypnotizable range. And she told me nothing" (Vogt, *Supermind* 99).

Barbara feels tired in the afternoon. She experiences energy flow from various areas of her body to other areas. She comes to Scientific Liaison and Investigation. As she rings the bell, Hammond summons Helen Wendell who measures Barbara as nine-point-two in the life-range indicator. Helen doubts that Barbara is the subject of Point Omega stimulation for Dr. Gloge and she decides to keep Barbara with herself for the night. She adds, "I'll give her the conditioning that overwhelms twelve point-oh and higher. She'll never know what hit her" (Vogt, *Supermind* 100).

Barbara feels several blackouts that she reports to Helen Wendell. For this, she is given a spare bedroom to rest. She is under the supervision of Hammond and Helen. By the time Dr. Gloge comes to the residence of Barbara but finds that she is out of place.

During the night the servicing agent reports that the life-range indicator appears to be nine-two and is working appropriately. The servicing agent says, "Since nine-two is no real threat to us, perhaps we might even use a little ESP on her occasionally" (Vogt, *Supermind* 102). Gloge goes to the apartment of Strather and releases the second gas. This time he is annoyed than before. He injects the second needle into Strather's body.

Barbara comes to the office of Dr. Gloge and during this time he takes advantage of the opportunity and shoots the second needle gun. But the girl behaves normally. Barbara senses physical weakness after the second dose. She informs Helen about her illness. When she wakes up from her sleep, she feels that her sensitivity has increased. She can control her breath involuntarily. Her brain seems "like an invisible eye stalk that could reach through walls and bring back visual images to the light-interpretation centers" (Vogt, *Supermind* 104).

She also comprehends that Dr. Gloge is listening to her through the earplug. As she tries to sense him, he shuts off his devices and flees from the place. She feels a sudden shivering inside her body. There are more changes that she can see in her. But she fails to control the sudden transformation in her body so she decides to take the third dose of the Point Omega stimulation.

The doctor says that Barbara has undergone a major change in her personality since he examined her a year back. She is suffering from multiple illnesses such as dysentery. Hammond says that Dr. Gloge gave them the first and second injections a week ago and the third injection is supposed to be given today.

Dr. Gloge is anxious contemplating both of his specimens as he has not spotted them since yesterday. In the entire human history, this experiment is regarded as the greatest. However there are no scientists who can review the consequences of the second injection. He also opines that Vince has failed in responding to the serum due to "the signs of internal malaise, the sick appearance, the struggle of the cells visibly reflecting defeat in the efforts and chemistry at the surface of the skin" (Vogt, *Supermind* 109).

Then he moves out of his workplace to take a look at both of his specimens. He goes to Vince's living quarters and scrutinises the audio recordings to be sure that he is lonely at his place. He identifies that Vince struggles while breathing. The couch makes squeaking sounds when he changes his sides on it while sleeping. Gloge is afraid and based on his past examinations, he decides to murder Vince. And this signifies that he also has to get rid of Barbara.

Gloge decides to meet Vince so he goes to his room. Before Gloge arrives, Vince has a dream of getting murdered by a man named Gloge with whom he got into a squabble a few days back at the Research Alpha. He sees Gloge sneaking through his main door. His sleeping body compels him to perform the defensive action. As a result of this:

> …millions of tiny, shining, cream-coloured energy bundles were emitted by his nervous system. They resembled very short straight lines. And they passed through the wall that separated the living room from the kitchen, and they struck Gloge. Great masses of the energy units unerringly sought out nerve ends in Gloge's body and darted in their scintillating fashion up to the man's brain. The energy units were not the result of conscious analytical thought. They were brought into being solely by fright, and carried pressor messages. (Vogt, *Supermind* 110)

These energies urged Gloge to abandon the place. But Gloge endeavours to go back to Vince's room as the force of energy lessens. He stares at the sleeping body that is dripping with sweat. He handcuffs Vince's hands and legs. When Vince awakes from his sleep, Gloge says that he has injected two doses of serum to quicken the evolution of cells. For that reason, he has come to check on the health of Vince. As Vince feels 'exhausted, weak and numb'. This combination is also visible in animals. Gloge wraps Vince's body in a blanket and lifts him to the van. And throws him inside the pool till he is dead. Now, Gloge plans to murder Barbara but he comes to know that Hammond is in search of her. So, he runs to the office and hides the remaining amount of serum.

When he returns to his office, he sees Barbara waiting for him. Subsequently, Neural acclimation occurs in his brain and he exclaims that she is his dead sister. Based on this fact, it is unethical to murder her. She demands the third injection so that she can carry the device and a quantity of serum for Vince. She interrogates if he has drowned Vince. Dr. Gloge suggests she wait till morning for the third injection to increase the efficacy of the dose. After getting injected with the third dose, they see Hammond advancing towards them.

Hammond commands Wesley Ames, head of the security personnel to not allow Barbara to touch any object or leave the room before he returns after having a secret conversation with Gloge. He is hypnotised by Hammond with the metal object and provides him with the information about Vince's drowning. During this time Barbara flees the place by tricking Ames. She takes Ames' mind eight years back and he is hypnotised which forces him to go back in time when his mother is alive. She makes Ames imagine her as his mother and he guides her to the elevator. Ames says, "She reached to that deep of the heart where the pure, unsullied dead are enshrined. And I thought she was only trying to read my mind" (Vogt, *Supermind* 116)! She goes to the roof of the apartment where she has discerned that a helicopter is about to take to the air. She plays mind games with the pilot and makes him think that she is his beloved. And, as a result, she flees from the place. Later this incident is erased from his mind.

Hammond orders Helen to switch on all the trapping screens and defences so that Barbara can be easily traced. He adds that "Gloge's drowned Strather—as an experimental failure. But the other one's awake and functioning. It's hard to know what she'll do next, but she may find it necessary to get to my office as a way of getting out of this building fast" (Vogt, *Supermind* 116).

Hammond declares that Vince is alive as water couldn't enter his entire body. In the case of Barbara, her body is not in her control. She half-kneels on the ground. It is impossible on her part to lose consciousness. She perceives that her body is getting transformed. There is a flow of energy from every direction inside her body. She feels that "Something of Barbara seemed to disappear with that awareness. "I'm still me!" the entity thought as it lay there on the floor. But she had the distinct realization that "me" even in these early stages of the five hundred-thousand-year transformations was ME PLUS. Exactly how the self was becoming something more was not yet clear" (Vogt, *Supermind* 117).

Hammond inquires Helen about Gloge and Strather. Helen says that she has let Gloge talk to the office assistants and now he is asleep. But regarding Strather, the MD machine has given its opinion that "some newly developed brain mechanism shut off breathing and kept him in a state of suspended animation. Vince himself has no conscious memory of the experience, so it was evidently a survival act of the lower brain. MD reports other developments are taking place in Vince, and regards them as freakish in nature. It's too soon to tell whether or not he can survive a third injection. He's under sedation" (Vogt, *Supermind* 119).

Helen says that she has a few transmitter messages for Hammond from New Brasilia and Manila. They acknowledge Hammond's opinion concerning Gloge that an error might occur if he stays in the Research Alpha for a long time. Although Gloge is 'role-perfect' he is intractable and he can receive the ultimate conditioning at the Paris centre. Hammond also adds that Gloge is of much use to seize Barbara. So, he plans to let Gloge leave beyond the defence screens. Barbara might be enduring the effects of the third dose. And, if she is alive after getting injected with the third dose, she will definitely come to take the fourth one. She will search for the person who might get the serum ready for her.

Barbara has developed a new type of consciousness that will let her brain perform acts automatically without letting the conscious part of the brain become aware of it. As she rests there, she feels:

> ...a new nerve centre in her brain reached out and scanned a volume of space 500 light-years in diameter. It touched and comprehended clouds of neutral hydrogen and bright young O-type stars measured the swing of binaries, and took a census of comets and ice asteroids. Far out in the constellation of Ophiuchus a blue-white giant was going nova, and the new, strange linkage in Barbara's mind observed its frantic heaving of spheres of radiant gas. A black dwarf emitted its last spray of infrared light and sank into the radiationless pit of dead stars. Barbara's mind encompassed it all, and

reached farther [. . .] reached out effortlessly until it touched a specific Something [. . .] and withdrew. (Vogt, *Supermind* 120)

Barbara is overwhelmed by the thing she touches but she knows that the mechanics of the brain have let her touch it. She is conscious of the fact that the nerve centre won't perform its scanning. And, conscious sensitivity is not associated with it.

She realises that the shifts in energy inside her body have initiated its course of action. Then, she slowly enables her mind and body to descend into the receptive condition. She lay quietly in the locked room curving her body to the other side as the sun peeps in. She gazes at the Research Alpha through the dirty window. She circulates her eyes through the entire institute and stations on the 'Scientific Liasion and Investigation'. She discerns energies winding and creeping like smoke inside the room. She cannot enter the energy barrier so she accesses the place from the living quarters of John Hammond. Her vision gets stabilised here. She is now well-informed about the location of the serum. It is present "in a strong room of Hammond's quarters, heavily screened, seemingly inaccessible" (Vogt, *Supermind* 121).

Her perception rolls out again from Hammond's living areas to the main office. She sees the hazy picture of Helen Wendell speaking, "Lift-off for the nonstop jet to Paris" (Vogt, *Supermind* 122). The crew members and the passengers have gone through the measuring radius which records the life energy volume remarkably more than six, the required range for an Earther. This implies that one who has a greater evolutionary faculty cannot travel to Paris.

Helen Wendell imitates the voice of Barbara and says "There seems to be a group of extraterrestrials on this planet, and I still do not have any clear idea of what they are doing here. That's our immediate task—to find out" (Vogt, *Supermind* 123). The jet heading towards Paris halts for a few repairs. At that time, Hammond sees Gloge accompanied by an unknown girl. He hurriedly demands for an off-planet observer to keep a watch on Gloge and his companion.

Hammond goes to his office and asks the machine about the efficacy of the fourth injection. The machine answers that "the evolutionary trend remains the same, but would be very much advanced. The resultant form would stabilize within twenty minutes. It would again be a viable one" (Vogt, *Supermind* 124). Hammond turns the screen off and decides to inject his patients with the fourth dose.

Dr. Gloge rings up to Hammond from Pennsylvania. Helen begins to record the entire conversation. Gloge says that the fourth injection has been administered to Barbara. Besides constraining the process of evolution and creation of a monster in the next level, the fourth dose will lead to the devastation of the monster. Helen Wendell thinks that Barbara has compelled Gloge to make the call to Hammond. She doubts Barbara wants them to know that she is arriving at the office within no time.

Hammond gazes at the control panel and gets a glimpse of the glimmering indicators. He sees the reaction of energy and anti-energy scrapping it. The energy strives to maintain its state of equilibrium. An erratic electric storm is glaring through the indicators. The defensive energies stationed in the office come closer for the test. The computer screen and the chair reiterate the name of John Hammond. His name vibrates from every nook and corner of the office room.

Being the chief, he knows the design and its

consequences. He uses external sources of energy to deal with it. He darts the projection with his hand and fastens it to place. A harsh sound comes out of it. And the voice of the ghost repeating his name grows fainter. Hammond winks at the screen and opens the door where his subject for experimentation is lying. He orders to injection of the fourth and the ultimate dose of Omega stimulation. The machine also acknowledges his command.

On the desk, the telephone rings and Gloge is on the other side saying last time the call is unknowingly cut. And, he says that he has understood the definition of evolution. Further, he utters, "The universe is a spectrum. It needs energies in motion at all levels. This is why those at the higher levels do not interfere directly with individual activities at the lower. But this is also why they are concerned when a race reaches the point where it can begin to manipulate large forces" (Vogt, *Supermind* 128).

Barbara's face is being reflected on the check screen innumerable times. Hammond lets Barbara enter the control room. He safeguards himself from any effort of meddling with his mind. The girl standing near the door is a shape created for this conversation. She is not the real Barbara. She voices that Hammond heralds from the race of the Great Galactic and is not an inhabitant of Earth. And, they will be exterminated soon. Hammond says that the Great Galactics have military agents who will help them take over the Earth. She presses him to release Gloge.

In the next moment, the Omega serum will be available endlessly. Everyone will go through the full process of evolution. If this situation prevails then the military servants of Great Galactics will not be able to take charge of Earth. Hammond says that the Omega serum won't be utilised again. He goes forward to prove his point.

The rose haze that was before him is now behind him. The energy radiance is cut out for the moment and the room is barrierless. She goes near the door and visualises it from outside. The energy flow seems to have disappeared. A dark figure is seated on the couch and cries in a shrill voice, "Bar-ba-ra!" (Vogt, *Supermind* 130).

Hammond discusses the two theories of Dr. Gloge. He states that at this level there is a possibility for growth and the Omega serum stimulates any one of these and is naturally bound to adhere to the path of development. He continues by saying that when the Great Galactics came to the planet, they never intervened with the basic traits of other races surviving here.

He thus reveals that:

> ...they interject selected bundles of their genes by grafting into thousands of men and women on every continent. As the generations go by, these bundles intermix by chance with those that are native to the people of the planet. Apparently, the Omega serum stimulates one of these mixtures and carries it forward to whatever it is capable of, which, because of the singularity factor, usually leads to a dead end. (Vogt, *Supermind* 131)

On interrogating the singularity factor, he states that men took birth after the consummation of a man and a woman. An intermingling of genes took place. The race advanced because of this sort of chance intermingling that occurred. In the case of Vince Strather, overstimulation of Omega serum has led to the whipping up of one bundle of genes. This bundle has restricted possibilities. He says that Barbara and Strather are an excellent variety of inbreeding, "life surviving through one line, a kind of incest carried to some ultimate sterility, fantastic, interesting, freakish" (Vogt, *Supermind* 131). Barbara rejects Hammond's statement and says that the galactic seedling variety of genes are instilled in her. She also asks the meaning of Omega and Hammond states, "When man becomes one with the ultimate, that is Point Omega" (Vogt, *Supermind* 131).

Barbara voices, "Mr. Hammond, what you said about being born of man and woman has another, greater meaning. When the right man and the right woman achieve togetherness, they simultaneously achieve fulfilment and the final expansion of being. That is the real completion" (Vogt, *Supermind* 132). Barbara looks up and asks William Leigh, the Great Galactic if he has any message for Hammond. Then, Hammond wishes a perfect marriage to William Leigh and Barbara Ellington.

While many writers reject the concept of time travel in Critical Posthumanism, but the concept is equally important as it reveals the processes that effectuate the merging of humans with other than humans. The concept of time travel to spaces is possible with the deployment of time machines and other technologies. These particulars are evident in the third novel of A.E. Van Vogt named *The World of Null A*.

The narrator is Gilbert Gosseyn who perceives the city of the Machine from his hotel room. The machine was placed on the mountain peak that sparkled with its glory. Gosseyn was least apathetic to the surroundings and exhibited a sense of fascination concerning the games of the machine- "the games which meant wealth and position for those who were partially successful, and the trip to Venus for the special group that won top honours" (Vogt, *Null A* 10). He had always desired to come. Formerly, when power and wealth were significant, he burned the midnight oil with his deceased wife, Patricia. And presently, the power and wealth were meaningless but the aloofness and inscrutability of Venus was influential for him. "It was the remoteness, the unthinkableness, the mystery of Venus, with its promise of forgetfulness, that attracted. He felt himself aloof from the materialism of Earth. In a completely unreligious sense, he longed for spiritual surcease" (Vogt, *Null A* 11).

His reverie broke with a knock on the door. A boy entered and invited him to go to the sitting room where people were conversing over the protection of the inhabitants on this floor as "the world's greatest city would be entirely without police or court protection during the period of the games" (Vogt, *Null A* 11). For about a month, there would only be a negative defensive law of the faction. And, those who do not come downstairs are not secured in any manner.

As he moved into the sitting room, he observed a man named Nordegg, a storekeeper from his own locality. The man behaved peculiarly as if they were not known to each other. Gosseyn gave his personal details to the old man who sat adjacent to the main entrance. "Gilbert Gosseyn, Cress village, Florida, age thirty-four, height six feet one inch, weight one hundred eighty-five, no special distinguishing marks" (Vogt, *Null A* 12).

The old man retorted with a smile, if Gosseyn's mind matches his countenance then he will be permitted to go a long way in the games. Another cheerful man stated that everyone existing here is obligated to repeat the information in the lie detector instrument that they shared with the doorkeeper. In addition to this, before the initiation of the game if anybody has suspicion on the legitimacy of any other member then he/she is free to declare it.

To which, Nordegg questioned the presence of Gilbert Gosseyn probing that he hails from Cress village but there is no person named Gilbert Gosseyn as such residing there.

Gosseyn was stunned to hear Mr. Nordegg's assertion. After repeated arguments, Gosseyn said that there is a strangely-shaped house towards the west of his store to which Nordegg adds, "The world-famous Florida home of the Hardie family" (Vogt, *Null A* 14). Gosseyn said Patricia Hardie is his wife who departed this life a month ago. He also proposed that the lie detector would certainly verify his proclamation. The lie detector answered in the negative that he is neither Gilbert Gosseyn nor an inhabitant of Cress village. Furthermore, it stated that there is a spirit of distinctive strength and there is no information available in his mind concerning his identity. Following the lie detection test, the staff of the hotel compelled him to leave as they could not accommodate any suspicious person during the policeless period.

Gosseyn spent the whole night wandering outside. The city of the Machine glittered and radiated far away. He was ostensibly affected by semi-amnesia. And to break out from the emotional effects of his condition, he must try to understand its signification. He visualises this escape as an 'event' in the exegesis of Null-A. This event designates himself, "as he was, his body and mind as a whole, amnesia and all, as of this moment on this day and in this city" (Vogt, *Null A* 16).

Gosseyn encountered a young girl named Teresa Clark who came darting from the alleyway to get rid of two men trying to attack her. They took shelter under a spreading shrub for the night. Gosseyn asked her whether she was present here for the games. The girl interrogated, "What is all this games stuff, anyway? In a way, it's easy enough to see what happens to winners who stay on Earth. They get all juicy jobs; they become judges, governors, and such. But what about the thousands who every year win the right to go to Venus? What do they do when they get there" (Vogt, *Null A* 20)? Gosseyn responded that these games demand knowledge and acute skill consolidated over a long period of time. The ultimate fifteen days call for suppleness in discerning that only the ambitious and refined brain can contest. One who completes the seven days is rewarded with the lowest job with a remuneration of ten thousand per annum.

Further, he elaborated that the human brain is more or less split into two segments- the thalamus and the cortex. "The cortex is the center of discrimination, the thalamus the center of the emotional reactions of the nervous system" (Vogt, *Null A* 21). Both together have efficient capabilities and should be highly trained to work in synchronization. With cortical-thalamic homogenisation, the nervous system can resist any trauma. If this functionality is not present in any brain, then the person experiences an entangled personality, neurological dysfunction and over-emotionalism.

Gosseyn and the girl walked through the streets of the city and arrived at a place where the machine was clearly visible. The base of the machine seemed gigantic. The first floor of the machine comprised the game rooms. It consisted of seven floors and corridors adjoining them. All the floors accommodated the games for individual contestants. The machine stood magnificently at a great height. It was systematically designed based on the semantic training of humans but no one is aware of the location of its electron-magnetic brain. It stands antiquated unsusceptible to any deception and competent enough to prevent its demolition.

It is an unmoving mechanical brain having both creative and rational faculties. Since the last three hundred or so, the inhabitants accept as to who should govern them.

Teresa Clark went downstairs for the second basement while Gosseyn moved to the third. He got into an empty examination cubbyhole in the G segment. It harbors a transparent panel desk with cabinets, and a folding chair, beside it with electron conduits glinted in a diverse range of flame-yellow and crimson patterns. The core of the panel incorporated an aerodynamic speaker of semi-transparent plastic from which the voice of the machine erupted. It echoed, "Your name? And please grasp the nodes" (Vogt, *Null A* 26). Gosseyn uttered his name and the machine accepted it. Gosseyn was astonished to hear that the machine knew his true name.

At a later point, Gosseyn was ordered to pick up the writing materials from the cabinet containing a few questions. "The questions were as Gosseyn had expected: What is non-Aristotelianism? What is non-Newtonianism? What is non-Euclidianism" (Vogt, *Null A* 26)? For the sake of answering the questions, one is expected to show awareness of the multi-ordinal signification of the stated words as each answer could signal an abstraction.

Gosseyn wrote down the abbreviated forms for each expression- "null-A or – A, null- N or N, and null-E or E" (Vogt, *Null A* 27). After the completion of the task, Gosseyn proleptically sat there. The machine reverberated that he should not be astonished at the directness of today's examination as "the purpose of the games is not to beguile the great majority of the contestants into losing. The purpose is to educate every individual of the race to make the best possible use of the complex nervous system which he or she has inherited" (Vogt, Null A 27). This feat can be achieved where all and sundry can sustain oneself the entire thirty days of the games. One who does not excel in today's test is prohibited from participating in rest of the games of the season.

The papers of the contestants were scanned and scrutinised by the television tube. Instantaneously, Gosseyn questioned whether the false notions were implanted in his mind with any external motive. The machine affirmed that due to logical reasoning, it is suggestive that his hallucinations were focused on Patricia Hardie. Further, the machine states that the practice of hypnosis brings about strong opinions. Consequently, the aforesaid conditions took place in his case and as a result, he was able to abandon his grief when he first learnt that Patricia was alive. The machine regurgitated after a pause, "I am only an immobile brain, but dimly aware of what is transpiring in remote parts of Earth. What plans are brewing I can only guess. You will be surprised and disappointed to learn that I can tell you nothing more about that" (Vogt, *Null A* 28).

The machine suggested he consult a psychiatrist to have the cortex of his brain photographed. Gosseyn walked through the city and reached the Medical Arts building owned by the psychologist, Dr. Enright. The psychologist has authored numerous books on the human body and mind, targeting the audience who want to pass the tenth day of the games. Gosseyn was hopeful that he could recollect Enright and his oeuvre. This reveals how gingerly the amnesia has encroached on his memory. Gosseyn booked an appointment with Dr. Enright. As he sauntered down the street, he saw Teresa Clark alight from the car. But a stranger surprisingly glanced at him and said that the girl was Patricia Hardie. "Why, that's Patricia Hardie, daughter of President Hardie. Quite a neurotic, I understand" (Vogt,

Null A 30).

Gosseyn sat next to her and began to talk gently as the night crept upon them. He narrated his plight from the hotel, his misapprehension of being married to Patricia Hardie, the amnesia that masked his brain, and lastly, "she turned out to be the daughter of the President, and very much alive" (Vogt, *Null A* 31).

A group of men emerged from the bush, seized and forced them into a car. Gosseyn tried to converse with one of the men who sat next to him but the man responded that they were not authorized to talk to him. They passed through a tunnel and assembled near a gateway. Patricia Hardie made an appearance and got into an anteroom. Gilbert Gosseyn is an upskilled null-A who has an impaired brain caused by amnesia. He might be capable of Venus in the games but he will be one of the many similarly victorious contestants. For this, he is supposed to manifest a unique type of structural differentiation in comparison to other contestants. Jim Thorson drawled, "your present predicament will have been integrated into control of your cortex, and semantically clever words will sound forth" (Vogt, *Null A* 34). Gosseyn followed Jim Thorson to the palace of the machine where Patricia and the President resided.

As they entered the President's chamber, Gosseyn's attention was directed towards a monstrous man possessing a plastic arm and leg with a plastic cage at his back. His head was earless and was designed like an opaque glass. "His nose, mouth, chin and neck were human. Beyond that, his resemblance to anything normal depended partly upon the mental concessions of the observer" (Vogt, *Null A* 35). The creature proclaimed himself as 'X'.

The president, Michael Hardie was a disciplinarian

and sensitive man showcasing a pleasurable smile. He stated:

> Gosseyn, we are men who would have been doomed to minor positions if we had accepted the rule of the Machine and the philosophy of null-A. We are highly intelligent and capable in every respect, but we have certain ruthless qualities in our natures that would normally bar us from great success. Ninety-nine percent of the world's history was made by our kind, and you may be sure it shall be so again. (Vogt, *Null A* 35)

He ordered Thorson to collect the required instruments to handcuff Gosseyn's wrists to the arms of his chair. Thorson fastened six cup-shaped gadgets to his face and head and another six to his shoulders, throat and back. Gosseyn inquired about what was taking place at the present moment. "This can't be happening to a law-abiding human being on the peaceful Earth of 2560 A.D." (Vogt, *Null A* 36). He added that in this sphere of Null-A, no one is important to a degree that his plans, inventions or disposition can be utilised for the deterioration of humankind. He recounted that "Individual machines cannot sway the balance against the accumulated mass of science as employed by determined, courageous men in the defense of civilization. That has been proved. Unique science cannot win a war" (Vogt, *Null A* 36).

Michael Hardie regarded Gosseyn as a psychoneurotic who is falsely of the opinion that he is married to his daughter, Patricia. Consequently, his surfacing must be examined. Jim Thorson nodded that he wanted to get into the memory and detect who the person was. He turned on the power switch and the machine vibrated and pulsated. It contains electron tubes so as to manage the momentum of the motors. Some of them sneaked through the plastic box. Gosseyn's eyes were hurt resulting in blurring of vision. His head was hit by an object and it was followed by a severe headache. He sensed as if he had plunged into a pool of water. He was under pressure because of the energy that circulated inside his body.

Gosseyn could hear Thorson giving a lecture:

> The medically interesting characteristic of this artificial flow of nervous energy is that it is photographable. In a few moments, as soon as the movement of artificial energy has penetrated the remotest easy paths, I'll obtain several negatives and make some positive prints. When enlarged in segments through a projector, the prints will show us in what parts of his brain his memory is concentrated. Since science has long known the nature of the memory stored in every cell group, we can then decide where to concentrate the pressures that will force the particular memory we want onto the verbal level. (Vogt, *Null A* 38)

Further, the machine will combine power with the word-association mechanism to perform the operation. Thorson paused the machine and dragged the film from the camera. Both X and Thorson examined the prints and babbled that Gosseyn should be immediately killed. They dragged and placed him in a dungeon.

Gosseyn sat motionless and frightened in the dungeon. He contemplated that a human is made up of a physico-chemical pattern whose consciousness towards life results from a complex nervous system. Following the person's death, the body gets fragmented and the personality continues to exist as a series of deformed impulse memories in another person's nervous system. With an advancing age, the memories in the person fade. So far as possible, Gosseyn would exist as a nerve impulse in another human for a semicentennial, as an emulsion on microfilm for the next hundred years, and as a photoelectric model in a sequence of cathode-ray tubes for several centuries. As he thought that he was going to die, he realised that his nerve was getting shattered.

After a few minutes, Patricia Hardie entered the hall freed him from the clutches of President Hardie and ordered him to hide in her bedroom. From her private chamber, Gosseyn could visualise the atomic lantern of the machine. It sparkled so near that he thought of grasping the light with his hand. Patricia unlatched the door and asked if he wanted to capture the machine to save the world. She added, "This plot is bigger than Earth, bigger than the solar system. We're pawns in a game being played by men from the stars" (Vogt, *Null A* 42). In this case, the monkey theory appears to be credible as to how men invaded the Earth. The sound of the footsteps ended the discussion as a few men came in search of Gosseyn. He desperately went to the ground floor and crawled along the pavement when he was shot with the first bullet and subsequently lost his senses.

He lay unconscious behind the trunk of a huge tree. He had turned into an insentient being who could hear noises coming from the functioning machine. As he regained his senses, he found himself on the soil of Venus. His stream of thoughts transformed with the awakening of his memory. The drizzle of impulse metamorphosed into a stream. "The fact that he was alive with the memory of having been killed became less a thing of remembered agony, more a puzzle, a paradox that had no apparent explanation in the null-A world" (Vogt, *Null A* 45). He witnessed several gigantic trees whose trunks were as thick as high-rise buildings. He came across a Venusian house made up of stone. It had become obscure with shrubbery. He landed up at the veranda where the names of John and Amelia Prescott were engraved on the floor.

Gosseyn could recollect these names once used by Patricia and Eldred Crang, "that Eldred Crang, commander of the local galactic base, and John Prescott, the vice-commander, have both been converted to null-A, then" (Vogt, *Null A* 46). And then Crang had said, "I've been intending to warn you. I no longer trust Prescott absolutely. He's been shifting and squirming ever since Thorson's arrival" (Vogt, *Null A* 47). He realised that John Prescott had acquired the A philosophy judiciously but never attempted to make it a fundamental part of the complex nervous system. He is a galactic agent disguised as a medical professional. He possesses a muscular body but this is essential if he has never received any A muscular guidance. "People who were not conditioned had difficulty understanding how strong human muscles could be when they were temporarily cut off from the fatigue center of the brain" (Vogt, *Null A* 47).

As he came close to the house, he heard John annotating on a recorder. The woman named Amelia stood near the entrance of the house and yelled, "John, it's less than a month since you returned from Earth, yet now you want to be off again" (Vogt, *Null A* 47). With a sense of dejection, John replied, "I'm restless, Amelia. You know I have a high energy index. Until the mood passes, I've got to be on the move or build up silly frustrations"

(Vogt, *Null A* 47). Gosseyn managed to hit John and Amelia when they saw him with persistent blows. He carried the comatose creatures to their private chamber and departed to investigate the house.

The house gave the impression of being a hospital with a surgical room and laboratory in the basement. The hospital was built on a lower peak and one can arrive at this place by air i.e., by a Roboplane. For summoning a plane one can dial their number. "All public roboplanes are connected with the dial system. That goes by pattern. The planes follow the electronic pattern and come to the videophone" (Vogt, *Null A* 51).

As Gosseyn moved into the private chamber, John and Amelia recovered from the trance. John Prescott made inquiries about the videophone who was in a state of impairment. His wife reported, "But isn't there supposed to be automatic warning long before anything is worn out, whereupon a repairman comes along and fixes it up" (Vogt, *Null A* 52)? Gosseyn tiptoed to the room and asked for the maps of Venus. He spread out the maps and "found it about four hundred miles north of the city of New Chicago" (Vogt, *Null A* 53). Amelia warned that the Venusian authorities were planning to capture him. Gosseyn examined the woman's mind and touched the lie detector to verify whether she is uttering the truth. The lie detector said, "That's the way it is" (Vogt, *Null A* 53). She disclosed, "We have no police system on Venus, and no ordinary crimes. But the cases requiring detective work that come up are always solved with extraordinary speed. You'll be interested in meeting a null-A detective, but you'll be shocked by the swiftness with which you are captured" (Vogt, *Null A* 53).

After hearing this remark, Gosseyn drops his plan

to meet the Venusian authorities and at once decides to leave the place. He has an intricate conversation with John Prescott mentioning to him that his life story is a flawed one. Gosseyn abruptly rejects this point of view, "My story is true according to my memory. And any lie detector will bear out every word of it. That is, unless all the memory I now have is of the same category as my earlier belief that I had been married to Patricia Hardie, but that she had died, leaving me grief-stricken. What is this flaw you have detected" (Vogt, *Null A* 54)?

John prompted thalamically that he should not forget his identification and memory of himself with the man named Gosseyn who was murdered by the bullets that struck him. He added that according to null-A, two ideas or things in this universe can't be identical at one time. Gilbert Gosseyn being alive claims a resemblance of his physique with a dead man named Gilbert Gosseyn I because this identification was stored in his memory. For this reason, his moniker is Gilbert Gosseyn I. In ancient philosophy, it is clearly stated that two ostensibly similar chairs are dissimilar in a thousand manners that are undoubtedly not visible to bare eyes. Likewise, a nerve impulse in the human brain can take multitudinous paths and is of twenty-seven-thousandth potential. The delicate structure that is created based on individual experience can never be mimeographed. This is evident that "why never in the history of Earth had one animal, one snowflake, one stone, one atom ever been exactly the same as another" (Vogt, *Null A* 55).

Now Gosseyn didn't believe in the picture that was painted by him. He went on to test this in the lie detector to which the lie detector, an inhuman object answered in response, "It is impossible for me to prove or disprove your story. My judgments are based on memory flow. You have the memory of Gilbert Gosseyn I. That includes a memory of having been killed so realistically that I hesitate to say it couldn't have been death. There is still no clue as to your real identity" (Vogt, *Null A* 55).

Gosseyn unknotted Amelia and took her along with him a few steps ahead. He informed him that John's faith in null A is more powerful than his allegiance to the government. He also made inquiries regarding the functioning of the hospital. In answer to this, Amelia explained when a person is injured and needs to be hospitalised, the robot exchange informs the nearby unit and after that, they admit or deny the patient.

As the night fell, Amelia left Gosseyn in that sequestered place. A flash of light beamed on his face and it was followed by a voice that ordered him to board the plane. To make the situation hassle-free, many guns were pointed at him. With utter silence, he walked to the door leading to the roboplane and the machine acquired its speed in the dead of night.

The roboplane vocalised, "During the next ten minutes you may ask any questions you please. After that I must give you landing instructions" (Vogt, *Null A* 58). Gosseyn realised that the voice that he heard is one of the agents of the Games Machine speaking indirectly to him. The agent added, "The Machine can receive messages from Venus but cannot itself broadcast on interplanetary wave lengths" (Vogt, *Null A* 58). Gosseyn requested for information about his identity and past about which the machine had no particulars. In its calm voice, the roboplane urged him to interrogate only regarding Venusian conditions. The machine explained to him in detail the prevailing situation on Venus. The planet has no dominating power such as any president or council members. Everything is left to the discretion of the people living here. People have the right to choose their profession based on personal choice. And not everyone selects the same profession as the population is responsible enough to carry out the work that is to be done.

For instance, when a detective plans to retire from his job he advertises his position and interviews the people who want to opt for his position. Finally, his next-in-line is chosen. But presently, the gang of Prescott has taken charge of all the judicial and detective positions. Consequently, the videophones of menacing creatures are being tapped by Thorson's detectives. For this reason, the machine had to build up an interference against his use of the videophone at Prescott's place.

Thorson wants to capture Gosseyn as his survival and his mysterious mind has led to a great war machine to take the record of time. And his only rationality lies in letting himself fall in the hands of Thorson so they can analyse his peculiar nervous system. Lastly, the machine instructed him, "In a few moments you will be landed beside the forest home of Eldred Crang. Go to him and tell him your story of the threat to null A as if you do not know anything about him. You're on your own from the moment you land. Don't underestimate the potentialities of a man who has been killed but is still alive" (Vogt, *Null A* 60).

Gosseyn stepped down and did as he was instructed by the roboplane. He saw a bright light glimmering from a house that belongs to Eldred Crang. As Crang was away from his home, he rested for some time. Then he went to the living room where he came across several books that fascinated him: *The Aristotelian and Non-Aristotelian History of Venus*, *The Egotist on Non-Aristotelian Venus*, *The Machine and Its Builders*, and *Detectives in a World without Criminals*.

He lifted the book entitled Venusian History. It narrates the story of the first men who landed on Venus. It inculcates the affiliation of the Institute of General Semantics in 2018 A.D. setting its foot on the governmental stage of the A capabilities. After a hundred years, the machine selected the colonists who were the emigrants from Earth.

He read another book named *The Egotist on Non-Aristotelian Venus*. It contains an excerpt that the author named Dr. Lauren Kair, Ps.D. who, 'would be practicing on Earth in the city of the Machine from 2559 A.D. to 2564 A.D. (Vogt, *Null A* 65).

A few moments later four men entered the house with guns pointing at him. Gosseyn realised that Eldred Crang, the galactic agent, detective of Venus and a patron of null-A had finally arrived at his apartment. He is cognizant of the fact that Patricia Hardie is in love with Crang. One of the men named Blayney babbled, "Mr. Crang, Why, if he had escaped, the big boss would have" (Vogt, *Null A* 68). Gosseyn countered Blayney saying that he lacks null A consolidation. Gosseyn explains, "His nervous system is beginning to react as strongly to things that might have happened as it would if they had actually occurred. It's a purely functional disorder, but its outward form is distressing to the individual. A gradual loss of courage. Sadistic outbursts to cover up the developing cowardice. By the time he's forty he'll be having nightmares about the damage he might have suffered in some of the danger spots he was in as a youth" (Vogt, *Null A* 68). This clearly indicates that Blayney is deficient in null A.

Ensuingly, Gosseyn was dumbfounded to see John and Amelia Prescott handcuffed and dragged to the living room. It was the outcome of Amelia's faith in her husband being more A than belonging to the gang. Notwithstanding the faith in the A philosophy, Eldred Crang intends to remain a part of the gang that demands displeasing compromises where a person's life is in danger.

In the dark of the night, a spaceship appeared from nowhere containing one woman and another four hundred men. Crang accompanied by Gosseyn climbed the spaceship and after a space expedition of three days, they reached Earth and paid a visit to the official headquarters of President Hardie i.e., the city of the Machine. Gosseyn was directed towards a guest room where he would spend the entire night. Patricia came with a bang on the door asking him why he left without informing. She remarked, "You did leave, got yourself killed, and now here you are again" (Vogt, *Null A* 71).

She retorted that Gosseyn must what his real identity is. Gosseyn was surprised and stung when she finally said:

> This second body of yours actually knows nothing more than the first. You're really just a pawn. The truth is that your very lack of knowledge has startled all groups. Thorson, the personal representative of Enro has postponed the invasion of Venus. You'll want to know about 'X'. So do the rest of us. The man has a will of iron, but no one knows what his purpose is. He seems to be primarily interested in his own aggrandizement, and he has expressed the hope that some use can be made of you. The Galactic League people are bewildered. They can't decide whether the cosmic chess player who has moved you into this game is an ally or not. Everybody is groping in the dark, wondering what to do next. (Vogt, *Null A* 72)

Another visitor was President Hardie, who acquired this position by commissioning a gang and demeaning the rules of the games of machines. Gosseyn posed a question about his identity. Hardie said that a couple of nights ago he received a letter that the author of the letter knew the best hidden fact about the solar system. The conspiracy that is being designed against Venus. In addition to this, Gosseyn will reside in the Tropical Park Hotel and save the planet from being attacked.

The next question that Gosseyn asks is what shall happen to him. Hardie answered, "You will be made an offer, just what I don't know yet. Thorson and 'X' are talking it over. Whatever it is, I think you would be advised to accept it for the time being. Mind you, you're in a strong position. Theoretically, if you can have two bodies, then why not a third" (Vogt, *Null A* 74)? He further remarked that, "Even as we plot to destroy the null A philosophy, we adopt its logic. The map is not the territory. Your belief that you know nothing is an abstraction from reality, not the reality itself" (Vogt, *Null A* 75). Hardie inspected if any time Gosseyn felt that he is dissimilar to other humans. Gosseyn said that Thorson's discovery relates to the possibility that he possesses extra brain matter. Prescott confesses that Amelia is captivated until the ensuing attack on the planet Venus is successful. And that Thorson and X have planned something for Amelia in relation to Gosseyn. He also offers some antidotes like pills for his safety which Gosseyn double-checks in the lie detector. After the lie detector approves of the pill, he swallows it.

Eldred Crang plunges into the room and escorts Gosseyn to a locked room for the sake of showing the dead body of Gilbert Gosseyn I. Gosseyn oscillates between life and death, thought and action, abstract and reality.

His organs endured a deep metabolic alteration. He had anticipated a scorched body. The body was damaged with the machine bullets but the head part remained intact. It was separated from the body. Gosseyn did not make any attempts to know whether the brain was inside the head or not.

Amelia was dragged inside the room. The half-human named X peered at Gosseyn and uttered that Gosseyn had put them in a quandary. They are allocated with "nine thousand spaceships, forty million men, gigantic munitions factories, yet this but a fraction of the military power of the greatest empire that ever was" (Vogt, *Null A* 82). He spoke again, "Nevertheless we prefer to play safe. We'd like to invite you, the unknown quantity, to join us as one of the top leaders in the solar system" (Vogt, *Null A* 82). "But you can understand that it would be useless even to begin such a relationship if you turned out to be unwilling to accept the realities of our position. We have to kill, Gosseyn. We have to be ruthless. Killing convinces people as nothing else will" (Vogt, *Null A* 82). This implies that millions of Venusians must be slaughtered.

X persuaded Gosseyn to be decisive so that he could perform a lot of transformations. But Gosseyn refused to make such kind of deal. His voice clamoured, "No deal. And may all of you burn in an early Christian hell for even thinking of such murder" (Vogt, *Null A* 83). At that moment, X ordered Thorson to kill Amelia. A syringe was plunged into her arm and she fell to the ground. In a trice, everyone except Gilbert Gosseyn, present inside the room dashed to the ground into a state of senselessness.

A few minutes later John Prescott appeared and asked Gosseyn, "Aren't you glad you took that antidote? I put Drae powder in the airconditioning machine, and you're the only one who" (Vogt, *Null A* 84). The drae powder operates in the nerves of the upper nostril hence making its way to the brain. Then John Prescott injected a syringe containing fluorescin into the thigh of Amelia. If she is breathing then the colour of her lips will change to greenish but the lips appear to be dead. Prescott fired two bullets against X and Michael Hardie.

After an hour they fled from the place by car. On the way, they heard the news of the assassination of President Michael Hardie by Gosseyn whose escape was facilitated by some Venusian detectives. Gosseyn searched for Dr. Kair's house. Kair is a semanticist who has acquired specialisation in the human brain. Gosseyn wants his brain to be diagnosed by this psychiatrist to find out how and for what reason his brain contains additional matter and as a result classified as peculiar.

Gosseyn went through dozens of tests. Some machines dazzled with galvanic eyes and others heated his skin. The sensitive rays of the machine investigated the additional matter in his brain. Eventually, the psychiatrist declared that there was no room for insanity in him.
The psychiatrist started explaining that Gosseyn does not own an additional brain matter. He stated that:

> The human brain that created the Games Machine and similar electronic and mechanical organisms has not even theoretically an intellectual equal in the universe. People sometimes think that the electronic brain system of the Machine constitutes a development superior to that of man. They marvel at the machine's capacity to handle twenty-five thousand individuals at once, but actually, it can do so only because twen-

ty-five thousand electronic brains were set up in intricate series for just that purpose. And besides, these operations are all of a routine nature. (Vogt, *Null A* 90)

He clarifies that:

...it is not to say that the machine cannot think creatively. It is located over a multimetal mine, which is completely under its control. It has laboratories, where robots work under its direction. It is capable of manufacturing tools and does all its own replacement and repair work. It has a virtually inexhaustible source of atomic energy. The machine, in short, is self-sufficient and superlatively intelligent, but it has limitations. These limitations were implanted from the beginning, and consist of three broadly based directives. (Vogt, *Null A* 91)

These include, "It must operate the games fairly, within the framework of the laws laid down long ago by the Institute of General Semantics. It must protect the development of null-A in the broadest sense. It can kill human beings only when they directly attack it" (Vogt, *Null A* 91).

Dr. Kair gesticulated that Jim Thorson, galactic agent of Enro is going to be next in line to Michael Hardie i.e., the President of Earth. Gosseyn wanted to know about the doctor's family. The doctor answered that Venusian children are permitted to come to Earth after they attain the age of eighteen. For this reason, his family is residing in New Chicago, Venus.

Prescott mentioned after hearing from the psychiatrist he was undoubtful of the fact that Gosseyn cannot gain control of his additional brain matter. Gosseyn questioned him "Where did X or the gang get the instrument, they use to corrupt the Games Machine? And where is that instrument now" (Vogt, *Null A* 97)? With an uneven tone, Prescott said that the 'Distorter' lies in Patricia Hardie's apartment and it was built to look like a wall. This is brought by Jim Thorson and is illicitly used. After this session was over, the roboplane arrived shortly and Gosseyn in the company of Kair left the place.

Inside the roboplane, Gosseyn asked Dr. Kair to elaborate on Venus and how it is different from Earth. The doctor riposted Venus has a mild climate due to the high clouds. Rainfall occurs only near the mountainous regions. But in matters of research, Earth is superior to Venus as "there are more people here, and specialization makes it possible for minds of middling intelligence- even unsane minds- to invent and discover" (Vogt, *Null A* 98).

After an hour, Gosseyn decided to abandon the roboplane as he had less time to save the solar system from being seized by a galactic empire. He fastened the ingravity parachute and adjusted the control into a circular arc and pulled the entrance door.

The ingravity parachute is an outcome of the null-A mechanism. It works within the range of Newton's law of gravity which states that in the universe every single particle attracts the other particle and the smaller of the two does the work. Gosseyn landed on the balcony of Patricia Hardie's apartment to have a look at the games machine.

He briskly lowered the parachute to the ground and got out of it. He went to Patricia's bed chamber and tied her and apologised for being rough with her. With her assistance, he desired to flee from the palace. In nanoseconds, Eldred Crang, the hidden A caught him with handguns.

He pronounced calmly that Thorson is of the opinion to imprison him but "I maintain that death and imprisonment are but facets of the same thing. And that either would be the signal for the appearance of Gosseyn III. We don't want that. And if we don't kill you. Then no one else will except you yourself- or some other agent of the invisible chess player" (Vogt, *Null A* 102). Correspondingly, they have resolved to free him so that he can protect himself.

He detailed further that the man who is at his back will never have two living bodies at once. As this might lead to the possibility of each body creating more potent equivalents of itself resulting in various complexities for the other body. Subsequently, he was free of all the charges and abandoned the palace.

Gosseyn went back to his hotel where he had left his possessions. He went through the reports of the radio exchange that asserts that no contact could be initiated with Venus. The machine mentioned that the Venusian cities had already been attacked but it failed to warn them as the gaze of the distorter was on him. The machine kept going:

> An electronic system of brains is a very curious and limited structure. It works by a process of intermittent power flow. In this process the denial of power at the proper split instants is as important as the flow during other split instants. The Distorter permits only movement of energy, not the hindrances or the variances. When it is focused on any part of me, the particular function to which it is attuned ceases to have inhibitions. In photo-electric cells. Thyratrons, amplifiers, and in every part of my structure, the flow of energy becomes

uniform and meaningless. My system of public communicators is constantly under this baneful influence. (Vogt, *Null A* 106) The machine added that it can declare the truth only to three persons at one time. Gosseyn had an appointment with Patricia. He was escorted to the top floor where he encountered John Prescott who had come to meet Eldred Crang, an advocator of null-A. He elaborated on his conversation with the machine and how it wanted Gosseyn should destroy himself so that a third Gilbert Gosseyn might take birth. Prescott took his leave for Venus. Gosseyn went to Patricia's chamber and tied her. He took out the atomic cutter and lacerated the wall that contained the Distorter. After slashing the wall, he impetuously took the Distorter into the sitting room. A few minutes later, three men arrived and packed the Distorter. They placed the Distorter on the crate of a truck and disappeared from the place.

Gosseyn left Patricia's apartment. While going back to his hotel room, he took a hypnotic drug from the nearest drugstore to prepare himself for next year's games. He borrowed a voice recorder for a week from a nearby firm. He went to his room and recorded the thing as he had planned. There was only a single sound of his voice reiterating, "I'm nobody. I'm not worth anything. Everybody hates me. What's the good of being alive? I'll never make anything of myself. No girl will ever marry me. I'm ruined... no hope... no money... kill myself... Everybody hates me... hates me... hates me..." (Vogt, *Null A* 114). He gulped down the hypnotic drug and rested himself on the bed to hear this recording repeatedly. He attempted suicide so that his triplicate i.e., Gosseyn III could emerge.

After an hour, he heard a deafening voice from a

distance. Then, he could hear the firing sounds of guns and cannons. He crawled to the window and discerned that the massive sounds were coming from the machine. He switched on the broadcasting radio in his hotel room and the voices came, "The dastardly machine! Mechanical monstrosity, treacherous inhuman! The Venusian plotters who had foisted its poisonous alien will upon men. Straitjacket… assassin… massacre…" (Vogt, *Null A* 116). Gosseyn assumed that the Machine with the Distorter under its possession is trying to broadcast the impending ambush on Venus as a result the gang attempted to knock it down.

    Gosseyn got back to his bed and dozed off. Instantaneously, he heard the Machine's voice admonishing him to not kill himself as his third body had already been destroyed. He must train himself to use the additional brain matter that he owns. The Machine also states that its ninety-foot steel barricade has been attacked by atomic torpedoes that were fired from the location of Venus. Within a short span of time, the Games Machine was dismantled.

    Gosseyn struggled to regain his consciousness from the hypnotic state. But a memory struck him of the purpose of his coming to the hotel room. He thought of grabbing the automatic that he had brought from Patricia and shooting his brain immediately. However, the impulse to murder himself did not occur to him. As he struggled to get off the bed, he glanced at Patricia seated beside him. When asked the reason behind her coming here, she answered that his attempt at conveying the Distorter to the Machine had misfired. She also informed that the Distorter is even now positioned inside the Machine where he had placed it. The Distorter being among the few accessible astronomical devices, must have it for the sake of accumulating evidence.

Further, she expressed that a general warning could have prevented the devastation that took place. However, due to the lack of government in Venus, it is dominated by the gang. The only remedy is to build up an upgraded Machine after the situation subsides. The Semantics Institute is working on highly efficient lie detectors that can scrutinise the mind and body of a person and quantify the amount of his null A grounding. This will in turn lead to the abolishment of the laborious games and safeguard the Machine from any further disturbance. She also warned him that as his third body is damaged, he has again become a wanted human. And an agent in this hotel named, Dan Lyttle will help him out of this.

He demanded ocular connectivity to the robot of the phonolibrary that brought about an image on the videoplate. He desired for recommendation on how to train his additional brain matter.

Gosseyn and Dan Lyttle walked through the passageway that led to the Machine. As they came out into the open, two guards rushed with guns. Gosseyn attacked them like they had "unhuman qualities, they were barbarous entities, to be destroyed like attacking beasts and forgotten" (Vogt, *Null A* 125). The dead machine stood there in a dilapidated condition. Gosseyn considered the Machine as a superior organism. He voiced his opinion:

> In all the man-known history of the world, there never had been an organism with so much memory, such a vast experience, such a tremendous knowledge of human beings and human nature, as the Games Machine. He was shocked to see men schlepping metal plates and machinery through the passageway hinting at the end of an epoch.

They advanced to the projection where the Distorter was placed. There were many doors near the platform. But the outhouse was left unoccupied and the crate with the Distorter in it stood off by itself as if waiting for them. (Vogt, *Null A* 126)

It contained an address on it, "Research Department The Semantic Institute Korzybski Square City" (Vogt, *Null A* 127). This implies that the machine was legally controlled by this institute.

They carried the Distorter, "bright, steely, alien metal-world destroyer" (Vogt, *Null A* 127) to the Dan Lyttle's cabin and examined it. To acquire it, astronomers have reached faraway regions of Earth. His seizure of the object is evidence of his final hassle in A. He located the origin of energy that is utilised by the tubes for switching it off or on. He gathered a few instruments that were used in null-A physics. He perceived, "the world of A, which he had once thought he was supposed to save, was crashing, had crashed, around him" (Vogt, *Null A* 127).

Shortly, Lyttle called from a pay phone and informed him that Patricia had been arrested. Gosseyn keenly observed the Distorter and pushed the tube. He felt a strain on his eyes. He vibrated as if a stone had been rigorously tossed. He opened his eyes to see that there was complete darkness. The scent reminded him of the tunnel behind the Venusian house of Eldred Crang. He was doubtless of the fact that "he was in a tunnel in the roots of a gigantic tree of Venus" (Vogt, *Null A* 130).

He touched the four edges of the tubes and the final edge was lowered. He muttered, "The Distorter had been set by people who had their own purposes and destinations. Some of the tubes were designed to interfere with the Games Machine, but a few surely could transport him to other parts of the solar system, possibly to key centers of gang activity- military headquarters, the secret galactic base, storehouses of atomic torpedoes" (Vogt, *Null A* 131). He cautiously carried the Distorter and walked through the murkiness. He came across a metal pothole that glinted faintly. At the extreme end, there lay an interstellar ship that was only imaginable by the Earthmen in their wildest of dreams. He saw tiny creatures crawling on the metal body of the ship. Within no time the gigantic ship vanished. Carrying the Distorter, he went down to the pit.

He came across a Distorter kind of elevator that was more complicated than expected as it not only moved up and down but also towards twelve directions. He investigated each of the tubes of the elevator. Each tube headed towards different paths. He pressed the tube downwards. This time his senses became hazy with the anaesthesia and when he regained his vision, the scene in front of him had transformed. There was a room with a hole in the ceiling from which light spattered down. He concealed the Distorter in the room and ascended the hole for the sake of contacting the Venusians. There was a thick Venusian jungle in the opposite direction. Using his cortical-thalamic impulse he climbed the limb of the tree. He found a robogun with the scream of Jim Thorson to surrender himself.

The Minister of Foreign Affairs of the Greatest Empire and the ambassador of the League landed on the beast's planet. He desired to go for a hunting business. They had guns and silent machines for each variety of beasts. Ensuing this, Enro the Red and the league officer have a conversation on the league that was formed by "nineteen galactic empires at a time when they were destroying each other in futile and indecisive wars" (Vogt, *Null A* 137). The motto of the league is to maintain peace and stability.

The league officer curtly said that many years ago a transportation base was entrenched near the sun system named Sol without the consent of the league. So, that should now be destroyed and made out of place as Sol is the system that was discovered after authorisation and agreement with regard to the findings and exploitation of the new stars. As per the charter of the League, the transit base must be removed from that sun system.

Jim Thorson set his foot inside the bedroom of Gosseyn. After a light conversation, the room was filled with darkness. Thorson showed him a video scene that was in the form of a virtual reality. This scene was shot using radaric cameras during the night time. Gosseyn saw galactic soldiers resting and had dressed themselves in green uniforms. They were conversing in a language that he failed to understand. Thorson entitled them as Altarians who were not permitted to speak the local language and that is why they had the language of their own. Gosseyn was surprised to learn that the galactic beings also had their language. As, "in his mind whenever he thought of a galactic empire and its myriad peoples were on a non-verbal level" (Vogt, *Null A* 141). He also spotted machines wandering in the clouds spinning and rotating with guns targeting all the sides.

The creatures were so tiny that they could jump from the trees like monkeys and carry clubs with them. They were attacked by the automatic machines during the night and thousands of them were killed because they were unaware of how to operate the device that makes the darkness visible. Thorson angrily moaned, "It's enough to drive you mad, to watch those stupid fools acting like all the stupid soldiers that ever were" (Vogt, *Null A* 141). He felt devastated as "no one expected unarmed hordes to attack one of the best equipped armies in the galaxy" (Vogt, *Null A* 142). He reiterates, even after the passage of the fourth day of invasion their spaceships have been seized and up to two million men have been assassinated. Gosseyn confusingly asked, "What are you trying to put over? How could a galactic empire with more soldiers than there are people in the solar system be defeated in four days? Why shouldn't they be able to supply virtually endless armies and if necessary, exterminate every null-A on Venus" (Vogt, *Null A* 143)? Jim Thorson answers, The Greatest Empire is associated with the galactic league having few obligations and signed treaties that prohibit the use of the Distorter and atomic energy that they utilised against the Machine. And if they fight for a few more weeks, they will be contingent to severe penalties.

Gosseyn was filled with resentment towards the galactic empire for frolicking power politics with human lives. He thought of supporting the inhabitants of Venus. But for him the spirit of A is that no two circumstances are similar. He is Gilbert Gosseyn II and is the sole owner of additional brain matter in the cosmos. Thus, his aim must be to train this special brain.

Jim Thorson added that Gosseyn is here to end this invasion. He narrated that they killed him at first. Then, Gosseyn made his reappearance on Venus to capture him Thorson ordered Prescott to allow him to escape so that he can be easily caught later on. Subsequently, Dr. Kair helped them to find his additional brain. In due course, Gosseyn reappeared in a second body as Gilbert Gosseyn II on the grounds of immortality that occurs "except the kind of accidents that can happen to bodies on Earth, where outsiders and their weapons have access everywhere" (Vogt, *Null A* 145).

Thorson reckoned that Gosseyn's third body was found at the Semantics Institute owned by 'X' whose real name is Lavoisseur. He did not intend to destroy the third body of Gosseyn but when his men were trying to get the body out of the container of Games Machine it exploded. He said, "That's the picture, my friend. I assure you there was a Gosseyn III. I saw him with my own eyes, and he looked exactly like you a nd exactly like Gosseyn I" (Vogt, *Null A* 146).

Darkly, he said, Enro is against the galactic league and desires war conspicuously and has instructed him to do away with the null A Venus as an intentional stimulation. But for the sake of Gosseyn, he refused to obey Enro's orders.

He suggests that they must find out the 'cosmic chess player'. Additionally, Gosseyn is a pawn, a partial version of the prototype. He adds:

> No matter how much you develop, you can probably never know who you are and what is the real purpose of the person behind you. And, Gosseyn, you must realize that he was only temporarily caught off base. Wherever he gets these additional bodies, you can be sure that he needs you for a short time only while he puts others into- production. It sounds inhuman, I know, but there's no point in fooling yourself. Whatever you do now, whatever success you attain, in a very short time you'll be scheduled for the scrap pile. And because of the accident that

happened to Gosseyn III, it just may be that the life memories of I and II will be lost. (Vogt, *Null A* 147)

Thorson requests Gosseyn to help them to which Gosseyn agrees but on one condition which is to initially train his additional brain matter. Gosseyn began to train his extra brain by joining two chunks of wood that were three centimetres away. The thought waves of his additional brain have administered this matter. It signifies the dominancy of the human brain over matter. The heat generated from his body would have made this possible. "It had similarized the blocks to nineteen decimal places. It quieted the molecular movement of the air, partially similarized the table on which the blocks rested, Gosseyn's chair, and Gosseyn himself" (Vogt, *Null A* 149).

Jim Thorson examined the photographs that revealed minute impulses ascending to the exceptional brain. Gosseyn was tired as the tests prolonged. As he started moving towards his apartment, he observed a little, circular metal ball containing a vibrator hovering behind him. Dr. Kair stated, "It will be used to make tiny changes in the atomic structure of the walls, ceilings, floors, ground everything-wherever you've been. It is a precaution against the time when you will be able to transport yourself from your apartment to any piece of matter, the structure of which you have previously memorized" (Vogt, *Null A* 149).

Gosseyn found Patricia in the living room of his apartment. He warily informs Patricia that the people of Earth and Venus have encountered a ravenous intergalactic empire attempting to overpower other astronomical systems despite the disapprobation of an pure Aristotelian league. It is evidence of "how neurotic a civilization can become when it fails to develop a method for integrating the human part of man's mind with the animal part" (Vogt, *Null A* 151). This is turn has resulted in wastage of their ancillary advances in science due to their overindulgence in achieving power.

Patricia says that she is his wife. She went on calmly that Thorson might murder them when he desires, pertaining to the way he killed his father and 'X'. She utters that her father despite having desirable qualifications was deprived of advancement in Null A by the machine. Patricia was also disinterested in this case. But when Eldred Crang came after a long gap she had her first encounter with the Galactic League which took place after a meteoric ascendency in the diplomatic affairs of the Galactic Empire.

Patricia reckons the league has varied imperfections. The League members are aware of the workings of null A but have failed to stimulate it elsewhere in the cosmos. The permanent League personnel have long been aware of null A but have been unable to promote it anywhere in the galaxy.

After an interval of two days, he twisted two rays of light together in the gloomy room without any assistance of the Distorter. The sensation that he felt was like "a floating arm in hypnosis" (Vogt, *Null A* 154). With time, the impulses in his body grew stronger and manageable. He tried to distinguish his personal feelings for Eldred Crang, John Prescott and Jim Thorson. He realises that Prescott furiously dislikes him because of the fright that he got when Gosseyn duped him by going to the palace for the second time for the sake of getting the Distorter.

Jim Thorson is a Machiavellian and purposeful human. He has no attachment to his prisoner. Eldred Crang is an unbiased person who is playing the game safely and intricately. Gosseyn tried to connect to Patricia's nervous system unsuccessfully. He comprehended that a man cannot get in on a woman's nervous system. In due course, Gosseyn tried to meddle with the vibrator's divergent energies. He was victorious in administering it as it was a tiny machine and the parts were near in space-time continuum. Later on, he was offered a metal rod "with a concave cup made of electron steel, the metal used for atomic energy" (Vogt, *Null A* 155). He attracted with his mind the power source that was present in his cabin. The electric force scintillated in the concave cup and sputtered against the wall and the ground. After twenty days Thorson decided to discontinue this brain training. Ensuingly, he saw three guards relieve the vibrator in the escalator and Prescott ordered him to enter. As Prescott speeded up to the control room, Gosseyn planted a hard blow on his face. A few moments later, four dead men lay on the floor.

Gosseyn flaked off Prescott's suit that was entwined with electronic devices. He took the next step by opening the entrance of the escalator to do away with the vibrator. He plunged it out and piled up the dead bodies mercilessly. He pushed a tube that led him to an unknown passageway. He retained the formation of the floor near the shafts of the elevator. He raced towards the turn near the passageway. Then, he retained the series of floors and named it A. He returned to the shafts of the elevator and punched the third tube. The words mentioned were "2" and "B". He achieved the aim that he had set for himself, "Nine pattern keys and as far as 'I' in the alphabet of alternative patterns. And every electric socket on the way was 'memorised' by a system of mathematical symbols" (Vogt, *Null A* 156).

He pressed another tube that escorted him to Patricia's apartment. His additional brain can draw on forty-one energy sources. His hands palpitated at the thought of the impediments. Within thirty minutes he will be set afloat to the military movement and following this either he will return victorious or he will die. He intends to kill Thorson and if he becomes unsuccessful in the endeavour, he will demolish the base.

The city of Machine had transformed after the invasion. The palace was in a dilapidated condition. Everywhere there were disintegrated buildings. Thorson returned from Venus and they went to Patricia's living room. They reached the wall on which the Distorter opened widely. The widows seemed out of place. Gosseyn gazed at the place where the games machine stood like an ornament crowning the Earth. Crowds of men led their way to Dan Lyttle's little cabin.

CHAPTER IV

Intertwining Human Subjectivities: Hybridising the Idea of Man in the Novels of Don Delillo

This study embraces a Critical Posthumanist approach to look over how Don Delillo's *Zero K* aims to reestablish and belatedly disassemble binary opposites so that a relatively posthuman cyborg can spring up. Concurrently, their spirited evolution provokes a crucial conflict between the German philosopher, Jurgen Habermas and American political activist, Francis Fukuyama, who consider it a menace to society. Regardless of the deep mistrust of the schools of transhumanism and posthumanism, a brand-new epoch seems to have come to light. It is considered to be the next level in the process of evolution of man.

To illustrate, the American theorist, N. Katherine Hayles' conjecture appears to have derived from the contemplations on technology and cybernetics. She states, "I understand human and posthuman to be historically specific constructions that emerge from different configurations of embodiment, technology, and culture" (*How We Became Posthuman* 33-34).

Hayles essentially signals 'the liberal subject' as a subject for reference and assumes that Critical Posthumanism initiates "when computation rather than possessive individualism is taken as the ground of being, a move that allows the posthuman to be seamlessly articulated with intelligent machines" (*How We Became Posthuman* 33-34).

A distinct perspective is appropriated by the Professor of Cardiff University, Neil Badmington, who searches for a description by inquiring into man's apprehension towards aliens in movies. He contends that "the confident humanism of the past seems not to apply at the beginning of the twenty-first century. The line that once absolutely divided and distinguished humans from aliens has become blurred. There is no invasion and, more strikingly, no apparent enemy" (*Alien Chic* 30).

Regardless of the fact that Badmington and Hayles belong to different areas, they have an identical point of view, i.e., reevaluating the concept of man. This implies that man has approximately or partially arrived at a stage and deals with absolute oppressive structures that plague mankind. It is indispensable to consider that man has been victorious in creating unerring narratives explaining the repressive power structures that have handled humanity for ages. These narratives shall act as an example for upcoming generations against submitting to any deplorable institution. Supposedly, Melzer clearly states, "the embracing of difference, in which these two mechanisms (deconstruction of existing structures and acceptance of that which is not-I) are combined, makes a clear demarcation of 'I' and 'not I' (the dualism of 'us' versus 'them') impossible" (69). In the view of the theorist, Neil Badmington, "They're us... We're them" ("PodAlmighty" 22).

Peter Boxall, a Professor at the University of Sussex, in his seminal work, *The Value of the Novel*, contends that the questions on the eradication of death and the purpose and language spoken by the deathless self are incessantly answered in his work. It reviews "under an emerging global regime that is almost unreadable to us," the 21st century novel, "allows us to imagine and to make new worlds, to fashion new forms of accommodation between art and matter, or even to live in a condition of worldlessness" (15). The paradigm shifts from historiography to the arena of futurography in the writings of Don Delillo such as *Zero K* is quite evident.

The narrator, Jeffrey Lockhart is a dissatisfied and purposeless being who was into several insignificant and disconcerting jobs and involved in various frustrating and futile relationships. At the beginning of the novel, he is journeying to a strange and isolated place to convey his final tribute to Artis, his stepmother. She is an archaeologist and is suffering from an auto-immune disorder known as multiple sclerosis.

Multiple Sclerosis is an enfeebling neurological disorder for adults under the age group of forty years. The term 'Sclerosis' signifies a lesion or injury. The immune system that protects the human body by producing antibodies against any virus inadvertently attacks myelin, the insulating coating of the nerves, in the nervous system comprising optic nerves, spinal cord and brain. Few people affected with this undergo a light course with negligible impairment while others show an unwavering deteriorating impairment with time. The symptoms are for a short time superseded by elongated idleness or inaction with full or fragmented recovery.

It strikes the white matter located near the nervous system. It also destroys the nerve cells that transfer photographic images from the eye to the brain. With the onset of fatality of the disease, the outer part of the brain known as the cerebral cortex dwindles due to a procedure called cortical atrophy. The disease can be recognised through a proper MRI or Magnetic Resonance Imaging. The lesion can be pointed like a pin or larger than the golf ball.

His father, Ross Lockhart is in his late sixties and is quite robust and energetic. He is much older than Artis. Jeffrey arrives at his father's facility known as 'The Convergence' and pleasantly greets him. Ross, an affluent business person has built this office by investing large amounts of money. Jeffrey is aware of the fact that "he'd put major sums of money into this entire operation, this endeavour, called the Convergence, and the office was a gesture of courtesy, allowing him to maintain convenient contact with his network of companies, agencies, funds, foundations, syndicates, communes and clans" (Delillo, *Zero K* 7).

During Jeffrey's adolescent years, his father deserted him and his mother, Madeline. Ross briefs Jeffrey that Artis' body is going to be frozen i.e., Cryonic suspension, and conserved up to the period of her medical recovery so that her life can be restored. He says, "The time will come when there are ways to counteract the circumstances that led to the end. Mind and body are restored, returned to life" (Delillo, *Zero K* 8).

Cryonics is the procedure of preservation of bodies of animals and humans at a certain temperature for their reconditioning and rejuvenating them into a physically fit condition. Presently, the procedure of cryonics can be carried out post-obituary of the man or animal.

The scientific vindication for the implementation of cryonics is contingent on numerous concepts, there is a deceleration of metabolism due to low temperature and this can further lead to the cessation of chemical modification for years. The formation of ice can be diminished or entirely eradicated with the utilisation of vitrification concoction. If someone is declared dead, it doesn't mean that death is irreversible. Death is a longer process than one is convinced. The destruction related to lower temperatures, clinical death and its preservation, although is not undoable in the present times but reformable in the near future.

Once the person's death is declared, cryonics stages can take place immediately. The series of steps for preservation have set out to safeguard the tissues of the body while freezing it below $-120°C$. There is a minute modification in the structure of tissues after the coronary infraction. In the initial level of cryostorage, the breathing and blood circulation of the subject are technically restored. The subject is orchestrated medicines and is instantly made to freeze to between $9°C$ and $0°C$. The blood is cleaned and the water inside the body is restored with a cryoprotectant blend to turn aside the formation of ice. Then the subject is made to freeze below $-120°C$ and gripped in cryostasis.

Jeffrey has a proclivity for fancifully naming people and objects surrounding him. He calculates and labels objects persistently, presenting himself as a spectator rather than a participator. Ross and Jeffrey squabble over The Convergence following Ross' disclosure regarding his failure to sustain without the presence of Artis in his life. For this reason, he aspires to freeze himself through the procedure of "Zero K" notwithstanding any health problems.

Jeffrey notices various peculiar features in the facility. He witnesses screens that unsystematically exhibit calamities and dreadful incidents globally. He watches mannequin-like beings scattered here and there. Jeffrey monikers a man as 'The Monk' who is dressed in monk's robes and communicates with the people getting ready for freezing but appears to have a lack of faith in the case.

Artis rests in an armchair inside her solitary suite. Subject to clinical experimentation, she will perish within a day. Ross makes it certain that the cryonic procedures are undertaken without delay. Due to a lack of networking in the suite, Jeffrey's mobile does not function. He performs various stretching exercises to keep his blood pumping. The ambience of the room is quite complicated. Then, Jeffrey leaves the room and moves in the direction of the hall.

He knocks on the door and three people come near him. A ten-year-old boy advances towards him on a mechanised wheelchair that looks like a toilet. The upper part of his body is leaned to one side but his eyes seem vigilant. He goes down the hall and reaches The Convergence. Jeffrey asks his father whether Artis' death is natural or her final breath is being roused. He answers that the procedure is pain-free, quick and secure. It is required that this procedure is undertaken in full synchronisation with the techniques that are being calibrated. It should also be taken utmost care that the methods befit her body that will ultimately allow her to survive for many weeks more.

Ross adds that although there are laboratories and divisions in other countries, the Convergence is the base and nerve centre for all these tasks. There are substantial energy resources and hard-wearing technical systems due to the utilisation of firewalls and toughened floors. It also accommodates digital security and sentinels. In this office, the employees are creating a future, "A new idea of the future. Different from the others" (Delillo, *Zero K* 30).

Peter Boxall elucidates science fiction and the conjugation between the novel, the body and the real:

> We have language to guide us out of dire times. We are able to think and speak about what can conceivably happen in time to come. Why not follow our words bodily into the future tense? If we tell ourselves forthrightly that consciousness will persist, that cryopreservatives will continue to nourish the body, it is the first awakening toward the blessed state. We are here to make it happen, not simply to will it, or crawl toward it, but to place the endeavour in full dimension. (253)

Based on this assumption, the extension of life is a kind of narration of the body. The finality of marriage between matter and art relates to the continuation of life, living beyond the end of the story, and the creation of the real future against just the representation of it.

Later Ross smiles and says, "What's happening in this community is not just a creation of medical science. There are social theorists involved, and biologists, and futurists, and geneticists, and climatologists and neuroscientists and psychologists, and ethicists, if that's the right word" (Delillo, *Zero K* 33). He thus adds:

> Some are here permanently; others come and go. There are numbered levels. All the vital minds. Global English, yes, but

other languages as well. Translators, when necessary, human and electronic. There are philologists designing an advanced language unique to the Convergence. Word roots, inflections, even gestures. People will learn it and speak it. A language that will enable us to express things we can't express now, see things we can't see now, see ourselves and others in ways that unite us, broaden every possibility. (Delillo, *Zero K* 33)

The Convergence is also funded by government and various corporations as they have realised that this is the time for all the organisations to surmise and survive uniquely. The man who was in the monk's attire said to Jeffrey that he didn't accept the cause behind the whole endeavour. He enumerates that he wants to die, "What's the point of living if we don't die at the end of it" (Delillo, *Zero K* 40)? He cites that there is a hospice present in the hall where one talks to the dying people. It contains all the technologically advanced types of machinery and trained personnel.

The characters in the novel think how their bodies will seem after their death. In this case, they perform the task of recuperating matter and designing the future. For instance, Jeffrey observes the difference between Artis' profession as an archaeologist and the bodies that are conserved inside the pods, which seem "nearly prehistoric", like "archaeology for a future age" (Delillo, *Zero K* 256).

Jeffrey recollects that his father, Ross once alluded to the pilgrims who came from various regions of the world in search of a transcendental being or a biological process that will prevent the tissues and organs of their body from decaying.

One fine day Artis recounts that long ago she underwent surgery in her right eye. She was prescribed an eye shield to use for a short time. She rests on her armchair for about an hour. And, as she woke from her nap everything seemed unalike. She says, "The bed spread and pillow cases, the rich color, the depths of color, something from within. Never before, ever" (Delillo, *Zero K* 45). She utters that when one visualises something, one gets a semblance or imitation as the optic nerve does not let one catch sight of the entire truth. The remaining is our reinterpretation of what is visible to us. Many researchers are conducting research on futuristic replicas of human perception and vision on robots and experimental animals.

She says that she just consumed eyedrops five times a day and everything appeared quirky. She delves into the memories and states, "Is this the world as it truly looks? Is this the reality we haven't learned how to see" (Delillo, *Zero K* 46)? She expresses that she wants to be a clinical sample that will make progress by replacement and reconstruction of the body parts with the passage of years. It will seem as if there is a reassembling of part by part or atom by atom resulting in rejuvenation or enlightenment of the body to a renewed sense of perception of the cosmos. This signifies "The world as it really is. And this is what I think about when I try to imagine the future, I will be reborn into a deeper and truer reality. Lines of brilliant light, every material thing in its fullness, a holy object" (Delillo, *Zero K* 47). This holy object represented as futuristic world is an abstract entity or transcendent era found in all places disseminated in its purest form, "the promise of a lyric intensity outside the measure of normal experience" (Delillo, *Zero K* 48).

Jeffrey interrogates whether she has immense knowledge regarding the future. And, whether the one and the same body will return after death or an enhanced form of it. He further asks "Is consciousness altered? Are you the same person? You die as someone with a certain name and with all the history and memory and mystery gathered in that person and that name. But do you wake up with all of that intact? Is it simply a long night's sleep" (Delillo, *Zero K* 48)?

Artis answers that metempsychosis will make these things possible. Ross remembers the old times and says that Artis will be elevated to the numbered levels that will make her lose her life. Then she will be "chemically prompted, in a subzero unit, in a highly precise medical procedure guided by mass delusion, by superstition and arrogance and self-deception" (Delillo, *Zero K* 50).

In this narration, there is a belief in language's capability to reclaim and proffer the world readable underwrites. One of the critics expresses, "We will emerge in cyber-human form into a universe that will speak to us in a very different way" (Delillo, *Zero K* 67).

This interpretation of the world expands to The Convergence's scheme to create a language for upcoming times. It is obvious at the personal strata, in Jeffrey's fondness for allocating names to persons he is unknown to, including his childhood inclination towards pharmaceuticals "impacted jargon of warnings, precautions, adverse reactions, contraindications" (Delillo, *Zero K* 50).

As he walks towards the hall, he sees a woman in her forties gazing at him. He is escorted to a long room where he finds a large human skull placed on the plinth. The skull is worn out and blemished with age. The eyelets are fringed with precious stones and the spiky teeth are silver washed.

He sees an elderly couple seated at the table discussing the process of contorting of the body, "But is there a link to older beliefs and practices? Are we a radical technology that simply renews and extends those swarming traditions of everlasting life" (Delillo, *Zero K* 64)?

Jeffrey is part of a gathering in which he comes to know that the persons engaged in The Convergence prophesize that a dreadful apocalyptic future will momentarily arrive. They consider that the destructible years can be avoided by adapting the process of body freezing.

A man effortlessly declares "This is the future, this remoteness, this sunken dimension. Solid but also elusive in a way. A set of coordinates mapped from space. And one of our objectives is to establish a consciousness that blends with the environment" (Delillo, *Zero K* 64). He puts a question to the audience whether humans live beyond space, time and history. The anticipation of the future time often dwindles to reckon the quality of life as it prevails on the earth. They discuss the end of the world. The lady who escorts him to the hall keenly looks at the speaker. She reiterates that humans are under the heel of the starry system while the sun is an unascertained structure.

They debate on the solar flares, coronal mass ejections, and the heavenly bodies such as asteroids and comets. They gather at the hall to prepare a blueprint that will liberate the earth during any natural havoc. They plan to imitate the apocalypse to examine it for any possibility of survival. As in the future times, life will be insubstantial and death unacceptable.

The speaker outrightly says, "We are here to learn the power of solitude. We are here to reconsider everything about life's end. And we will emerge in cyberhuman form into a universe that will speak to us in a very different way" (Delillo, *Zero K* 67). Jeffrey has a habit of naming persons and places so he names the speaker as Miklos Szabo because his voice is similar to the programmed speech in translation.

The stenmark twins present their views that they intend to straighten the borders of the definition of human. They utter, "We want to do whatever we are capable of doing in order to alter human thought and bend the energies of civilization" (Delillo, *Zero K* 71). They add that they wish for a reworking of the future. They are not really dead. For them "Death is a cultural artifact, not a strict determination of what is humanely inevitable" (Delillo, *Zero K* 71). Their bodies will be colonised with nanobots. The internal organs and systems will be reinvigorated and regenerated. The enzymes and stem cells will be replenished.

Raising objections against the supposition regarding the finiteness of man's life, the stenmark twins lay stress on the dimension of human civilisation to expand the span of life beyond the restrictions of the biological body. The essence of our self is the result of the neurochemistry of matter of the brain that can be preserved.

In the non-permanent slumber of profound freezing, the mind can transcend the body so that the subject of man can be restored in former unrevealed types of embodiments. The stenmark twins are advocates of what Hayles in her book, *How We Became Posthuman* states, "the posthuman view," which considers "embodiment in a biological substrate [...] as an accident of history rather than an inevitability of life" (2).

Jeffrey discloses the fact that his father's real name is not 'Ross Lockhardt' but Nicholas Satterswaite. He changed his name to Ross after college as he thought that this name would match his position as a business giant and a change-agent as "It was a challenge, he told her. It was an incentive, an inducement. It would motivate him to work harder, think more clearly, begin to see himself differently" (Delillo, *Zero K* 81). In the company of the Monk, Jeffrey advances towards an alleyway to the atrium. He sees the patients lying on padded stools. It is difficult for him to distinguish between anaesthetic and sleepy patients. The paramedics diagnose the patients by examining instruments on the headboard. He strolls around the hall gazing at the patients in waiting. He sees the same boy with a mechanised wheelchair on the other side of the hall. He is positioned on a carrel with the upper part of his body twisted to one side and lower to the other side. He tries to speak that is incomprehensible. In his physical disability, Jeffrey harks back to the new technologies "that would one day be applied to his body and brain, allowing him to return to the world as a runner, a jumper, a public speaker" (Delillo, *Zero K* 94). Jeffrey asks the Monk about the procedures to which he answers that everyone assembles here to die. "The dead do not sign up beforehand and then die and then get sent here with all the means of preservation intact" (Delillo, *Zero K* 96).

Jeffrey goes to Artis's suite and finds her resting on the bed. She is all set to put her future on trial. He comes across a series of associations such as "The cryonic pod, the tube, the capsule, the toll booth, the phone booth, the ticket booth, the shower stall, the outhouse, the sentry box" (Delillo, *Zero K* 99). Jeffrey interrogates whether his father, Ross has regular health check-ups or not. Ross answers indicating to Artis that if one person dies, the other is destined to die. Jeffrey queries if his father has committed any blunder, "Enormous frauds. Doesn't this happen all the time in your line of work? Investors get swindled. What else? Enormous sums of money get transferred illegally.

What else? I don't know. But these are reasons, right, for a man to disappear" (Delillo, *Zero K* 112).

Additionally, he questions the consequence if accidentally he perishes before the procedure of freezing is completed. Ross replies that there is a particular unit known as Zero K that will allow him to get uplifted to the next level. He requests his son to freeze his body. The resolution both Artis and Ross have made to freeze their bodies will allow them to live together. Jeffrey remembers the dialogues of the Stenmark twins who talk about becoming immortal by taking a single leap. They utter, "Give the futurists their blood money and they will make it possible for you to live forever" (Delillo, *Zero K* 117).

Jeffrey stands anterior to the art that demonstrates the afterlife. He goes to his room and ruminates over the matter. Ross may fail to go inside the chamber for a renewed consciousness before the malfunctioning of his body. So, Jeffrey decides to remain apace with his father when Artis and his father are sent to the chamber for self-renewing themselves.

Ross says:

> We understand that the idea of life extension will generate methods that attempt to improve upon the freezing of human bodies. To re-engineer the aging process, to reverse the biochemistry of progressive diseases. We fully expect to be in the forefront of any genuine innovation. Our tech centers in Europe are examining strategies for change. Ideas adaptable to our format. We're getting ahead of ourselves. This is where we want to be. (Delillo, *Zero K* 126).

He believes that existence on this earth is considered

delicate due to food deficit, change of seasons, deforestation, irregular climate changes, shortage of drinking water and threat to water bodies. Furthermore, biological warfare has led to mass destruction as people fail to return to their homes and die at sea. For that reason, Ross remarks, "We reverse the text here, we read the news backwards. From death to life, our devices enter the body dynamically and become the refurbished parts and pathways we need in order to live again" (Delillo, *Zero K* 128). This will in turn examine the feasibility of man by demeaning all the former ideas.

The humans who will arise from the capsules will be considered as ahistorical humans. These humans will be liberated from the circle of time i.e., past and present. They will enounce a newly discovered language. This type of language is isolated from others and is taught to the ones who sustain the procedure of cryopreservation. It will entirely rejuvenate humans by enhancing their perception of reality and intensifying the reach of the mind by offering "new meanings, entire new levels of perception" (Delillo, *Zero K* 130). Humans will perceive themselves as a revived entity with the application of logic and mathematics in colloquial speech.

Artis is being prepared for cryopreservation by the team of Zero K. The doctors are diversely dressed for the procedure. Some are operating, adjusting and scanning the monitor screens. Artis is made to lie flat on a table. The team operated by encircling her to chemically induce her to die. Jeffrey fails to evaluate whether Artis is still alive or it is simply her physical 'body'. He is also unaware of what comprises the end of one's life either "the body withdraws from one function and then possibly another, or possibly not- heart, nervous system, brain, different parts of the brain down into the mechanism of individual cells" (Delillo, *Zero K* 139).

Three persons are lying dead in the open space inside body pods and cases. The heads are shaved and their outfits are made up of plastic tubes that are highly insulated. The organs are removed from the body and are preserved individually in insulated containers known as organ pods. The bodies seem hairless and are not rightly placed. The eyelids are open and arms are suspended at the sides.

Ross wonders which stage Artis might have arrived at in the body-freezing procedure: Vitrification, cryopreservation or nanotechnology. He talks to the guide regarding the naming of these figures to which the guide responds as 'Heralds'. The Heralds are efficient for "showing the way, making the path, being early, being first" (Delillo, *Zero K* 142). They wait for none and perform before they are required to do it.

Jeffrey has several questions concerning the bodies lying on the table regarding their identity and the procedures that have been undertaken on them. He ruminates on the nature of the beings that these are laboratory beings cleanly shaved and placed naked in the pods and collated as a single unit for freezing and curing. Later, they are kept in an empty space for the healing procedure to occur.

The guide describes the term Zero K as "a unit of temperature called absolute zero, which is minus two hundred and seventy-three point one five degree Celsius. A physicist named Kelvin was mentioned, he was the K in the term" (Delillo, *Zero K* 142). He also adds that the temperature involved in the cryostorage does not advance towards zero K.

In the meantime, there is continuous lingering in

Artis's treatment that makes Jeffrey wait in the facility for multiple days. He has an exasperating experience as he is detached from the outside world. And, Ross also informs Jeffrey that he cannot follow Artis anymore due to which Jeffrey feels disgusted. The staffs of the facility are queer. And, the procedure of freezing is quite tenuous for Artis.

The dissimilarities between the two demonstrate how one person ponders and expresses himself at the prior and post-cryopreservation stages. When Jeffrey locates Artis at The Convergence, he sees himself on her side. He tries to motivate her. With hesitation, she explains how she remains immersed in thoughts of the minutest sensations of the body in day-to-day life, "I think about drops of water. How I used to stand in the shower and watch a drop of water edge down the inside of the sheer curtain" (Delillo, *Zero K* 17).

Artis' pre-cryonics reminiscences are both alluring and enigmatic as she struggles to persuade how her life story is formed by the essence of becoming a body in place of possessing a body. This reflects the severity of the transformation that Artis is dealing with, which is both a type of death and birth to her. She perceives this fissure in her own voice, in a sense of self-consciousness that appears to be interrelated to the language she utters as a sort of embodiment. She ascertains: "My voice is different. I hear it when I speak in a way that's not natural. It's my voice but it doesn't seem to be coming from me" (Delillo, *Zero k* 52). But Ross objects and says that this condition is because of the medications that she is taking. Artis continues to say, "It seems to be coming from outside me. Not all the time but sometimes. It's like I'm twins, joined at the hip, and my sister is speaking. But that's not it at all" (Delillo, *Zero K* 53). Artis is quite excited for the procedure as she presents, "I'm so eager. I can't tell you. To do this thing. Enter another dimension. And then return. For ever more" (Delillo, *Zero K* 53).

In part two of the novel, Jeffrey is again found in the physical world. He is seen attending an interview for a position in his father's firm. Ross is attempting to enroll Jeffrey into his business for a while but Jeffrey abandons this idea. Jeffrey's present beloved's adopted son, Stak, is passionate about numbers. But Stak is mysteriously nowhere to be found.

And, later Jeffrey finds that his father, Ross, has decided to attain the procedure of body freezing. As Jeffrey accompanies his father to the facility for the process of cryopreservation, he visualizes a war scene on the screen and Stak is killed in the battle.

In this context, Hayles writes that Critical Posthumanism contemplates, "consciousness, regarded as the seat of humanity in the Western tradition long before Descartes thought he was a mind thinking, as an epiphenomenon" (3). She continues, "Extending or replacing the body with other prostheses becomes a continuation of a process that began before we were born" (3).

This ambition of the theory of Critical Posthumanism, with origins in Cartesian Dualism, is demonstrated in the digressive differentiation between possessing and remaining a body as Hayles suggests, "Identified with the rational mind, the liberal subject possessed a body but was not usually represented as being a body" (3).

Bernadette Wegenstein, the Professor of Media Studies, observes that the incarnation of man can be represented through the phenomenological distinction between remaining and possessing a body, "the former, insofar as it designates the process of living the body, the first-person perspective, coincides with dynamic embodiment; the latter, referencing the body from an external, third-person perspective, can be aligned with the static body" (19).

Furthermore, Thomas Pynchon's instinct fabricates a collective space which is ultimately usurped by other dominants. It emanates the cessation of man that at the beginning made this collective space feasible. Don Delillo's instinct begins from the ultimate part of Pynchon's concept. He opines that man is nothing special than what the corporates of America have pronounced.

By deeply engaging with this perturbing reality, Don Delillo exhibits how man can be restored under certain circumstances, thereby constructing the types of individuals who can participate in Thomas Pynchon's collective space.

Delillo both enlists and attempts to persuade the creation of a method of artistic perception constructed around computer or information technologies that is otherwise named as 'Cyberspatial Paradigm'. This structure gets hold of human and computer interactions as a representation of all sorts of experiences and visualises the world as created from the concealed set of information or data.

This idea is illuminated in the novel, *White Noise*. It narrates a pedagogic year in the life of Jack Gladney, an academician at the College-on-the-Hill. He is an instructor in the school and executes his duties as the department chair of the Hitler studies, a discipline that was introduced in the year 1968. He resides in the town of Blacksmith with his family, namely his wife, Babette and four offspring from previous marriages, namely, Wilder, Heinrich, Steffie, and Denise.

For the last many years, the narrator observes

the wagons loaded with students at the College-on-the-Hill premises. He has been perpetually surprised by the students' exhilaration and idiosyncrasies of their more opulent and satisfied parents.

As Jack returns to his house, he recounts the picturesque Blacksmith town with its dilapidated houses, the mental asylum and the grotesque church building. As he reaches his home, he converses with his wife, Babette, an unkempt tall lady with messy light-coloured hair. He takes great solace in her. Babette is proud of doing a lot more work than thinking about her appearance. She nurtures their children, reads to old man Treadwell, a blind and gives lessons on adult education. Projecting his former spouses, Jack comments, "self-absorbed and high-strung bunch, with ties to the intelligence community" (Delillo, *White Noise* 7).

All three children from Jack's former marriages, Steffie, Denise and Wilder appear in the kitchen to have lunch. Heinrich arrives at the kitchen but passes from sight. Denise scorns Babette for purchasing food and not utilising it. But Jack safeguards Babette in this case.

Jack gives an account of the sweeping cloak he dresses in while lecturing and later talks of his colleagues. The Department of Hitler Studies and the Department of Popular Culture are present in the same establishment which is in conjunction with the American environments.

In the 1960s, the nascent transmission networks had become many times ingrained in day-to-day life. The personal computers were in their infant stages. In 1985, when Delillo published *White Noise*, computer networking transformed the lives of people. There is an interlace seen in American's corporation, technology and culture. These information technologies ensnare humanity in the vicious cycle of acquiring more technologically developed and advanced commodities. In the novel, the characters are lured by the communication processes to purchase them. Delillo's reciprocation to this buildout of a cyberspatial system, thus, is to attempt to search a few areas that are left uncolonized by the communication systems. He speculatively answers that when one is away from the high-yielding sets of collectivity, the only way is to get back to man as the origin of creativity that may arise from the downpour of techno corporate apparatus.

Murray Jay Siskind, an erstwhile sports critic turned instructor is unique to this depiction. At the luncheon meeting, Murray informs Jack with respect to his residing as a lodger in a lodging house. He also makes it clear that he has arrived at the tiny academic station of Blacksmith to get rid of the obstacles of living in the city. He applauds the efforts of Jack about the Department of Hitler Studies and desires to do a similar kind of thing for Elvis Presley.

After a couple of days, both of them travel by car around the country to pay a visit to the often-photographed farmhouse in the USA. They come across an assembly of tourists who are deeply absorbed in writing notes and positioning the camera to take a picture of the barn. Murray asserts that the barn is in itself insignificant but the only noteworthy thing is the accumulation of all energies at one place. The aura that has been created by the victim is high-powered and cogent which is worthy of consideration.

Jack encounters his wife at the secondary school where she is found exercising to and fro on the staircase. As he observes her working out, he catalogues the humdrum particulars of both of their life altogether. He records that in their daily affairs, the primary question is who will depart this life first between both of them.

Jack ponders the fact whether death swings in the air one inhales like a noble gas. He also thinks that the terror of death is curative of innocence from their marital life. The same night the family members assemble to watch TV. She believes that switching the television on is beneficial as a household chore as it lessens the negative effects.

The expression 'cyberspace' includes any type of intercommunication between computers and humans. It is originally explicated by William Gibson in his text *Neuromancer* published in the year 1984. Cyberspace classifies a certain type of interrelationship between computers and humans, "A consensual hallucination [....] A graphic representation of data abstracted from the banks of every computer in the human system. Unthinkable complexity. Lines of light ranged in the non-space of the mind, clusters and constellations of data. Like city lights, receding" (51).

William Gibson's concept of cyberspace is a confluence that transfigures information into a graphical representation. This combination utilises man's awareness of spatial systems to enable them to sell across data structures that are literally unimaginable. Thus, Cyberspace is basically an abstraction or a rendition of an elemental and non-human entanglement. N. Katherine Hayles represents it as "a level playing field on which humans and computers can meet on equal terms [....] Cyberspace is created by transforming a data matrix into a landscape in which narratives can happen" (38).

This explanation reinforces cyberspace as a recompense outlined to conciliate between uncooked, computer-decipherable information and the cooked, human-comprehensible abstraction of the data. It is this interpretation of 'cyberspace' as the construction of a technological 'consensual hallucination,' that makes it plain an inconceivable complication to enable Man to reflect in methods that they in other ways could not have comprehended. The cyberspatial subtlety is indicated in this novel which is best appreciated in conjugation with information technologies. The technologies impinge on brand-new areas of experience. These experiences are an expression of complex, concealed data.

Jack recollects and discusses with Babette how he created the Department of Hitler Studies in the year 1968 and the chancellor of the college-on-the-Hill suggested he deliberately create an intense and high-powered atmosphere around him to be assumed as an academician of much significance. He attaches an initial to his official name and calls himself J.A.K Gladney. He realises that he has now turned into an artificial character who plainly complies with his new nomenclature.

He is afraid of the conception that his life is accelerating at a faster pace. In its course, he relates to a day when Babette was going through the horoscopes and he acquired a sudden terror of dying. Both Jack and Babette collide with Murray at the marketplace.

Murray puts forward the marvels of generic wrapping. He records the sturdiness of transparent wrappers and his experience of inner peace with generic products. They leave Murray at his apartment as Jack discerns that Murray has confidently built up a personality that will compel women to admire him.

Heinrich's hairline has been receding which becomes a cause of concern for his father, Jack. He ponders if his son's condition is because of him or if the toxicants in the atmosphere are to be held responsible. He escorts Heinrich to school and starts an earthly conversation regarding the day's weather conditions.

In the theatre of college-on-the-Hill, Jack arranges for the broadcasting of a documentary for his seminar on Advanced Nazism. Indeed, the documentary has no raconteur. Jack has assembled extracts from Nazi propaganda movies, promoting extensive snapshots of rally, conference and congregation scenes.

After the completion of the screening of the documentary, the audience informs Jack about his strategy to assassinate Hitler. But Jack restricts him by saying, "All plots tend to move deathward. This is the nature of plots" (Vogt, *White Noise* 30).

In the novel, Jack Gladney is bewildered and made wretched by the universe around him. He is disrupted by his connection with the idea of death. He fails to ascertain the real meaning of what he is involved in. He is also unable to comprehend his self-utterances. A literary critic, Tom LeClair comments on Jack Gladney's lack of certainty, explaining his narration as jotted down in "a primer style, an expression not of ignorance...but of something like shock, a seeming inability to sort into contexts and hierarchies the information he receives and the thinking he does" (387-411).

Babette takes a class on posture for the aged people in the basement of the church. Jack conjectures that Babette's tutees perceive that they can fend off death through conventional conditioning. Both Jack and Babette spend time together and go through the family photographs for hours altogether. Jack again thinks about who is going to die at first.

Regardless of chairing the Department of Hitler Studies, Jack has little knowledge of German. So, he plans to learn the language from Howard Dunlop, a man who has rented a room in Murray's apartment. For Jack, the language appears to be unpleasant. But the College-on-the-Hill is convening a conference on Hitler in the upcoming spring and it shall be disgraceful for Jack if the chairman himself is ignorant of the German language. The grad school of the children of Jack, Steffie and Denise is evacuated as both the students and educators are showing strange symptoms such as head pain, and irritation of the eyes and their taste buds had a metallic taste. One of the educators rolled on the ground while uttering some kind of remote language. The grad school remains shut for more than a week so that there could be a proper inspection of the school building. The investigators had put on suits designed in Mylex, a material that mystifies the detecting instruments and, in a way, furnishes enigmatic and indecisive outcomes.

There is another aspect of the way Jack tries to elucidate what appears to be unexplainable. This can be stated as a transcendental idea by focusing on Paul Maltby's perspective that Delillo has embraced a metaphysics on Romanticism or has used Osteens' magic to elucidate the point of view. Of course, Jack's mysticism is important for the enhancement of his creative faculty. He chooses the ATM to authenticate his survival as intrinsic to the flow of information:

> Waves of relief and gratitude flowed over me. The system had blessed my life. I felt its support and approval. The system hardware, the mainframe sitting in a locked room in some distant city.... I sensed that something of deep personal value, but not money, not that at all, had been authenticated and confirmed. A deranged person was escorted from the bank by two armed guards. The

system was invisible, which made it all the more impressive, all the more disquieting to deal with. But we were in accord, at least for now. The networks, the circuits, the streams, the harmonies. ("The Romantic Metaphysics of Don Delillo" 498-516)

After Jack's daughter returns from school, all of them pay a visit to the market. They meet Murray there and Jack exclaims that he has encountered Murray the similar times as in the premises of College-on-the-Hill. He overhears the noise of humans shouting whose location is untraceable.

Babette finds Denise going through the Physician's Dictionary to acquire particulars regarding a drug that Babette has been consuming. In the ensuing moment, Murray assists Babette in thrusting the load into her cart. Later, he discusses Tibetan beliefs about death. He adds that he gets spiritually energised by the sounds, hues and mysticism of the market.

For him, the supermarket holds boundless quantities of secretive symbolism. Examining these symbols acts as a way of studying how to pull off the sheets of ambiguity. Babette listens to Murray's views on death. As they move out of the supermarket, they get the news of the death of one of the inspectors in Mylex suits who passed away during the inspection of the school.

The ATM is a prototype of both the financial and technological systems. It works more than assigns to the value of his mechanical assets. It even decides his placement in the arrangement of cultural values. By associating himself with these organisations, Jack manages to temporarily relieve his anxiety for death.

After arriving home, Denise berates Babette for her gum-munching habits enlisting the detrimental effects of gum which causes cancer in animals like rats. She also argues that Babette has been experiencing a loss of memory due to this addiction. In the upstairs of their house, Heinrich has been learning the chess moves to play with a murderer named, Tommy Roy Foster. Heinrich informs his father that Babette wants to meet him during the summer at the abbey where she resides. On being asked, he answers that he might go but that may be due to the accidental misfiring of neurons inside his brain.

Jack and Babette arrive at the house of Murray for dinner. Murray sets forth the theories based on television. He states how his tutees regard television as valueless. But he is of the opinion that television is indispensable and crucial to America's way of life. If one showcases himself in television then one can perform all unique and impossible things.

After dinner, as they return, Babette communicates the loss of memory matter to Jack that Denise affirms to have observed. Jack comforts her by saying that she is probably alright. Later, they talk over the various pills that Denise confirms she has witnessed. But Babette asserts that she is not consuming anything that could lead to her memory lapses.

Jack's involvement with the ATM associates him with the virtual congregation of persona which Stephen doCarmo conceptualises as 'object strategy'. Regarding *White Noise*, doCarmo in his article "Subjects, Objects, and the Postmodern Differend in Don DeLillo's *White Noise*", contends that his "characters are caught between two equally seductive urges, one toward autonomy and individuality, or 'subjectness,' as we can call it, and another toward absorption and dispersal of the self into larger systems—a diametrically opposed 'objectness'" (32-33).

Jack learns German with Dunlop and blames him that he is breaching nature's law while talking in the German language. After the class, Jack escorts Babette to the residence of old man Treadwell for reading the tabloid but they find the old man missing.

And was ultimately found in the shopping mall. The police summoned Adele T, a psychic to discover them. Although she didn't help the police in this matter, but helped them locate bags full of heroin and a handgun.

Denise appears in the bed chamber of Jack and poses questions regarding the improvement of Babette's loss of memory. She also informs him that she has discovered a drug named Dylar thrown into the dustbin. She also puts in that the references to this drug are nowhere to be found.

Then they converse about German and Jack says that there is something extraordinary in both the language and ethnicity that he is intent on knowing. Then all the family members go to watch TV as a ritual every Friday night. The children are immersed in watching the video of a disastrous and tragic plane crash.

The next morning Jack asks Alfonse Stompanato, a charismatic chairman the reason why everyone is interested in watching calamities on television. He answers that as people are flooded with news each day for this reason it is essential that calamities can step into the continual circulation of information. People desire calamities on account of regaining their attention as these days they are in great trouble. They are affected by brain fade and their perceptions have become tired due to overuse or misuse.

Jack runs in to attend Murray's lecture on Elvis. Murray starts by mentioning that Elvis had a strong relationship with his mother, Gladys. Jack also puts his statement that Hitler admired his mother, Klara as well.

Jack and Murray reiterated anecdotes about both of the personalities. Then they discuss how Elvis was devastated learning about his mother's demise. On the contrary, Jack states that Hitler had arranged a grand funeral after his mother died.

Both talk about the death of Elvis and Hitler where there were crowds of people. Jack says remaining unidentified in a large crowd is a procedure of framing a guard against death. As the lecture ends Jack finds students crowding around him. Seeing this he restricts the students from gathering there and utters that death is a professional affair in the class. And he is at ease with the conception of death.

In the mid-afternoon, Wilder starts crying. His parents take him to a doctor who prescribes him a dose of aspirin and recommends him to rest. As they leave, Babette goes to take a posture class. Jack keeps on waiting inside the car and holding Wilder on his lap. He is absorbed in the wailing sound of his boy. His loud wail makes him nostalgic. It gets a tinge of something primaeval and eternal.

As the family moves to the mid-village Mall, Denise asks Babette about the drug named Dylar. But the conversation gives way to a conflict. Jack shops prodigiously in the mall which makes him feel more powerful.

Dylar is an investigational drug created to weaken an individual's apprehension of death. It is the only solution for Jack that strikes him as "Technology with a human face" (Vogt, *White Noise* 243). But the drug fails in its experimentation similar to Eric's mechanical lifestyle. The plan of consuming pills to find answers to problems is a kind of lampoon in the same way as searching for a quick technological solution to the existential conundrum in the present times.

Jack finds Willy Mink having a never-ending reserve of Dylar. He also shoots him out of jealousy when he finds Willy having an extramarital affair with his wife. Jack's apparent impulse to be submerged in technological networking is comprehended as closely related to the distinguished culmination of such networking; by identifying himself through the process of technical interpellation. This attitude can be considered a tenet of Critical Posthumanism in the way that he identifies himself and is co-dependent on technology. In this regard, Laist asserts that the characters in the novel exhibit "doubleness concerning the relationship between a romantically stable cogito and a destabilized postmodern condition of radical alienation" ("Technology and Postmodern Subjectivity" 2). He refers to Stephan N. doCarmo's article 'Subjects, Objects, and the Postmodern Differend in Don Delillo's *White Noise*' and says that Jack is "caught between two equally seductive urges", one absorption and dispersal of the self into larger systems and other autonomy and individuality" (32-33).

Of course, when Jack encounters technological sublimity, he greets interpellation in technological networking. However, he is filled with fear and decides to leave his self-identity at a time when he declares his death and gets rid of all his possessions to "say good-bye to himself" (Delillo, *White Noise* 337).

Jack travels to the Iron City to get his daughter who is on her way to pay a visit to their home. But he finds Bee's mother in the airport. Her mother, Tweedy Browner has been patiently waiting for him near the entrance. Her mother notifies her that Bee will be landing in three hours from Indonesia. She is residing there with Malcolm Hunt, her stepfather. As they stroll around the Iron City, they discuss their respective life and marriages.

Tweedy reveals her dissatisfaction with her current husband, Malcolm Hunt. They move back to the airport. Another aeroplane landed before the arrival of Bee's aircraft. The voyagers inform Jack about the close hit that they pulled through. While the aircraft was plummeting from the sky, it recovered its pace and control. Bee queries regarding the presence of media during this incident. But Jack informs that there is a lack of media persons in the Iron City.

Jack accompanies Bee to the airport. While returning home, he stops near a cemetery titled, 'The Old Burying Ground'. This cemetery is beyond the humdrum of city life. He pauses there for a while to sense "the peace that is supposed to descend upon the dead" (Delillo, *White Noise* 116). He discerns that the dead possess a kind of energy by which the mortals can locate their presence.

Old man Treadwell's sister, Gladys demise occurs due to a "lingering dread" as the doctors have named it. This resulted in their disappearance for four days. Jack expresses that at any moment he goes through the obituaries, he abruptly draws a similarity between the departed soul's age with himself. He conjectures how historical legends such as Attila, the king of the Huns, perceived the idea of death. He encountered death fearlessly, considering it as a natural phenomenon.

Jack and Babette again converse about who is going to die first. Babette deliberately thrashes out that she will perish before Jack. But she is quite confident until their children are near them nothing unfavourable will occur to them. But Jack contradicts her by saying that he wishes to lose his life first as he will be isolated and fragmented after her death. Throughout the night, they keep on debating and arguing on this topic.

Later, Babette leaves for her posture class and Jack talks to his children. They see Babette on the television broadcast by a cable station and are filled with awe. They conceive that they are being punctured and illuminated by her image.

Jack discovers Heinrich standing on the terrace and looking at a faraway distance through her binoculars. He visualises a smoke fog emanating out of a derailed train. He says that the chemical burning in the atmosphere is Nyodene Derivative, which is otherwise known as Nyodene D, a chemical which is toxic and causes bumps in rats.

The health department has already stated that palmar hyperhidrosis or sweaty palms, nausea and irritation of the skin are the common symptoms of being exposed to the toxic substance. Jack attempts to dispel Heinrich's fear that the chemical cannot reach them and acts comfortably and nonchalantly. He sits calmly and notes their monthly expenditure while the warning is issued on the radio and television. He says that he is a professor at a college and should not run away from an airborne chemical such as this. The cloud of chemicals is provided with a new nomenclature: 'the airborne toxic event'. All the members have their supper and the warnings come nearer.

No sooner did the fire commander's coach issue a notice of evacuation, than Jack's family filled their stuff inside the car and moved near an encampment of Boy Scouts as advised. Half of the population escaped the town dressing in plastic kits and luggage sealed in briefcases and loaded on shopping baskets. Babette is seen chewing something but she avoids it when she is interrogated by Jack.

Acute symptoms of exposure to the toxin at a growing rate are declared. The initial symptoms of nausea and palmar hyperhidrosis are replaced by constant premonition of Déjà vu which is at a later stage superseded by miscarriages, seizures and comatic state. Denise and Steffie show few symptoms but Jack wonders if they are really affected by the toxic chemical or simply affected by the media experts.

On the route, Jack saw military helicopters lighting up a black mass which he exclaims as "some death ship in a Norse legend, escorted across the night by armoured creatures with spiral wings" (Delillo, *White Noise* 148). They reach the Boy Scout camp where massive effects of Nyodene D start to spread. Heinrich gives a lecture on airborne toxic events to the masses gathered at the camp.

A consultant examines Jack for the presence of Nyodene D in his body he might have come in contact with while filling the gas. An expert from SIMUVAC or Simulated Evacuation elucidates the harmful effects of the chemical on Jack in vague terms. He informs Jack that the organisation is recording their experiences to prepare a simulation of the calamity. He informs Jack that Nyodene D survives in the body for three decades and in the next fifteen years it will be possible for them to provide detailed data regarding the consequences.

When Jack comes near Babette after having a thorough discussion with the chief of SIMUVAC, he sees his wife reading the tabloid to a blind man. In one of the articles, a young girl who is believed to be a metempsychosis of a KGB murder case states that she was fearless about the concept of death in her previous life.

Heinrich and Jack converse about what kind of wisdom will be communicated if the entire population is sent back to the past. Jack informs Murray regarding his meeting with the SIMUVAC and how the idea of death has taken its place in his mind. They explore the notion of death concerning modern civilisation and how death adjusts to the current advancements in technology.

As they fall asleep, they notice that the wind has changed its direction and a cloud of chemicals is nearing them. Everyone escapes the encampment and reaches the Iron City at twilight. They get to know that the microorganisms that have the potential to eat the harmful chemicals circulate in the air. The entire population look bewildered and apprehensive.

Jack expands the time of his German lectures as the conference date comes nearer. Although he has developed his fluency in vocabulary, but his way of speaking was not up to the mark. Dunlop adjusts the tongue of Jack while speaking.

Meanwhile, the city is being examined by sniffer dogs and men in Mylex kits. Heinrich remarks that the officials aren't revealing every single thing they are aware of. They proclaim that the toxic chemical is not harmful to humans. As the inhabitants of Blacksmith Town are affected by Déjà vu, multiple counselling helplines are built. Jack records that the local people are nonetheless feeling lonely without any reason or context to which they can deviate their apprehension and hatred.

Jack finds a container of pills tagged as Dylar and hands it over to Denise, who unearthed Babette's hidden secret of medication that not a single pharmacist could recognise the pill. He contacts Babette's doctors but gets to know that none of them has prescribed such medicines to her.

Jack gives the medication to Winnie Richards, a neurochemist at College-on-the-Hill. For the next two days, Winnie examines the Dylar pill and elaborates on the efficacy of the pill. She explains that the pill is a kind of psychopharmaceutical that she has never come across.

The other night Jack presses Babette to tell him about the pill. She says that she is in a state from which she is unable to come out. While interpreting the National Enquirer to Treadwell, she came across an advertisement for a pharma firm that had a vacancy for the post of volunteers to undergo research confidentially. After conducting many tests of the drug, the company declared that the drug is life-threatening for humans. However, Babette managed to get the drug from the Project manager, Mr. Gray. She ultimately says that she is consuming this drug to overcome the inevitable fear of dying. Both of them conclude that they possess the fear of dying.

She describes how the drug, Dylar abandons the neurotransmitters that take charge of the fear of dying. Although she has consumed all her pills, she has to wait for the visible effects of the medication. Jack goes to the washroom but finds that the bottle of pills has disappeared from the radiator.

He finds the bottle with Denise and presses her to give him the bottle by saying that Dylar might prevent the spread of Nyodene D in the bloodstream. Jack lets Winnie know what he knows about Dylar. But she says that she doesn't want to abandon her fear of dying as it provides consistency and meaning to her life.

As the entire family go for dinner, they discuss that the Russian psychics are effectuating these patterns of weather that they are presently coming in contact with. Jack notifies that the UFO have been spotting the matter lately. The children sitting in the backside of the car sense a surly threat hovering over them. Babette calms them by saying that UFO spotting always takes place in the upper regions.

To this Denise adds that as the mountains are located in the upper regions and when the melting of the snow occurs the water moves to the reservoirs situated in the southern regions of the country.

Babette mentions two things that she desires, the first one is she doesn't want Jack to die first and the second is, that she wants Wilder to remain the way currently he is. While loitering on the premises of College-on-the-Hill, Jack and Murray discuss the improvement in Jack's learning of the German language. Murray says that Howard Dunlop is behaving strangely. He further adds that Dunlop is the kind of person who in the course of time developed carnal desire while visualising the corpses. Then, Jack decides to discontinue his learning of the German language.

The other night, Jack hears the TV sound emerging from the bed chamber of Denise. He enters Denise's room and sees that she has consumed the Dylar pill. After she is awake from her sleep, Jack persuades her to hand him the bottle of pills but she says that she has thrown the bottle away.

Jack begins his search for the bottle of pills in every nook and corner of the house including all the material objects that are a part of their life. With this, he discerns a relationship between his mortality and the material objects that his life is surrounded with.

While Babette is listening to the radio, Jack asks how she is coping with the fear of death. She says that she feels solace with Wilder and the less he communicates the more she admires him. Jack invites Orest Mercator to dinner to know his views on death but to no avail. Jack presses Babette to let him know about the whereabouts of Mr. Gray but she doubts that Jack might take revenge on him.

In the meantime, the SIMUVAC imitation of a

poisonous smell takes place. A few days later, there was a really unhealthy and pungent smell in the town. But there was no process of evacuation rather the people paid no attention to the smell and the smell vanished within a short period.

After the Airborne Toxic Event, a team of evacuees are replaced by the toxic cloud eclipsing Blacksmith. But there was no media to record the event. One of them shouts due to the negligence. Concerning this, Duvall puts forward:

> What is perhaps most horrifying about this absence of mediation is that, for those who experience the disaster, it is precisely this mediation (and this mediation alone) that could make their terror immediate.... DeLillo's postmoderns seek affirmation through television, the GRID who/that really cares and affirms the legitimacy of their terror. Those who encountered the airborne toxic event intuitively know that television is not a mediation; it is the immediate. Television, the intertextual grid of electronic images, creates the Real. (432)

The graphics that the technology creates is the ultimate reality. Jack and the other characters perceive the world as immersed in the cyberspatial or the computer system. When the information is processed across the electronic grid and illuminated by the Machine, it turns into an experience.

As the conference on Hitler initiates, Jack gives the inaugural speech in German and later views the conference from his private chamber at College-on-the-Hill to keep himself away from the people of Germany.

Jack pays a visit to the Autumn Harvest farms to conduct bodily tests with advanced equipment. The technician asks him if he has come in contact with the toxin, Nyodene D but Jack repudiates it. He hands him over an envelope and asks him to show it to the doctor.

Emphasizing the central point of the subject of technology in the novel, Susanna S. Martins focuses on the ubiquitous essence of technology in the article, "White Noise and Everyday Technologies." She asserts that the novel, *White Noise* is "a seminal literary exploration of ordinary, banal (but not trivial) interactions with technology in everyday life" (87). She states that the novel depicts technology as it "suggests the possibilities of a new sensibility, one that can be reduced neither to dystopian visions of brainwashing nor to Utopian celebrations of liberation from the constraints of ideology" (113).

Furthermore, she adds that "White Noise also provides insight into the pleasures of technology" (92) and thus "This acknowledgement of the pleasures of technology in the midst of anxieties and questions about its effects is critical . . . for an understanding of how Americans think of technology and negotiate its representations" (111). The Professor of Literature, Michael Valdez Moses contrasts the novel, *White Noise* with the concepts of German thinker, Martin Heidegger in the essay "Lust Removed From Nature" and asserts that "significant antecedents to the novel's treatment of the theme of technology can be found in the philosophical works of the latter" (63).

Based on this, he expostulates that "The greatest threat of technology is its promise of immortality", which in White Noise is showcased with the drug Dylar" (75).

Jack in the company of Murray strolls in the town of Blacksmith for an evening walk. During the walk, Jack discloses all his trepidation and exasperation that comprises his powerlessness to get along with the notion of death. He fails to lead a life full of meaning in the idea of death. He accounts that turning to Hitler studies was the only reason for him to get rid of death as he believes that, "Hitler is larger than death" (Delillo, *White Noise* 330). And, losing oneself in the force and aura of Hitler allows him to protect himself from the energy of death.

Murray says that the only possible way to get rid of the fear of death is to murder himself. He contradicts Jack's proposition which is "every plot is a murder in effect" (Delillo, *White Noise* 335). He says that life is proclaimed by plots which leads to advancement in consciousness. Further, he states that in every human there is a fit of rage that is deeply inherent and that will to a larger extent make a murderer. After the conversation, Jack reaches him and throws every material object that is not required for his survival, holding these articles responsible for his inescapable fear of death.

While resting in his bed chamber, Jack informs everything that he talked with Murray. The next day he meets Winnie Richards who informs him that he has found out the project manager of the Dylar pill from a newspaper article. Jack comes to know that his actual name is not Mr. Gray but Willie Mink. He also learns about his illegal procedures of enticing people to his hotel room. He also finds that the man has lost his job and is residing in the same hotel located at Germantown of which he is unaware. Jack recklessly drives the car all his way to the Germantown.

Jack arrives at the Roadway Motel and enters the private chamber of Willie Mink. He discovers a clumsily dressed person gazing at the television and popping the Dylar pills one after another. Willie seems to be indifferent to the appearance of Jack as male people come to meet him seeking the pill. Jac yells and shoots Willie. A splash of blood falls from him. Jack cleans the gun and positions it in Willie's hand. When Willie is lifted to the hospital, Jack enquires if he will be alright and the doctor answers in the positive.

With the help of technology, the characters in Delillo's novels seek answers to questions concerning life, death, immortality and the extension of life span. The apprehension for death in the life of Gladneys is conciliated as they keep themselves engaged in the television screen. Technology assists them in eliminating the fear of 'who will die first?' (Delillo, *White Noise* 17). This question is principal to the entire novel. Nevertheless, technology fortifies fear in Jack as he visions his death, "It is now official, according to the computer. I've got death inside me. It's just a question of whether or not I can outlive it" (Delillo, *White Noise* 175).

The postmodern character, Murray Siskind, a professor, advises Jack to deviate himself from the idea of mortality by saying, "You could put your faith in technology. It got you here, it can get you out. This is the whole point of technology. It creates an appetite for immortality on the one hand. It threatens universal extinction on the other" (Delillo, *White Noise* 328).

Through the character, Murray Siskind, Delillo calls attention to the disaster that dwells in technology. This has also led to the want to get rid of death. A contemporary approach towards the 'technological sublime' can be traced to Burke's concept of the sublime. Delillo presents how one believes in technology to put an end to the terror of death.

Delillo explicates in the article, "In the Ruins of the Future", how "technology has become 'our fate, our truth' and technology is something that has to be trusted as a type of religious symbol" (12).

The literary theoretician, Joseph Tabbi puts forth that, "the emergence of science and technology has put to flight former metaphysical, religious and political certainties" ("Postmodern Sublime"10). Other critics, Behrooz and Hossein point out that "technology has substituted religion in terms of 'faith,' producing feelings of 'awe and bewilderment' due to unexplainable events that take place" ("The Ridiculous Sublime" 188). As Laist states it is the hunger for technology that Jack aspires to transform to produce a "version of the future in which there is no death" ("Technology and Postmodern Subjectivity" 180).

In addition, Delillo in the novel *Cosmopolis*, clearly mentions, "Humans and computers merge [...] And never-ending life begins [...] Why die when you can live on a disk" (105)? This technology provides a solution to the fear sensed by Babette and Jack.

Additionally, Jean Baudrillard declares that the present epoch is 'hyperreal' which implies that the instances of real are disoriented and the world is approached by 'simulations'. In the book, *Simulacra and Simulation*, Baudrillard argues, "The era of simulation is inaugurated by a liquidation of all referentials" (2). When these simulations get enlarged in computers and TV, their allusion to historical, social and political reality is eradicated and later they allude to one another. Thus, the definition and significance are lost. The individuals experience the performance with a loss of reality.

He expresses that in this era of 'ecstasy' of explanation, subjects are presented with plentiful information and redundant meaning produces a sort of 'nebula'. The collapse of immoderate details and media news ensues the fading of information. It also leaves the subjects befuddled and saddened as they cannot comprehend the genuine significance of it. Baudrillard adds that due to the 'Moebius spiralling negativity', the inspection of genuine objects appears to be out of the question:

> The facts no longer have a specific trajectory, they are born at the intersection of models, a single fact can be engendered by all models at once. This anticipation, this precession, this short circuit, this confusion of the fact with its model...is what allows each time for all possible interpretations, even the most contradictory—all true, in the sense that their truth is to be exchanged, in the image of the model from which they derive, in a generalized cycle. (*Simulacra and Simulation* 17)

In this world of hyperreal that Jean Baudrillard presents, the technologies and objects are in a quite advanced and intelligent state. This expansion and complication of objects which he defines as 'ecstasy', produces a kind of disaster for the concerned subjects as the 'ecstasy' of a particular object is bolstered by the 'inertia' of the concerned subjects. The smart technologies are replicating and progressing at an uncontrollably faster rate. This leads to their outshining of the utilisation and exchange rate. "The only revolution in things is today no longer in their dialectical transcendence, but in their potentialization, in their elevation to the nth power, whether that of terrorism, irony, or simulation. It is no longer dialectics, but ecstasy that is in process" (*Fatal Strategies* 63).

The subject is surrounded by the ecstatic protuberance and starts to decelerate till he becomes motionless. In his work, *Fatal Strategies*, Baudrillard converses about a man who surrenders to the schemes of the objects and is surprised by the complication. With respect to this, Baudrillard's idea of present-day man is moreover contradictory to the idea of man depicted by the French scientist, Teilhard de Chardin.

Teilhard gives utmost credence to the metaphysics of man's evolution. In this postulation, he puts forth that the cosmos is expanding and someday cross the limits of complexity of material world. The humans are on the verge of the ultimate coalition known as the 'omega point'. This is the premier ramification of consciousness. He maintains that far off the proclivities of the physical world towards manufacturing and urbanity, humans are becoming more composite and merged.

He suggests that man unfolds satisfactorily with an enlightened nervous system to allow rationality and self-consciousness. The idea of 'omega point' for humans, according to Teilhard, is in disparity with how Baudrillard depicts subjects in the epoch of the hyperreal. Baudrillard opines that "as information starts to circulate everywhere at the very speed of light. There is no longer an absolute by which to measure the rest. But behind this acceleration something is beginning to slow down absolutely. Are we now slowing down absolutely" *(Fatal Strategies* 37-38)? As a result, he questions man's evolution and asserts that man does not accompany the complexities and 'ecstasy' of technologies and objects. Delillo appropriately portrays Richard Elster, the protagonist, who is convinced by the 'omega point' and desires to achieve it in the isolation of the desert.

Richard Elster is a mature intellectual of seventy-three years. His academic undertakings captivate the attentiveness of eminent government and armed forces. He is invited to a meeting in which the planners of war are a part. In this meeting, the assembly queries regarding the strategies of war. Fundamentally, they hope for Elster to frame the blueprint by which they can be aware of the stationing and retribution. "There were the risk assessments and policy papers, the interagency working groups. He was the outsider, a scholar with an approval rating but no experience in government" (Delillo, *Point Omega* 23). Elster goes through the documents related to the military and eventually delivers the blueprint of war set down similar to a haiku. He states, "I wanted a war in three lines…" (Delillo, *Point Omega* 23).

On being asked the meaning of Haiku, he answers, "Haiku means nothing beyond what it is. A pond in summer a leaf in the wind. It is human consciousness located in nature. It's the answer to everything in a set number of lines, a prescribed syllable count. I wanted a haiku war. This was not a matter of force levels or logistics. What I wanted was a set of ideas linked to transient things. This is the soul of haiku" (Delillo, *Point Omega* 37). He adds that he desires war as the future must be reconsidered. The world cannot be let to be shaped by others.

After the fulfilment of military endeavours, Elster withdraws himself to the Sonoran Desert under the auspices of San Diego. He is abandoned there and leads the rest of his life by ruminating and gradually entering into his old age. He says, "There was the house and then nothing but distances, not vistas or sweeping sightlines but only distances" (Delillo, *Point Omega* 22). He tries to find time and space and is enchanted by the concept of geological time. He pronounces that "he'd exchanged all that for space and time. These were things he seemed to absorb through his pores. There were the distances that enfolded every feature of the landscape and there was the force of geologic time, out there somewhere, the string grinds of excavators searching for weathered bone" (Delillo, *Point Omega* 24). He believes that the setting sun is man's invention. He reiterates that it is "our perceptual arrangement of light and space into elements of wonder" (Delillo, *Point Omega* 22). This time extended long ago the existence of human beings and progressed for generations afterwards.

The house where he resides in the desert is a bitter hybrid. It contains a ridged metallic ceiling with a weatherboard on the outer side and a deck that is tagged on the other side. From this place, the nearness of hills is observable in the noon.

Richard Elster withdraws from the hyperreal euphoric simulations as he desires not to succumb to the object's directives and be sedated by the convolutedness. As Jean Baudrillard describes Richard Elster is in a condition of inertia. He resides in the desert which is a remote location from the progress of technologies and momentum of objects. Elster says, "Time slows down when I'm here. Time becomes blind…I don't get old here" (Delillo, *Point Omega* 30). He claims that he has settled in the desert to "eat, sleep and sweat, here to do nothing, sit and think" (Delillo, *Point Omega* 30) and to refrain from "News and Traffic. Sports and Weather, away from the claustrophobic areas of the town (Delillo, *Point Omega* 23). He stays in a bleak house and notices "nothing but distances, not vistas or sweeping sightlines but only distances" (Delillo, *Point Omega* 22).

Richard Elster expresses that he visited this habitation before too, "to write, to think" (Delillo, *Point omega* 29) but now he names it a "spiritual retreat" (Delillo,

Point omega 29). He decides to simply recover his mind and body as he is 'inert' and is trying to break loose from the 'ecstasy' which has transformed him into 'inert'. An American writer and theorist Michiko Kakutani expresses that, "all three central characters in this novel [...] are alienated, oddly detached people. They are individuals dwelling in a limbo state, searching for something that might give order or meaning to their lives or simply shell-shocked by the randomness and menace of modern life" (1).

Richard Elster disappears to his isolation in the desert to refrain himself being susceptible to the avalanche of particulars. The filmmaker, Jim, chaperons Elster and targets to create a documentary starring Elster. He is also attracted by the lack of information and communication and chooses to access his vulnerability towards them, "I went inside to check my laptop for e-mail, needing outside contact but feeling corrupt, as if I were breaking an unstated pact of creative withdrawal" (Delillo, *Point Omega* 31). Later Jim utters, "I wasn't using my cell phone and seldom touched my laptop. They began to seem feeble, whatever their speed and reach, devices overwhelmed by landscape" (Delillo, *Point Omega* 82).

He is later accompanied by an associate and film-maker known as Jim Finley. Finley is preoccupied with the creation of on-shot movie during the time of Elster, searching for meaning in the region. He seeks to "make about his time in government, in the blat and stammer of Iraq" (Delillo, *Point Omega* 26). Finley finds the desert as beyond his range. He utters that "it was an alien being, it was science fiction, both saturating and remote, and I had to force myself to believe I was here" (Delillo, *Point Omega* 25). The landscape seems claustrophobic and spacious. Finley presses Elster now and then so as to record his experiences. To form a background, he arranges the books on the shelf. He asks Elster to position himself there and relate all his experiences, personages and emotions.

Finley asks Elster if he is in exile. To this Elster answers, "Wolfowitz went to the World Bank. That was exile. This is different, a spiritual retreat" (Delillo, *Point Omega* 29).

Teilhard communicates that Man's consciousness is culminating to the 'omega point' simultaneously, Elster remarks, "human thought is alive, it circulates. And the sphere of collective human thought, this is approaching the final term, the last flare" (Delillo, *Point Omega* 65). Teilhard's idea of the concept of 'omega point' is in disparity with Jean Baudrillard's perspective. It signifies the evolution and refinement of objects and technology that compels human to decelerate and anaesthetized.

The technology is advancing towards the verge of ecstasy and burgeoning to a stage which is on the farther side of the cognizance of man. This leads to the people failing in their understanding of cutting-edge machine age. Teilhard aims to achieve an 'omega point' to which man is moving at a faster rate but with regard to Baudrillard's point of view, the 'ecstasy' of technology and objects do not hold man, and man has to comply with the regulations of the advanced mechanism so as to become 'inert'.

In the meantime, Teilhard visualizes an 'omega point' of superior awareness and intellect towards which man is heading. Jean Baudrillard presents man being ensnared by the worldliness of the universe and as a result affected by the condition of 'inertia'. Teilhard is convinced by the metaphysics of growth of man till the ultimate confluence with mysticism.

Elster thinks about extinction of man in the isolation of desert. Humans are following the step of extinction as other species are. He observes the scenic beauty of the desert and contemplates about the species that have extinct aeons ago.

Spreicer presents, "Point Omega portrays the exhaustion of the complex system of American-style visuality and connects it to the space of the desert, where the retardation of time functions as an ominous foreboding of system entropy affecting the genuinely American sense of endless future development, the relentless self-perpetuation of the capitalist system" (qtd. in Parvaneh 172).

Richard Elster puts forward that man is drawing near the ultimatum, "Do we have to be human forever? Consciousness is exhausted. Back now to inorganic matter. This is what we want. We want to be stones in a field" (Delillo, *Point Omega* 67). Present-day humans reside in "the desert of the real" (*Simulacra and Simulation* 1) and Elster ponders on the extinction of man in a hyperreal arena.

Shortly, Elster's adorable daughter, Jessie accompanies Elster and Finley. She is astute and exceptionally intuitive. She can foretell what anyone says by interpreting the person's lips before the person utters the words. Elster describes, "She seemed attentive to some interior presence. She heard words from inside them" (Delillo, *Point Omega* 50). Finley relaxes in the company of Jessie and is charmed by her. He gazes at voyeuristically.

But Jessie feels abandoned and deadly by the world surrounding her. Meanwhile, both Elster and Finley learn that her mother is constantly disturbed by the thought of a man, Dennis with whom Jessie is in love and who is attempting to destroy Jessie's life. Dennis keeps on stalking Jessie and they one day find Jessie nowhere.

Nevertheless, Elster aims to arrive at the 'omega point' in the quietude and loneliness of the desert "where the mind transcends all the direction inward" (Delillo, *Point Omega* 91). He yearns for isolation by disconnecting himself from the outer world. It is opposed to the idea of watching which is a contemporary theme of the novel. Whilst, Mary K. Holland remarks "self becomes what self perceives" (10). She assumes that the novel is "a warning about the dangers of constituting the self purely externally, through image and representation" (10). The person who is glancing at 24 Hour Psycho hopes for "complete immersion" with the feature film. He takes a fancy to "bathe in the tempo, in the near static rhythm of the image [...] He wanted the film to move even more slowly, requiring deeper involvement of eye and mind, always that, the thing he sees tunneling into the blood, into dense sensation, sharing consciousness with him" (146).

In due course, Finley takes Elster to watch a movie namely, 24 Hour Psycho directed by Douglas Gordon. This movie is a theoretical piece of art. It is taken from Alfred Hitchcock's *Psycho*. It is decelerated to such a pace that it takes twenty-four hours for the completion of the movie. Elster discerns the movie as "watching the universe die over a period of about seven billion years" (Delillo, *Point Omega* 59).

Focusing on a Baudrillardian approach of the novel, it is clear that Teilhard's concept of 'omega point' is out of the question in the modern hyperreal generation as the objects are heading towards 'ecstasy' and the subjects are heading to a condition of 'inertia'. In the novel, Delillo proposes that man's evolution vaporises with the brutality and chaos occurring globally.

When Richard Elster is engaged in the misery of loss, he is far away from achieving the 'omega point'. On the contrary, in the age of the hyperreal, the objects appear to be victorious over subjects. The motionless subjects are devoid of the idea of going beyond the 'omega point'. Elster also fails to achieve the omega point as depicted by Teilhard.

CHAPTER V

Apocalypse of the Human: Human Mutation and the Practice of Critical Posthumanism in the Novels of Olaf Stapledon

It is quite ordinary that postmodernism is distinguished by the plight of liberal humanism i.e., the end of man, just as it is often regarded. The subject of the rights of man is primary to moral concerns. If a man is rapidly becoming Posthuman, the question is whether there is any importance of human rights morals in the upcoming topics spawned by advancements in science and technology with added shifts in culture.

The English Professor of History, Felipe Fernandez-Armesto concisely sums up the condition, "Over the last thirty or forty years, we have invested an enormous amount of thought, emotion, treasure, and blood in what we call human values, human rights, the defense of human dignity and of human rights. Over the same 30 period, quietly but devastatingly, science and philosophy have combined to undermine our traditional concept of humankind" (1).

Customarily, the frontiers of the ethical sections have coexisted within the confines of humanity. In the present times, there are advancements in science namely, stem-cell research, genetic engineering, Human Genome Project, cloning, palaeontology and an increase in neuropsychology has varied contributions to the field of Critical Posthumanism. These practices inquire into the concept of man and thus are indispensable to a radical ethical reestablishment of man. The concept of man is subject to modification based on biomedical science which is assisted by Weltanschauung, "the fact remains that technology is rapidly making the concept of the 'natural' human obsolete. We have now entered the realm of the Critical posthuman, the debate over the identities and values of what will come after human" (Vint, "Bodies of Tomorrow" 7).

The dimension of Critical Posthumanism adjures a different approach. The frontiers of humanity are contingent upon numerous political and religious beliefs. These ideologies are corroded by progress in information studies and biological science. The generous attempt of the reformers of human rights is futile as there is nothing palpable regarding humanity.

The prerogative of Critical Posthumanism rests on the emendation of the foundational standard by which morality is attributed to an institution. This standard is set by human rights in the age of Critical Posthumanism. The theory of Critical Posthumanism presents the insinuations and reverberations of advancements in informatics and newly discovered technologies. These developments have an influential effect on culture. Numerous central ideas of Critical Posthumanism namely, the hybridisation of humans and animals, cloning, cyborg, android, and aliens impart considerable importance. As the Professor of Media Studies, Sheryl Vint contends, "SF is particularly suited to exploring the question of the posthuman because it is a discourse that allows us to concretely imagine bodies and selves otherwise, a discourse defined by its ability to estrange our commonplace perceptions of reality" ("Bodies of Tomorrow" 19).

In spite of the fact that all these tenets are significant to Critical Posthumanism, the continuity of evolution of man/animal, Artificial Intelligence or non-biological subjectiveness, and the hybridisation of human and non-human are much focused in the novels of Olaf Stapledon. These subjects showcase how the frontiers of humanity are at first inflated and then detonated by way of radical immolation of the precepts of liberal humanism. Regardless of what new morals may spring up, all will be founded on the reconstitution of the idea of morality.

The subject of Critical Posthumanism serves both as a perception of the future and a reflection of the bygone times. In *The Order of Things*, Michel Foucault presents his statement, "It is comforting, however, and a source of profound relief to think that man is only a recent invention, a figure not yet two centuries old, a new wrinkle in our knowledge, and that he will disappear again as soon as that knowledge has discovered a new form" (23).

This expression supports the view of Roland Barthes who is a critique of universal humanism in his work *Mythologies*. It is feedback to the utopian intentions of the 'New Man' which is a core idea to the 20th-century beliefs of Fascism, Nazism and Communism.

Critical Posthumanism has come to light out of the genocide and cleansing of the self, based on morality and ethnicity. Both of these tried to constitute the sufferer as a non-human other. In *Faces of the Enemy*, a picturesque series by Sam Keen presents the enemy as "the other. The outsider. The alien. He is not human" (16). These expressions serve as rhetoric but have tremendous significance in restructuring the extremities of human beings and thus making way for utmost violence.

Humans have inherited 'brakes' in case of assassinating the creatures of their species. The discourse can incessantly overrule the brakes by transferring the everlasting blueprint of humanness. Assassinating is easier if the enemy is considered as inhuman or non-human other. In examining the discourse on Nazi biomedical, Robert Proctor and Robert Jay Lifton have presented how genetics and anthropology are misemployed to typify the Jews as "literally non-human, members of a parasitic alien species" ("The Nazi Doctors" 561).

A similar kind of scheme of dehumanization functions in disoriented ways in another massacre led by Stalin and Pol Pot. In "A Cyborg Manifesto", Donna Haraway displays the Posthuman or otherwise, she names it as cyborg is a new mode of human subjectiveness associated with a utopian restructuring of the world. Donna Haraway perceives the cyborg as "a cybernetic organism, a hybrid of machine and organism, a creature of social reality as well as a creature of fiction. Social reality is lived social relations, our most important political construction, a world-changing fiction" (149).

The concept of Cyborg is regarded as a communal metaphor that constitutes the subject of Critical Posthumanism as changeable, shattered and going beyond the disjunction of inorganic and organic, inhuman or non-human and animal, female and male. The French

Philosopher, Jean-Francois Lyotard, in his book, *The Inhuman* initiates a similar question, "what if human beings, in humanism's sense of the word, were in the process of, constrained into, becoming inhuman" (2)?

Both the philosophers Haraway and Lyotard attend to the Critical Posthuman as a literal creation, a metaphor that reviews postmodernism's revolutionary interrogation of the old definition of humanism. According to Lyotard, the notion of inhuman has been connected with man since time immemorial. The subject matter that suits mankind is owned by the inhuman faculty of the social strata along with the secret disparity of the unconscious in which the soul is a part. While, on the other hand, Donna Haraway, exhaustively employs genetics, prosthetics and biological evolution. Lyotard inscribes the likelihood of an artificial administration of man's body and mind. Lyotard and Haraway are inclined towards the political and philosophical reconsideration of humanity.

In the book, *How We Became Posthuman*, N Katherine Hayles, connects the political and philosophical interrogation of humans with the development in technology and science especially in "cybernetics, genetic engineering and neuropsychology" (199).

This quantum leap compels man to renounce the insolvent idea of a ubiquitous nature. It also reviews the likelihood of the exact manufacture of perspicacity sheltered in beings that are no longer regarded as organic species or human namely, the genetically engineered species and AI or Artificial Intelligence. These topics arouse deep political and moral concerns. An author, Thomas Foster identifies that Critical Posthumanism might work in two methods. One is, "posthumanism has critical potential, that it is or can be part of struggles for freedom and social justice, and the argument that posthumanism dismisses such struggles or even makes them obsolete" (27).

Another question that is asked in this context is what will be the consequence if the fight for liberty and equitableness becomes impracticable in the world of Critical Posthumanism. And, if such a fight takes place, then what will be the cause of this fight? Haraway speaks out that Science Fiction is the genre from which Critical Posthumanism emerges. She says, "Contemporary science fiction is full of cyborgs—creatures simultaneously animal and machine, who populate worlds ambiguously natural and crafted" (*Simians, Cyborgs and Women* 149).

Aristotle in his *Nicomachean Ethics* presents ethical conduct as an outcome of remaining a biological being. He states:

> For all things that have a function or activity, the good and the 'well' is thought to reside in the function, so would it seem to be for man, if he has a function ... Life seems to be common even to plants, but we are seeking what is peculiar to man. Let us exclude, therefore, the life of nutrition and growth. Next, there would be a life of perception, but it also seems to be common even to the horse, the ox, and every animal. There remains, then, an active life of the element that has a rational principle; of this, one part has such a principle in the sense of being obedient to one, the other in the sense of possessing one and exercising thought ... if this is the case, and we state the function of man to be a certain kind of life, and this to be an activity or actions of the soul implying a

rational principle, and the function of a good man to be the good and noble performance of these, and if any action is well performed when it is performed in accordance with the appropriate excellence: if this is the case, human good turns out to be activity of soul in accordance with virtue. (10)

Aristotle assigns the ethical subjects to humans alone and non-humans or animals are devoid of this. This homo-centric approach of Aristotle on ethics is opposed by critics of animal rights like Peter Singer. He is a proponent of the liberation of animals. He proclaims the expansion of utilitarianism towards non-human animals. Animals should be free from pain and suffering and it is "the vital characteristic that gives a being the right to equal consideration" (*Animal Liberation* 8).

In his discussion with Richard Posner, Peter Singer states his point of view,

> What ethically significant feature can there be that all human beings but no nonhuman animals possess? We like to distinguish ourselves from animals by saying that only humans are rational, can use language, are self-aware, or are autonomous. But these abilities, significant as they are, do not enable us to draw the requisite line between all humans and nonhuman animals. For there are many humans who are not rational, self-aware, or autonomous, and who have no language ... Like racists and sexists, speciesists say that the boundary of their own group is also a boundary that marks off the most valuable beings from all the rest. (1)

With the publication of Charles Darwin's Origin of Species in the year 1859, many philosophers have addressed the continuation of evolution between man and animals. They have also granted this conjugation with ethical consideration. These inferences are extended in the novels of Olaf Stapledon.

The narrator intends to write John Wainwright's biography. John Wainwright is a mutated form that resembles the upcoming level of evolution namely the Homo Superior. Some unknown people regarded him as 'spiderish' as his body seemed inconsiderable and "his legs and arms so long and lithe, his head all eye and brow" (Stapledon, *Odd John* 3). The narrator draws a clear picture of John's peculiar outward features, advanced intellect and quick education.

Similar to the other colonists, John moved by uncovering his body. Despite being at the age of twenty-three, he seemed much young as he didn't have the maleness in him. The texture of his skin was greenish-brown due to the effect of the Polynesian sun. His hands were gigantic in appearance. His head was huge but not inordinate to his extensive limbs. His head was much bigger than it seemed, "for its visible bulk was scarcely at all occupied by the hair, which was but a close skull-cap, a mere superficies of Negroid but almost white wool. His nose was small but broad, rather Mongolian perhaps" (Stapledon, *Odd John* 4). His lips were large and his eyes seemed queer and huge in comparison to his head which appeared to be like a falcon.

He was quite reluctant to attend the school but he was quite passionate about subjects like biology and maths.

Thomas Wainwright, John's father was convinced by the fact that the Moroccans and the Spaniards had come up with his making. He also had nuances of Arab and

Latin in his personality. Everyone believed that he was an intellectual but he was weird and as a result, condemned to be a failure. He practised in North Wales as a medical professional but his patients did not develop faith in him which is essential for a doctor's gain. His children have named him as Doc.

His wife, Pax, was also of a cross-breed kind as he. She is from Sweden and her forefathers comprise the Lapps and the Finns. Her appearance was a type of Scandinavian. The narrator is acquainted with John through Thomas' wife. Some talk over that she is a splendid female beast but subnormal in disposition.

John is the youngest of their children. His mother has suffered a lot of physical strain during his birth. She carried him in her womb for eleven months. And, when the baby was born it had a peculiar look of a foetus of seven months. With utmost difficulty, the foetus was kept living inside an incubator. The narrator ruminates that "such an inert and pulpy bit of flesh could ever develop into a human being. It was like some obscene fruit, more vegetable than animal, save for an occasional incongruous spasm of activity" (Stapledon, *Odd John* 5).

At the age of one, John's physical growth was unsatisfactory. He looked like a newly born child. He opened his eyes when he was eighteen months old. The eyes seemed as if "a sleeping city had suddenly leapt into life. Formidable eyes they were for a baby, eyes seen under a magnifying glass, each great pupil like the mouth of a cave, the iris a mere rim, an edging of bright emerald. Strange how two black holes can gleam with life" (Stapledon, *Odd John* 5)! After the opening of his eyes, Pax, John's mother names him as 'Odd John'.

The nomenclature 'Odd John' represents the oddity

in John's physical and mental stature. The adjective 'Odd' was attached to his name throughout his life. As time passed by, he became enthusiastic and focused. But his physical growth was quite slow in comparison to other babies of his age. This was a matter of concern for his parents. His attitude and appearance resembled a six-months baby. He failed to efficiently operate his toys with his fingers. Although he was intelligent, he showed no indication of talking and crawling.

Weeks later, he started talking and asking for milk. When his parents heard him talking, they learnt that he remembered how he was bereft of his mother's womb while taking birth. And, as he was unable to breathe, he was given artificial respiration for the purpose. From this, he acquired the skill of exerting control over the lungs. His heart was also under the voluntary mechanism so cardiac issues are common for him. The narrator also says that "his emotional reflexes also were far more under control than in the rest of us. Thus if, in some anger-provoking situation, he did not wish to feel angry, he could easily inhibit the anger reflexes. And if anger seemed desirable, he could produce it. He was indeed "Odd John" (Stapledon, *Odd John* 6).

At the age of nine when John was vocal, he got an abacus as a gift. Furthermore, John was so preoccupied with the child's abacus that he became completely silent and skipped his meals. He showed keen interest in the number system. Initially, he desperately played with it. And, in a while, he threw the toy flung himself to the bed and gazed at the roof.

His mother was concerned and made efforts to know what had happened to his boy. But John carelessly answered that he is absorbed in the number system. He asks Pax what are the numbers that succeed twelve and Pax counts till thirty. John regards Pax as stupid because abacus and she "count the numbers in tens and not in twelves. And that's stupid because twelves have 'fourths' and 'threeths', I mean 'thirds' and 'tens' have not" (Stapledon, *Odd John* 6). Pax justifies his point by saying that, "all men counted in tens because when counting began, they used their five fingers" (Stapledon, *Odd John* 6). Then, John admonishes all men as stupid. Even when John was five years old, he seemed like a newborn. He slept on his carriage the entire day motionlessly and practised mental geometry and arithmetic.

He always sat still which is bad for a nurturing child. The guests who arrived at their house didn't believe that John was mentally energetic. They thought he was in a comatic state on all occasions and was growing like an idiot. John's passion for geometry arose with his cousin's case of bricks and a disposable diaper. Then, he turned up with the slicing up of cottage cheese and daily soaps into shapes such as cubes, slabs and oval.

He cut his fingers at the outset. But in the next few days, he used his sister's geometrical set covering sheets with various designs. As he grew with age, he asked several questions to Thomas. One of them is, "If you went in a straight line, on and on and on, how far would you have to go to get right back here" (Stapledon, *Odd John* 7)? He also enquired about the theory of relativity that was confusing him with the presumed notions of geometry. Later, Thomas hired a mathematician from his university to clear the doubts of John.

One day Pax and John visited Thomas' clinic, one of the visitors noticed John and commented, "It's the child's imaginative power that is so amazing. He knows none of the jargon and none of the history, but he has seen it all already for himself. It's incredible. He seems to visualize what can't be visualized" (Stapledon, *Odd John* 7).

    Thomas looks at John as an extraordinarily noticeable case of an 'infant prodigy' and this kind of behaviour will disappear when he grows older. He was good at reading and writing. It took him no more than a month to leave behind his siblings in this task. He has an efficient memory-retaining capacity as he analysed each of the words with the letter sounds. Within a short period, he gulped down all the books that were present in their library. But he was not a bookworm. For him, "Reading was an occupation fit only for times of inaction when his overtaxed hands demanded repose" (Stapledon, *Odd John* 8).

When John reached the age of six, he was fascinated towards locomotion. At first, he worked on balancing his body and made a few acts with his mother's support. Consequently, he had a nervous breakdown and rested for many days. After his complete recovery, he moved into his bedroom and succeeded in his endeavour. But he was dissatisfied with this as his legs weren't mature. They were short and coiled. With constant exercise, his legs grew longer and stronger.

    He no longer looked like an infant but muscular enough to climb on the pipe and get the ball from the gutter of the roof. Everyone was panic-stricken seeing John performing such a type of act. When Thomas learns about it, he says, "The prodigy has advanced from mathematics to acrobatics" (Stapledon, *Odd John* 10). Every child in the neighbourhood is envious of John's tactics.

    In the course of time, Stephen, a school-going boy from the neighbourhood was battling with a grass-cutter. John glares at him for a few minutes then grabs the cog-wheel from his hand, assembles the sections judiciously and the work is done. Surprisingly, Stephen looks at John when he comments, "Sorry you're no good at that sort of thing, but I'll always help when I'm free" (Stapledon, *Odd John* 10).

For the next six months, John has two objectives, specifically, becoming an indestructible combatant and the next is comprehending his fellow mates. John performs the second task first by interrogating and then by observing the humans. He came up with two ideas firstly, the humans are shockingly disinterested in their motives and second, he was unique to the humans.

The children of the neighbourhood are heard talking about him, "John's a great little sport now", at the same time, their parents are influenced by his role as a warrior and discuss that, "John's a dear these days. He's lost all his horrid freakishness and conceit" (Stapledon, *Odd John* 11-12). Even Stephen feels sorry for the mower and praises John for his abilities.

After being demoralised now and then by his father, John has been reading books on physiology, anatomy, and other books related to medical science. As he did not have adequate knowledge in understanding the medical terms, he opened up a Dictionary containing medical \terms that helped him gain an understanding of medicine and anatomy.

He is proficient in 'microscopy and dissection' (Stapledon, *Odd John* 11). To everyone's horror, "he was found cutting up a dead rat on the dining-room floor, having thoughtfully spread a newspaper to protect the carpet" (Stapledon, *Odd John* 11). Thomas was amazed at seeing John's efficiency in anatomical theory and practice. Weeks later, John keeps Biology aside as he did with Mathematics as according to him "life doesn't hang together like a number. It won't make a pattern. There's something wrong with all those books" (Stapledon, *Odd John* 11).

John was sent to school but was quite unmanageable as the teacher declared that John required psychiatric treatment as he was abnormal. Henceforward, Pax begins to teach John. He pretends to read the books to please his mother, Pax.

John's digestive system was poorly functioning. It was still infantile as till the age of six, it failed to accept anything except milk and fruit juice. He was prone to digestive issues. But now he has charted out a diet plan for himself comprising fruits, cheese, whole bread and cautiously spaced with physical exercise. Over time, he developed unquestionably strong will and his bodily growth seemed compatible with his age. His cunningness allowed him to defeat his opponents who were much more powerful and muscular than himself.

John realised that he was dissimilar to other humans. He played with his companions but out of the group he was the youngest and of infantile type. John and his mother, Pax together resembled "a human foundling with a wolf foster-mother, or better, a cow-foster-mother" (Stapledon, *Odd John* 14). He showers his complete faith and love on her but he faces difficulty when his mother fails to comprehend his countless questions regarding the cosmos.

But his relationship with his father was distinct. It was filled with disgust and contentment. He utilised his father's bent of mind as a medical professional. Thomas, at times, contemplates lecturing his boy on the basic nature of humans or the universe.

The narrator thought that John had said to himself, "I have somehow to understand these fantastic beings who occupy the planet. Here is a fine specimen I must experiment on him" (Stapledon, *Odd John* 14). The narrator thought that John had preserved him for future use and was planning to capture him.

At the age of eight, John was still considered an infant of five years. Although he enjoyed playing the child games, he could be a part of any adult discussion. He either excelled in something or was entirely bad. But John was rapidly becoming sophisticated as he was reading many books at an impressive rate. It took him a few hours to develop mastery of any book or subject. He picked up nearly all the books, went through them for some time and disposed of them for being valueless.

He keeps on demanding his parents take him to visit a mine, a historic place, or a laboratory for the observation of an experiment. And, whenever they went to these places, they had to profess that John's appearance was a coincidence. John was enough able to initiate a discussion with an outsider to learn what kind of task they were performing and what will be the resulting outcome. He was independent of his parents to visualise the world. His parents also realised this and left him to manage his devices by himself.

John continued his observation on the nature of man. He utilised his time in designing the mechanical toys for instance the electric boats. The electric railway created by him has occupied their garden in the form of a maze. He was awarded prizes for producing model aeroplanes at home. In these endeavours, he seems to others as a school-going boy who is unusually experienced in this area. He had also built, "a minute but seaworthy canoe, fitted both with sail and an old motor-bicycle engine. In this he spent many hours exploring the estuary and the sea-coast, and studying the sea-birds, for which he had a surprising passion" (Stapledon, *Odd John* 20).

During summer he was more attracted to Philosophy. He said, "Philosophy is really very helpful to the growing mind, but it's terribly disappointing too" (Stapledon, *Odd John* 20). He was an avid reader of the works of Plato, Immanuel Kant, Spinoza and other realists of the modern age. For John, "Philosophy is an amazing tissue of really fine thinking and incredible, puerile mistakes. It's like one of those rubber bones' they give the dog to chew, damned good for the mind's teeth, but as food- no bloody good at all" (Stapledon, *Odd John* 21).

When John reached the age of nine, he was living a dual life. The other part of his life was exaggerated. The narrator visited the house of the Wainwrights to take Thomas' book on medical science. As John and the narrator have breakfast together, Matilda, the washerwoman of the house says that, this morning a policeman has been killed in Mr. Magnate's Garden. And, the narrator notices a scrape enveloped by dirt in the inner part of John's wrist. Recently, there occurred many thefts in the locality and the cops were incessantly searching for the culprit.

Momentarily, the narrator presents all the information regarding the murder and burglaries in John's words that he has given him.

The narrator is ignorant of the fact that John has committed a crime. Hereafter, significant transformations were seen in John's behaviour. He became both imperceptible and gentle to his friends and acquaintances. Most of the time, he remained in solitariness. He spent most of the time tidying his home. Gradually, he instituted a few labour-saving instruments in their home. For instance, "shifting a hook or a shelf to suit the natural reach of the adult arm, altering the balance of the coal-scuttle, reorganizing the larder and the bathroom. He tried to introduce his methods into the surgery, suggesting new ways of cleaning test-tubes, sterilizing instruments and storing drugs" (Stapledon, *Odd John* 27).

After several weeks, John spent his time reading a book on the shore. To keep warm, he preferred taking walks in the city during the winter. At the age of ten, John forced the narrator to accompany him to his workshop. They arrived at the shore and walked along the wet sands. They reached a steep slope where there was a "rusty sheet of corrugated iron, which lay derelict on the hillside. One end of it was buried under a mass of rubbish. The exposed part was about three feet square" (Stapledon, *Odd John* 28). The narrator had his fingers injured with the rusty surface.

There was a black hole between the gravel. It was quite easy for John to crawl inside due to his miniature body. But he had to displace one gravel for the narrator to pass. John used his flashlight to lighten the cave. The narrator exclaims, "So this was the workshop! It had evidently been cut out of the clay slope and lined with cement. The ceiling was covered with rough planks, and shored up here and there with wooden posts" (Stapledon, *Odd John* 28).

John lighted an acetylene gaslight which was placed in the outer wall. He shut its glass front and mentioned, "Its air comes in by a pipe from outside, and its fumes go out by another. There's an independent ventilation system for the room" (Stapledon, *Odd John* 28). There were several drainpipes too used for draining out the fields on the shore.

In John's compact den, there were various articles such as a blow lamp, lathe, bench and other tools. He picked one of them and showed it to the narrator and said, "This is one of my earlier gadgets, the world's perfect wool-winder. No curates need henceforth apply. The Church's undoing! Put the skein on those prongs, and an end of wool in that slot, then waggle the lever, so, and you get a ball of wool as sleek as the curate's head. All made of aluminium sheeting, and a few aluminium knitting needles" (Stapledon, *Odd John* 28).

He produced a partible and untearable leather pocket for males. He said, "The pocket itself clips onto this L-shaped strip, so; all your trousers have strips like this, firmly sewn into the lining. You have one pair of pockets for all your trousers, so there's no bother about emptying pockets when you change your clothes. And no more holes for Mummy to mend. And no more losing your treasures. Your pocket clips tight shut, so" (Stapledon, *Odd John* 28).

The narrator enquires if John feels cold in his workshop, then he says that he warms it with an oil stove. He goes to light the stove to prepare some coffee. Then, John gave him an appliance to cleanse the corners of the room. The appliance consists of a long tube with a handle on it. There is a brush attached to the handle like a cork screw that can be rotated by pressing it in the opposite direction. These labour-saving household appliances if displayed in front of the public will gain high popularity. But due to the secret pact between the Wainwrights and the narrator, he is restricted from publicizing John's inventions.

The narrator states that there are several other devices that John has invented such as, "a parsley cutter, a potato-peeler, several devices for using old razor-blades as penknife, scissors, and so on" (Stapledon, *Odd John* 29). But his inventions were kept a secret as he believed that, "Homo sapiens may be too prejudiced to use them" (Stapledon, *Odd John* 29).

John adjures the narrator to get all his inventions patented. He says, "You're going to launch all these things, sometimes under your name, sometimes under sham names. I don't want people to know they all come from one little brain" (Stapledon, *Odd John* 30). He also adds that he is a kid to interview the patent agents so in this case he wants the narrator to assist him. Further, he clears out that "there was not to be any regularized business arrangement between us, no formal agreement about profit-sharing and liabilities" (Stapledon, *Odd John* 30). He declares that "the payments will have to be made to you at your bank mostly, to keep me dark. These gadgets are to go out as yours, not mine, and as the inventions of lots of imaginary people. You're their agent" (Stapledon, *Odd John* 30).

The narrator invested his time in moving around the country in search of manufacturers and patent agents. John also went along with him and was introduced to everyone as a friend to him. In this way, he visited various factories and learnt the operations and limitations of various machines that allowed him to build manufacturable products.

In due course, they realised that these agents were trying to get more out of them than producing their articles. John was "as contemptuous of the morality as of the intelligence of Homo sapiens" (Stapledon, *Odd John* 31). He was astonished to see the money-making skill of Homo sapiens. He never had the echo of any business or economic independence in him. But at a later time, they become extraordinarily successful. They "launched scores of ingenious contrivances which have since become universally recognized as necessary adjuncts of modern life" (Stapledon, *Odd John* 31). Their bank balance accelerated at a high rate with minimum expenditure.

John gained a lot of financial knowledge from the books and the local stockbrokers as well. He plans to invest half of their capital in the British light industry, electricity and others as that will be profitable. He was able to make contact with the big financiers of London by captivating and reading their minds. With the adaptation of new financial techniques, he accumulated a huge amount of fortune. John made the narrator the benefactor of his wealth and named him 'The Bean'.

John's adolescence started with a delay. He seemed to be ten years old. And, when he died at the age of twenty-three, he gave the impression of being a young boy of seventeen. During these years, John was immersed in examining the strengths and constraints of Homo sapiens as exposed to modern-day world issues. Even though he was backwards physically his cognitive faculty was advanced.

As time went by, he sensed a change in attitude towards life. His face was already transforming from an infant to a boy.

Starting from the age of fourteen to seventeen, John absorbed himself in observing the world around him. This examination took the path of an exploration of the normal species concerning its nature, accomplishment and predicament. The extensive research should be accomplished confidentially as he didn't want to exhibit any of his endeavours in front of the public.

He succeeded in establishing his association with the cabinet minister by falling ill in front of his residence when the Cabinet minister's wife was making her way to the house. John had full control "over his organic reflexes, and could influence his glandular secretions, his temperature, his digestive processes, the rate of his heartbeat, the distribution of blood in his body, and so on" (Stapledon, *Odd John* 41). John developed a compassionate relationship with the minister before the arrival of the physician. The physician advised that John should be permitted to take proper bed rest. His methods of artificial illness were initially a success and he used this procedure to meet the Communist leader, the bishop and other gentlemen. He also became friends with engineers, clerks, dock labourers and so on.

When the time came to learn a new language, John went through the grammar, and the dictionary and took courses on pronunciation from any native or the records of gramophone and then visited any foreign country.

The narrator asks John whether the predicament of the universe is accidental or it is inherent to the Homo sapiens. John answers:

> Homo sapiens is a spider trying to crawl out of a basin. The higher he crawls, the steeper the hill. Sooner or later, down he goes. So long as he's on the bottom, he can get along quite nicely, but as soon as he starts climbing, he begins to slip. And the higher he climbs the farther he falls. It doesn't matter which direction he tries. He can make civilization after civilization, but every time, long before he begins to be really civilized, skid!
> (Stapledon, *Odd John* 52)

The narrator disregards John's statement and says that "Homo sapiens is an inventive animal" and his climb is altogether different from other species. (Stapledon, *Odd John* 52). He adds, "Mechanical power is a stickiness for his feet. And I believe his wing-cases are stirring, too" (Stapledon, *Odd John* 52).

John rejects the narrator's opinion and utters that Homo sapiens does not know how to use his mechanical power due to which he is backward. "Homo sapiens reached his limit a million years ago, but he has only recently begun to use his powers dangerously. In achieving science and mechanism he has brought about a state of affairs which cannot be dealt with properly save by capacity which is much more developed than his" (Stapledon, *Odd John* 52). Mechanical power is necessary for the growth of the human psyche but for the subhuman it is fatal. And if the entire population is spiritually enlightened then everyone's nature can become genuinely human at once leading to a state of wholeness.

John remarks during the advent of Christianity, the entire population was converted. The ancient Buddhists and the Christians were called subhuman regardless of the miracles they performed. The mental capacity of those populations remained the same as before but they envisaged a slight transformation in their will which was temporary.

They became saints but not angels. There was an inner conflict between the human and the sub-human in them. For this reason, "they mostly got obsessed with the idea of sin, and saving their souls, instead of being able to pass on to live the new life with fluency and joy, and with creative effect in the world" (Stapledon, *Odd John* 52). John thinks of taking the responsibility of man to redo himself into a more human. But he realises that an invasion of higher beings from a different planet can make it possible.

When John noticed the inefficacy of Homo sapiens, he succumbed to a state of loneliness and panic. In the company of Homo sapiens, he felt spiritually adulterated. As a result, he wanted to look out on the universe in complete nakedness to clarify that he is not dependent on any creature that controls the Earth. He walked to the high mountains, removed all his clothes and moved forward in absolute bareness.

As he traversed the wilderness, there occurred a spiritual awakening in him. His temperament towards the humans was going through a great transition. The narrator affirms that "his researches into the world of men had been too devastating for a mind which, though superior in quality, was immature and delicate. But the wild had cleansed him, healed him, brought him to sanity again. He could now put Homo sapiens at arm's length for study and appreciation. And he saw that, though no divinity, the creature was after all a noble and even a lovable beast" (Stapledon, *Odd John* 65).

John plans to develop contact with supernormal creatures. In his workshop, he was busy with his new kind of invention which was a generator-accumulator. His table was engulfed in test tubes, metal pieces, insulated wires, jars and stones. He aims to search the universe and find the species of his kind and later create a tiny colony for the supernormal to survive in any part of Earth.

For this work, he said, he requires, "an ocean-going yacht and a small aeroplane, or flying machine of some kind, which could be stowed on the yacht" (Stapledon, *Odd John* 74). He declares that he is designing a yacht at the present moment. And that, he has been going through the texts of nuclear chemistry that made him aware that there is a huge amount of energy sealed in the atomic nucleus. These energies can only escape with the help of an electric current to tame the pressure that binds the protons and electrons together. He hypnotizes these atoms so that they become numb and get separated from each other. As they come alive, they move forcefully and "all you have to do is to see that their barging drives your machinery" (Stapledon, *Odd John* 75).

To carry out this task, normal mud from the mouth of the river will do. Holding a pair of pincers, he extracted a small amount of mud from the test tube and placed it inside a platinum bowl and later the bowl was put outside so that the particles could come to rest.

They both sit for a cup of coffee and discuss that when John's plane is built, he will go around the world in search of the supernormals and once they are found, he will "voyage in the Pacific to find a satisfactory island for the Colony" (Stapledon, *Odd John* 75). For the next few months, he indulged in building the plane and the yacht, improving the power mechanism, and trying to fly. At the age of nineteen, John's remarkable venture was over. The narrator negotiated with the aeroplane and ship manufacturers to begin the real construction.

As both the narrator and John moved to Paris, they met a strange-looking lady named Jacqueline Castagnet, to whom John was deeply attracted. Although she met the standards of Homo sapiens, she seemed queer. Jacqueline' was raised in a peasant family but she possessed supernormal powers and intellect. Her parents were concerned as the age when other girls of her age are ready to get married, she remains a child.

John continues his search for supernormals and meets, "an older girl in Moscow, a boy in Finland, a girl in Sweden, another in Hungary and a young man in Turkey" (Stapledon, *Odd John* 82). John takes Lo, a supernormal girl from Moscow to his house.

Initially, Pax takes care of Lo but later she is tired of old age and wants to get rid of her. When the yacht and the plane were ready for a flight, they made a trial around the Western Isles. John persuades the other supernormal creatures to create a new society on one island of the South Pacific. He plans to build a territory over there where the inhabitants will be able to achieve complete spiritual enlightenment.

As the supernormal establish their colony, John asks the narrator to visit it. Unluckily, the island is found by a few British sailors. They sent warships to strike the island. The supernormals decide to destroy both themselves and the island rather than get killed at the hands of the British ships.

In the novel, *Sirius*, Stapledon develops the subject of consummation in interspecies i.e., human and animal. Sirius is a self-recognised being who has a human beloved named Plaxy. It contains numerous interactivities between genetic material and culture. His affection for Plaxy is subject to sympathy and recognition. He transfers the topography of ethical taste from the rights of man to what signifies the category of man. He despises the bitches who lack in intellect. All in all, this novel chooses the path of continuity in a conjugal evolution of man and animal.

Sirius represents a dog possessing a human-like intellect. He is brought up by a scientist named Thomas Trelone originated in North Wales. The scientist, Thomas Trelone undertakes an experimentation on the use of steroids and chemicals to swiftly develop the analytical faculty of dogs. This resulted in the creation of massive sheep-like dogs.

Plaxy's father, the great physiologist was involved in remarkable experimentation on the brain of mammals. As a result of this, he has created a few extraordinarily intellectual sheep dogs. The narrator, Robert, a civil servant by profession, meets Plaxy who is residing at Trawsfynydd in North Wales. He heard the voice of an inhuman. And, then Plaxy and a massive dog named Sirius appeared near the main entrance door. She released one of her hands that was placed on the dog's head and welcomed Robert. Sirius was an enormous dog of Alsatian breed with a "dash of Great Dane or Mastiff" (Stapledon, *Sirius* 3). He had a great height and seemed wolf-like.

Sirius' hair was thick and lustrous, especially around the neck. On the back of his body, it was dark. But on the thighs and feet, it was plain grey. There was a pair of patches of pale brown colour over the eyes that gave a masking appearance to the face. Sirius was unique to other dogs due to his skull. It was majestic but less than the beings having human intellect. Robert assumed that the technique of Trelone enlarged the mass of the brain and at the same time churned out a mechanism of self-cleansing of nerve fibres. He has a large head in comparison to any other dog. And to carry the weight of his enormous head he has a well-built neck and shoulder.

The beastly creature widely opened his mouth showcasing his ivory jaw in a way inquiring who the visitor was. He shook his fully plumed tail and gazed at him. Plaxy utters that both of them have been working on spending sleepless nights and the dog understands everything that is said to him. She adds, "You won't be able to understand him at first, but I shall, and I'll interpret" (Stapledon, *Sirius* 4). She adjoins that she cannot confide in her as she is indulged in her father's pursuits.

Plaxy proceeded to narrate the story of Sirius to Robert. In the interim, Sirius was interfering with the story displaying his human intellect and acting in accordance with the conversation. After becoming aware of the genesis of Sirius, he realised that the human-inhuman bonding of Plaxy and Sirius was pious. Sirius is created by Plaxy's father Trelone. He has been raised as a member of their family and is assisting them on the sheep farm. Before leaving, Plaxy gives Robert multiple documents including journals and articles by Thomas Trelone that contain the nurturing of Sirius.

Sirius' potential transcends the perimeter of an animal and infiltrates the human. His control over his forepaws and his performance in academics pertain to his emerging as an excellent specimen of the genetic research of a scientist. The humanimal explores the limitations of both the worlds of human and animal. Stapledon's Sirius serves as a reemergence of Mary Shelley's Frankenstein who is an artificial being created from the corpses and later made to survive.

As a young researcher, Thomas Trelone experimented on the "stimulation of cortical growth in the brain of mammals" (Stapledon, *Sirius* 7). It was accomplished with uncompromising secrecy as Trelone had an affinity for the limelight. Moreover, besides his wife and a few colleagues in Cambridge, he wanted to hide his research from the charlatans.

His research began with injecting a hormone into the mother's bloodstream that would in turn interfere with the growth of the unborn's brain. As opined by Robert the result of infusion is two-fold: "It increased the actual bulk of the cerebral cortices, and also it made the nerve-fibres themselves much finer than they normally are, so that a far greater number of them and far greater number of connections between them, occurred in any given volume of brain" (Stapledon, *Sirius* 8).

A similar kind of experiment was carried out by Zamenhof in America. But it differed in the case that Zamenhof nourished the animal with the hormonal medicine with the food but Trelone injected the hormone into the mother's body that entered the foetus. The only complication was that the hormone effectuated a substantial development both of the mother's and the unborn's brain. Since the mother's skull was matured and stiff, it might result in serious blockage of the brain resulting in death unless some way was there to envelop the brain from the effect of the drug. This complicity was also defeated with an assurance of a healthy and secure maternal condition.

After birth, Trelone regularly added dosages of the hormonal medicine to the food of the infant and moderately lowered the dose as the developing brain achieved its required size. He also formulated a method for slowing up the recovery of the stitches between the skull bones so that the skull might expand more. A huge population of laboratory animals like mice and rats were slaughtered to achieve the desired result of the experiment. The survival period of Trelone's rats, rabbits, guinea pigs possessing huge skulls was lessened by disease. They had high intellect as they could find their route through the puzzles without effort. The rats "excelled their species in all the common tests of animal intelligence, and had the mentality rather of dogs and apes than of rodents" (Stapledon, *Sirius* 9).

Trelone desired to create a healthy animal by adjusting the cadence of its life so that the animal would mature sluggishly and live a longer life than normal animals of its type. A massive brain requires an extended period of survival to work to its full potential. Further, Trelone started working on huge animals of higher levels. Although cats are believed to have an independent cast of minds, they were of smaller size. He worked on apes as they proffered striking success over other species. They were superior to the dogs in the sense that they were equipped with hands, stronger eyesight and a developed brain. But dogs were fortunate as they had free entry into society.

Trelone did not think of raising any animal's mental

capacity similar to that of a human but to create "a rather super-sub-human intelligence, a missing-link mind." (Stapledon, *Sirius* 10). To achieve this feat, dogs fit the most as the society of humans "afforded for dogs many vocations requiring intelligence at the upper limit of the sub-human range' (Stapledon, *Sirius* 10). Trelone chose a sheep-dog for his purpose and endeavoured to produce a 'super-sheep dog" (Stapledon, *Sirius* 10).

He estimates that the dog's disposition is capable of reaching the level of humans. Because the dogs are socially more aware, they can utilise their intelligence to its maximum. In due time, Trelone created a group of puppies with huge brains. Except for two, the majority of them lost their lives before growing to the fullest. The two puppies were raised by him and became big dogs. He implemented further research and ultimately "from an Old English Sheep-dog bitch, produced a big brained family, three of which survived, and reached a definitely super-canine level of mentality" (Stapledon, *Sirius* 11).

This novel can be interpreted as a reaction to the mistreatment of animals as Bullock describes it as an awareness for animals "may have come about only because we can imagine a world without animals, now that our powers of destruction have grown so monstrously" (Bullock 98-118).

For a long time, he conducted research on this subject. He was concerned more about the raw materials involved in the research. He did not ignore the fact that Border Collie, one of the most diligent of all the canine races was known for intellect and responsibility. All the canine races are the successors of the animal named Old Hemp born in the year 1893 at Northumberland. Trelone decides that the most suited raw material for the research would be "a cross between some outstanding champion of the International Sheep-Dog Trials and another intelligent but much heavier animal" (Stapledon, *Sirius* 11). For this reason, he chose the Alsatian breed.

After a great deal of deliberation with the keepers of sheep dog for Alsatian, he created various strains which were a combination of both types. He administered the method to the expecting mothers of this breed and later he provided his acquaintances with house dogs of "missing-link intelligence." (Stapledon, *Sirius* 10). But all the dogs perished before attaining the age of adolescence. Later, he made changes in his research that brought commendable success to him. He shifted to the sheep district of Trawsfynedd in North Wales with his family. They resided in an old farmhouse named Garth.

They carried two canine families with them that were later to be trained as super sheep dogs. They had huge brains in comparison to that of other canine animals. Three of them died while they were being displaced from the location. And the last one to survive was Sirius. Sirius fully developed at a slow pace. Trelone produced many super sheep dogs. And, these dogs adapted to and learnt the methods of the farmers who owned them sooner or later. They performed multitudinous tasks like, "They attached the right meanings to the names of particular pastures, hillsides, valleys, moors. Told to fetch sheep from Cefn or from Moel Fach or what not, they succeeded in doing so while their master awaited them at home. They could also be sent on errands to neighbouring farms or villages. They would take a basket and a note to a particular shop and bring back the required meat or haberdashery" (Stapledon, *Sirius* 13).

Trelone found that these dogs had an ability to understand language. Being subhuman, they failed to comprehend speech like humans do but they were more familiar with words and certain phrases than other dogs such as searching for wood from the garden or bringing the basket. Thomas published a monograph on super sheep dogs that coerced scientists from around the world to visit Garth and take a look at the dogs working on the farm.

At Cambridge, Sirius discovers himself in entirely new surroundings, having resided in a rural district during his childhood and youthful years. He is quite exhilarated by the development in learning and accepts the scientific temperament that is disseminated by the university. As he makes himself more associated with the scientific world, he feels a kind of boredom in contemplating that it diminishes one's logical thinking.

His act of retreating to the forest is introduced as a method of escape when he fails to resist the hubris of man. In this state of Wilderness of Sirius, Stapledon presents the creature as both a dog and a wolf at one time. He resorts to pursuits that are regarded as primitive. A balance of the genes of the human and the dog is efficiently carried out as it becomes difficult on the part of the dog to abandon his non-human or animalistic traits such as hunting.

Besides everything, Trelone was more concerned about the little Alsatian named Sirius who was in its infancy. He discussed his ideas with his wife, Elizabeth. He wanted Sirius to be raised as socially uniform to Plaxy, his daughter. He desired to give serious a soothing and healthy family environment. Elizabeth feared that this might affect Plaxy's life. But Trelone induced her saying that "the companionship of child and super-canine dog must be beneficial to both" (Stapledon, *Sirius* 15).

Elizabeth was advised by Trelone to teach Plaxy not to show her advantageousness of being a human over

Sirius. He adds that "everything possible must be done to prevent Sirius from becoming either unduly submissive or defiantly arrogant in the manner so familiar in human beings suffering from a sense of inferiority" (Stapledon, *Sirius* 16).

He was well aware that Sirius would not achieve the human's intellectual capacity but he suggested to Elizabeth that Sirius must be raised as a human and not as a pet. He must be treated as an individual who would in the later years survive independently. At a school-going age, he must get engaged in canine work like hunting and fighting. He must perform tasks in his adolescent years and learn to become self-reliant in his adulthood.

Sirius manifested a similar kind of refulgence as Plaxy in her cradle. But Sirius was deficient in hands which was a great drawback to him. Both played with rattles but Plaxy's infant hands defeated Sirius' infant jaws. When Plaxy started crawling on the ground, Sirius teetered after her. He was filled with pride after learning this new technique. He was now superior to Plaxy for this practice of locomotion suited his quadruped-shaped body than the creep to her two-footed form. Both of them were developing a sense of togetherness that would affect their lives deeply for the years to come. They performed their daily chores together such as playing, eating and bathing.

When one of them is unwell, the other feels dejected. When one is hurt, the other is empathetic. But Plaxy was incapable of developing the habit of smelling like Sirius. Sirius was jealous of Plaxy's versatile hands as one day Plaxy was trying to build a wall with bricks while Sirius put a brick on the top that shattered the wall. For this reason, he had to train himself to handle dolls and bricks in such a manner that his pointed tooth and saliva did not spoil them.

Although a normal puppy possesses the faculty of inquisitiveness but no creativity, Sirius owns both abilities of inquisitiveness and at times is creative. His temperament was mostly similar to that of a canine animal. Trelone believed that Sirius' crude vision had made him less creative which is customary in dogs. For this, he failed to differentiate between visual structures in which Plaxy was competent enough. For example, he failed to distinguish between oval, podgy and circles.

At times Plaxy made fun of Sirius' impuissance due to lack of hand. And she was made to realise her mistake of making fun of Sirius' helplessness. Sirius looked for Plaxy to assist him in things that he could not perform alone such as opening up of boxes. In his entire life, he couldn't lace the fabric of cotton. In speech practice, Plaxy was competent enough to understand. Sirius was also able to comprehend the words by making strange noises that Plaxy uttered. It is noteworthy that, "Like plaxy, Sirius began with a very simple baby-language of monosyllables. Little by little this grew into a canine, or super-canine, equivalent of educated English" (Stapledon, *Sirius* 19).

Gradually, the Trelone family followed Sirius way of uttering the syllables that were only whining and squeaking. Thomas Trelone was delighted to be informed about Sirius' development of speech as this is an indication of nurturing of human intelligence in him. Thomas plans to treasure Sirius' speech and his gossip with Plaxy through the gramophone discs. He hid the recordings from everyone except his family and two of his colleagues namely, Professor McAlister and Dr Billing who have procured funding for conducting this research.

Day after Day, Sirius foster mother, Elizabeth nurtured him and that assisted him to sharpen his skills. When Elizabeth took care of her child, Sirius was filled with enviousness and bit her leg. Plaxy was angry about this pitiless act of Sirius. Gelert, the super-sheep dog of the Trelone family punished Sirius by attacking him. Plaxy seized Gelert by snatching his tail. This incident made Plaxy and Sirius understand as how much they care for each other.

When his family was disappointed with him, he tried his best to impress Plaxy either bringing her a feather or a beautiful pebble. Later, he developed a high regard for Gelert. Sirius tried to lure Plaxy by acquiring about her human skills. As Plaxy was being taught to read and write, Sirius also showed interest in it. For instance, "Plaxy used to spell out simple words with her box of letters, but Sirius found it very difficult to distinguish between C, G, D, O and Q and also between B, P, R, and K" (Stapledon, *Sirius* 25). It is noticed that he has a sub-human intellect.

Elizabeth was quite biased towards Plaxy as she secretly wanted her child, Plaxy to excel than her foster child, Sirius. She constantly writes to Trelone that Sirius is no better than a fool. But Trelone motivates his wife by saying that dogs have a bad vision but they are superior to everyone in other fields. To sharpen his writing skills, he came up with a way. He convinces his foster mother, Elizabeth to sew a compact leather glove for his right fore paw so that a pen can be thrust inside from the back of the glove. At the next moment, he lay in the couchant posture "with his left foreleg on the paper to hold it in place, he kept his right elbow on the ground, and was able to scrawl out DOG, CAT, PLAXY, SIRIUS and so on" (Stapledon, *Sirius* 25). After a lot of practice for years, he succeeded in writing a letter.

Sirius was disadvantaged in another sphere i.e., he was completely colourblind. He was distressed after knowing this. While Trelone assures him that, "all dogs were colourblind, and probably all mammals but apes and men. And he reminded Sirius that dogs were at any rate far superior in hearing and smelling" (Stapledon, *Sirius* 28). Sirius was so sensitive to sound and smell that he thought human speech was incapable of elucidating the bounty of the cosmos.

The family made an effort to teach music to Sirius. He also showed interest in the musical instruments. Often, he struggled to play any of them to add harmony to his endeavour. Overcoming the sense of disability of his handlessness, he made an effort with high-spiritedness to triumph despite his helplessness.

In his adolescence, Sirius was of considerable size than other sheep dogs. It is often said that he has outgrown his robustness. He was engaged in minor fights with other dogs as his skull was unmanageable due to his huge cranium which posed a problem while taking hold of his opponent. This flaw was dealt with when he matured with age. He did various exercises of the neck muscles that made it adequately strong to hold the additional mass of his head.

Sirius was one day chased by an animal named Diawl Du, a black devil. But Plaxy shoved off the animal with a broom. Sirius hears Plaxy narrating the event to their mother and ends the narration with "I'm afraid poor Sirius hasn't much spunk" (Stapledon, *Sirius* 35). He wasn't aware of the word 'spunk' and incessantly searched the word in the Dictionary that stated 'courage, mettle, spirit, anger' (Stapledon, *Sirius* 35). He was disappointed with Plaxy addressing him in such a manner.

The very day Plaxy turned her attentiveness

towards Trix, the cat. This made Sirius envious and as a result, he attacked Trix. After two weeks, it was noticeable by the Trelone family that Sirius was desperately searching for an old spade handle lying inside the hovel. When Marice returns from the school, they both play together. When the holidays got over, Maurice asserted, "Sirius is getting damned strong. You can't tear the thing from him; you can't twist it from him" (Stapledon, *Sirius* 36). During these times Sirius had been hiding from Diawl Du and now he defeats him furiously. Presently, he feels stronger than ever. As he has now become unassailable, he should now focus on his mental faculty i.e., he should focus on being supremely guileful.

    The exchange of blows with Diawl Du was a life-changing activity for Sirius. He became victorious for the first time. Never in life would he be regarded as a coward or a half-wit. As days passed into years, "Sirius' self-confidence in relation to other dogs was greatly augmented. His increasing weight and strength combined with superior intelligence gave him not only freedom from persecution but also acknowledged superiority over all the sheep-dogs of the countryside, who were all much smaller than the young Alsatian. His combination of size and cunning put him in a class apart" (Stapledon, *Sirius* 39).

    Plaxy's parents decide to send Plaxy to the boarding school which turns out to be a great change for Sirius. Thomas Trelone plans to appoint Sirius as a full-time super-sheep-dog so that he can obtain the right training. He wants Sirius to become a great animal psychologist at Cambridge as he is as intelligent as the humans. To achieve this feat, Thomas takes Sirius to Llewelyn Pugh at the Caer Blai for the completion of his apprenticeship as a sheep dog.

    While escorting Sirius to Caer Blai, Thomas

RECONCEPTUALISING THE HUMAN | 263

discusses Sirius' future prospects with him. He says that while living with Pugh, he should divulge his attention towards the human world more than the sheep's. Sirius labels human beings based on their temperament towards the dog species and this labelling helps him to know more about the personality of humans. Some humans are dog lovers. They cuddle, and overfeed them.

At the sheep-farm, Thomas and Sirius were welcomed by the uproar of super-sheep-dogs from the shed. The farmer appeared and Sirius grew a kind of fondness towards him. Thomas and Sirius were escorted to the kitchen where drinks were served to them. Mr Pug gazed at Sirius and uttered, "He's really far too big for a sheep-dog, Mr Trelone. He should be herding rhinoceroses, or not the little Welsh mountain sheep, anyhow. But, my! What a head he has on him! If it's brain that counts, Mr. Trelone, he must be a genius, isn't it! I can see that it's he that'll be running this farm and me running after the sheep for him" (Stapledon, *Sirius* 51). Thomas acknowledges that Sirius has more strength in comparison to a normal dog and he will be helpful over time.

Mr Pug asks if Sirius is fifteen years old then the dog answers in the positive. Pug is surprised to hear this and says "but most dogs are dead long before that and this one is not much more than a puppy" (Stapledon, *Sirius* 52). He also adds that if Sirius stays with them then he will marry his daughter, Jane and take charge of the farm after he is dead. Pug decides to name him as Bran instead of Sirius. He became disheartened to learn that his name would be changed. He thought that he had to share many things like toys and pencils with Plaxy. He also had few personal possessions. But now he is a mere dog and having ownership over bones and bitches.

Thomas left Sirius behind and he was taken to a valley by Pugh accompanied by Idwal, another sheep-dog. Idwal raced towards the sheep and grouped them to move down the valley. Each dog stood in his respective arc. Idwal's arc was broader than Sirius' arc as he was less skilful and he had to get the sheep back who had slipped away down the hill. Idwal was made to find a castrated male sheep and gaze at it for some time. This was done to train the eyes and bring them under control. Idwal performed multiple duties as commanded by Pug in Welsh.

Now, it was Sirius turn to perform the duties. Sirius worked incessantly to follow the activities. He failed at sea as he kept on slipping due to fatigue. Sirius had difficulty in grasping the Welsh language in which Pug talked. In the case of control over eyes, he was quite skilful but required practice for perfection. During those times, he was assigned constant work with Idwal. With sincere practice, he invested less energy in realising his mistakes. He was successful in grasping the Welsh language and the names of the grasslands.

Sirius was sent to find the sickened sheep in the bracken zones. The sheep who fall sick become afraid of their opponents and hide in these bracken zones. If within time they are not retrieved from those zones, they perish due to lack of attentiveness. With time, Sirius had strengthened the control over his eyes.

As autumn came closer, Pugh assigned Sirius and Idwal to bring down the lambs from the mountains for sale. The dogs advanced towards the moors taking the animals with them to the valley. The sheep of Pugh's have their lower back marked red and the left ear contains three slits. Sirius was acquainted with each sheep of Caer Blai by its smell.

After the end of autumn, the dogs were assigned to protect the pastureland from the sheep in the valley. Sirius used to visit a stationery shop where he used to go through the posters with his paw hung outside the shop. Numerous dogs in the village were unequal to Sirius as by time he had grown stronger and harder. He studied the psyche of these dogs but realised that all were similar in their temperament.

One evening Sirius had fallen in love with a bitch from another village. He desired to visit the village again and again but dropped the idea at the thought of being beaten by his master. As "Sirius was determined that he would never do anything to incur such an indignity. He had never been thrashed in life, though occasionally hit or kicked in anger. To be deliberately thrashed seemed to him to be a mortal insult to his dignity as an intelligent and self-respecting person" (Stapledon, *Sirius* 59). But Pugh never beat his sheep-dogs. He preferred being compliant to ferociousness. He doubts that Sirius is more than a super-dog as he has a human attitude.

One morning Pug sent Sirius to a nearby village with a case and a ten-shilling note to bring back his boots from the cobbler that he had given for repair. Pug was amazed to see that the dog performed his duty well. He had brought the pair of boots and the leftover money with him. A few days later, Sirius wrote a letter to Plaxy by hiding inside the outhouse. It was quite difficult for him to put the letter inside the envelope although he did it. He licked the envelope to paste it. He held it with his paw and posted it. This incident was noticed by Dr Huw Williams who informed Pug appreciating the dog's human intelligence.

At the prep school, Plaxy's days seemed unending to Sirius. He went on counting the days by depositing one pebble per day in a case. Thomas talked to Pug regarding the improvement of Sirius as a sheep dog. Pug stated that Sirius is as robust as Idwal but in matters of craftiness and accountability, Sirius is superior to Idwal. But he is a daydreamer and was often caught sleeping. A sheep runs away before he regains his consciousness. He also hands over ten shillings to Thomas as an earning of Sirius.

Sirius returned home and was cheerfully greeted by everyone. Thomas didn't let Sirius get rid of his apprenticeship as a sheep-dog. But Sirius was engrossed in indoor activities like reading, gossiping and listening to music. He also performed varied olfactory experiments such as collecting things having different fragrances and mixing them. Plaxy had also returned home on vacation. Both Plaxy and Sirius didn't have the charm in their relationship that they previously had. Sirius was bored of hearing Plaxy's narration about her school life and Plaxy was as well wearied of the things that they formerly rejoiced in.

During these days, Sirius indulged himself in reading Wells' *Outline of History and The Science of Life*. He also irked his family members to recite poetry and stanzas from The Bible for him. He was thorough in prose, poetry and rhythmical quality of words. He was fascinated by Robert Browning, Thomas Hardy and T.S. Eliot. He was also desperate to learn the music composed by humans so that he could communicate with them.

Plaxy is now mostly preoccupied with her schoolmates and instructors who are now playing a pivotal role in her life. During this vacation, Plaxy and Sirius' relationship had deteriorated. They both were alienated from each other. Plaxy had a passion for painting but Sirius was disinterested in it. Plaxy was upset if he didn't appreciate her art. And if at all he appreciated her creation, she was disgusted with him. They both developed a tangled relationship.

One evening, Thomas and Sirius were discussing Thomas' latest developments in his experiment on "localisation of mental powers in the brain-centres" (Stapledon, *Sirius* 74). He was impressed by Sirius' cunning interrogation such as, "Even by human standards I really am fairly bright, am I" (Stapledon, *Sirius* 74)? Thomas answers in the positive. Then Sirius complains that his mind is inconstant. He starts thinking about one topic and ends up thinking about another. His mind keeps dawdling. And, Thomas says, "It's just that you're a rather complicated person, really, and there's too much diversity in you to be easily systematized" (Stapledon, *Sirius* 75).

Sirius adds that he is then a real person and not a laboratory animal. Thomas agrees to this within no time. Further, Sirius queries if he is a person then for what reason is he being trained as a sub-human that will in the end dehumanise him. Thomas annoyingly clarifies:

> It's true you have a first-class human intelligence, but you are not a man, you are a dog. It's useless to train you for some human trade because you can't do it. But it's immensely important to give you some responsible practical work until the time comes for you to join us at Cambridge. You are not to be an imitation man. You are a super-super-dog. This sheep-dog life is very good for you. Remember you are not yet seventeen. There's no hurry. Your pace is Plaxy's, not Idwal's. If you grow up too quick, you'll fossilize too quick.

> Stick to sheep. There's a lot in that job, if you give your mind to it. When you come to us at the lab we want you to have had experience of a normal dog's way of life. (Stapledon, *Sirius* 75)

Sirius angrily says that he is neither human nor canine. He has a canine cover and Thomas has a human cover. He remarks that if Thomas had a dog's body and a human mind, he would have expertly understood his situation. Thomas blatantly utters, "but the conflict is not really between your spirit and your canine body; it's between the canine part of your body and the super-canine part, that I gave you" (Stapledon, *Sirius* 76).

As the vacation was over, Plaxy was all set to return to her school life. But Sirius had doubts about his future. He pressed Thomas on not returning to Caer Blai. With Machiavellian elusiveness, Thomas convinces him to complete his remaining apprenticeship with Pugh which will ultimately strengthen his spirituality.

Sirius life at Caer Blai was a mixture of both peacefulness and hardships. When there was no work, he pretended to sleep but he was wallowed in thinking about man and his self. He tried to find out the similarity of spirit between them. It was strenuous for the old Welshman to travel to the high hills so Sirius was given the responsibility to escort the Welshman to the high hills. A saddler was hired to prepare two pairs of tiny crates that could be attached to the flanks of the dogs. These crates were packed with medications and lotions. Sirius was now able to travel far distances. Idwal considered him as his leader. They both kept a watch on the flock for fly-strike or foot-rot. Any sheep that was tired or bit his own back was affected by the fly strike. Like humans, Sirius hated revealing the larva with his teeth. By taking ardent care, the cases were reduced in number.

Sirius was in mental conflict with the ruling species of Earth i.e., man and himself. He was aware of the fact that man and himself were different species but they have a similar kind of nature. Man has made multitudinous inventions and discoveries with his efficient brain and hands. But Sirius is not competent enough to do anything with his inept paws and unclear vision. He is unworthy of the mental intelligence that Thomas has created in him. Everything that is contained in him has come from humans. He is saddened at the thought that his passion for arts, literature and humanities will glide into the study of canine beings. He has no aim for a life that humans usually have. He is designed to perform the job of sheep-tending or the vocation that Thomas has figured out for him i.e., of a "museum piece or a tenth-rate scientist" (Stapledon, *Sirius* 79).

Mankind has also bestowed the feeling of love on him. The Trelone family has always taken care of him. Thomas also has manifested 'man-to-man intelligent companionship' to him (Stapledon, *Sirius* 80). But he loves his experiment more than anything and can render his creation to any infliction for the furtherance of his experiment. Sirius has found the potion of love with Plaxy. All humans had a detracting effect on him except Plaxy. The only reason why Sirius had disregard for humans is that they treated him affectionately in front of humans of their kind but at other times they treated him harshly or with bad conduct.

Soon after Plaxy returned home, she learned that she had gained a scholarship for one of the affiliated colleges of Cambridge. Thomas expected her to pursue the profession of a doctor but she has shifted her interests from medical profession to humanities and English Literature in particular. Reading English Literature at Cambridge accommodates a scientific temperament in it. Plaxy asserts her liberty in choosing her career and toiling to gain a scholarship.

    Sirius develops the wolf in him and kills a pony. Thomas lectures him on this heinous act of his. Helplessly, Sirius cries out, "Unless you help me to be myself, you will force me to be- a sham wolf" (Stapledon, *Sirius* 91). He adds that he wants to experience the world the way he likes. He will fail to do so if he oscillates between Caer Blai and Thomas' laboratory. He denies being a mute subject for experimentation or a tenth-rate researcher. If he is restricted in becoming his sense of being, he will assume humans by disrespectful means.

    After having a thorough discussion with Elizabeth, Thomas plans to take Sirius to the laboratory. And, as planned he should be introduced to the world of the humans through the process of sight-seeing of factories, slums and concerts. He should be allowed to read books from the library. Thomas cautions Sirius that he should pretend as a normal dog. There should not be any kind of publicity. He should initially be accepted by the scientific world before the commercial world takes over him.

    Sirius was taken to the Lake District to make him familiar to McBane so that he could gain an understanding of the dog's speech before conducting research on him in the laboratory. Sirius was made to experience a sheep-dog trial and he was made to enter as a competitor. It was later known that Thomas is the creator of super-sheep-dogs. He has received offers from many to buy Sirius from him.

 Sirius was taken to Cambridge after the vacation ended. A sitting room was assembled for him within the confines of the laboratory. The senior staff acquainted themselves with Sirius as 'man to man' on the agreement that they must keep the dog's secret from the public. Sirius spent the initial days loitering in the streets and gazing at men and dogs. The dogs seemed hale and hearty. But they had ill mental hygiene as they had nothing to do besides sleeping, eating and strolling around. Now Sirius had to imitate them and make fun of himself in front of Elizabeth's friends. He was appreciated for revealing his human intelligence or for shaking his hands.

Thomas decides to uncover Sirius' special intelligence to the world. He exhibits Sirius in front of a few distinguished Professors of the university. They include biochemists, zoologists, biologists, philologists, philosophers and psychologists who might have a keen interest in the dog's speech. And, a few painters and surgeons who come under the category of Thomas' acquaintances. These people gathered at Thomas' house for lunch. After the lunch was over, Sirius walked inside the room. He seemed tall and slant.

The guests were astonished after seeing Sirius and thought that Thomas was deceiving them with his trick. The dog was asked to get a book which he successfully did. Thomas declares that Sirius can understand English and anyone present there can converse with him in the same language.

The earliest days of Sirius at Cambridge were extraordinarily amazing. Every single day some amount of research was conducted on him. Someday his sensory responses would be studied. And on other days his response to emotional provocations were taken into consideration. X-rays were conducted of his skulls and his speech was recorded by gramophones. With the assistance of a psychologist, he writes a tract on his aromatic experiences and his ability to detect the character of humankind. He also mentions his emotional changes after smelling an aroma and the change of tone in his voice that results from it. He also plans to write two books, *The Lamp-post, A Study of the Social Life of the Domestic Dog* and *Beyond the Lamp-post*.

Sirius feels honeyed to be the heart of the matter for everyone. Thomas got countless requests to meet the human-dog from people in and around his circle. When Sirius was seen loitering in the streets, the people gazed at and talked about him for this reason Thomas didn't allow him to roam lonely in the streets. He spent the autumn at Cambridge and the time was quite fascinating for him. After the vacation was over, he travelled back to Wales accompanied by Elizabeth, Plaxy and Thomas. While on the hills, he felt petrified as a result he indulged himself in long adventures.

After spending precious time with Plaxy, Sirius marches to the laboratory. On the way, he ruminates over the imperfection in humans, his solitariness and the lack of concern for the universe. These thoughts made him rise to the wolf mood. This type of mood was common in him whenever he felt frustrated or irritated. He yearns for individualism and self-expression but fails.

During the canine years, he had planned to station his human forces with superhuman expertise. He also transformed the entire scenario of human music adding with it the finer feelings of a dog. He had also acquired a longing for religion. But he didn't find anyone among Thomas' acquaintances who would assist him in strengthening his religious temperament.

Most of the time he would be seen hanging by his neck near any window of the church to listen to the prayers and sermons. But he was prohibited from entering the church as normal humans do. This aroused a sense of inferiority in him.

One fine day Sirius convinces Thomas to allow him to introduce himself to not many religious persons of Cambridge. But Thomas had no idea regarding this so he persuades his wife, Elizabeth to comply with Sirius' religious inquisitiveness. Elizabeth's cousin, Rev. Geoffrey Adams is a parson so both of them plan a meeting with him. Rev. Geoffrey Adams is among those Clerics who are more concerned about the parishioners than about self-development. Elizabeth informs him about Sirius but he says that he is extremely busy and that religion is not a matter that can be acquired by discussing it. Rather they should come to the East End to experience it.

They both travel by train to meet him. And Sirius was amazed to see the creation of man. He says, "What an amazing species it was, with its great buildings, its endless streams of cars, its shop-window displays, its swarming foot-passengers, with their trousered and silken legs!" (Stapledon, *Sirius* 117) Subsequently, Elizabeth wanted tea so they searched for a café where dogs are let in. She gives Sirius a bun and a bowl filled with tea. Someone in the café notices Sirius and says, "That dog's expression is almost human" (Stapledon, *Sirius* 117).

The eyesight is indubitably an important part of sensory organs on which the Homo Sapiens rely to achieve infinite progress. Literature is also dependent on this criterion when one reads the animal narratives using monosensorial impressions and later gets transmitted into multiple sensorial reactions. It permits the reader to travel across the boundaries of non-human species and parley with them. This in turn allows them to accept certain temperaments or attitudes as integral and necessary to the non-human contrary to what they would have regarded it as improper or disgusting. It is evident when he says, "This is real life, this is what I am for, not all that human twaddle" (Stapledon, *Sirius* 37).

At the outset, there is a kind of inquisitiveness on the side of the reader regarding the hunting faculty of animals. The humans can only conjure up hunting as they cannot consume raw meat. The Homo Sapiens also fear of being attacked and consumed alive by the animals. This is regarded by Bulliet as 'carnivore monsters'.

It also reminds us that the division of humans and animals should be eradicated. The human ought to synchronize themselves with animals. It precisely subverts the borders of species limitations. The Homo Sapiens regard themselves are core to everything are demoted to a situation of frailty and are later made to intermingle with the nonhuman other. As Jaques Derrida now and then prompts, "Mortality resides there, as the most radical means of thinking the finitude that we share with animals, the mortality that belongs to the very finitude of life, to the experience of compassion, to the possibility of this nonpower" (Derrida and Wills 396).

Rev. Geoffrey Adams received his visitors with a kind of awkwardness as he didn't know how to attend to a dog. Soon, he realises that Sirius is no less than a human and the weird noises that he was creating are an effort to speak the English language. He lives with Geoffrey for more than a week for there is a part of life here that he is unaware of. Geoffrey was taken by Sirius' passion for music. Sirius accompanies Geoffrey to all the places except death scenes or meetings with the councillors of the town. He was known as Geoffrey's lap dog.

He goes along with Geoffrey to "a canteen or mission hall in dockland, sometimes to a Men's Club, where, followed by the observant Sirius, he would pass from room to room exchanging greetings with the members. Sometimes the person took a turn at darts or billiards, or watched a boxing match" (Stapledon, *Sirius* 120). In these places, few people disregarded him and restored kindness on him.

Every night before retiring for the night, Geoffrey and Sirius discuss the occurrences of the entire day. Sirius has comprehended the fact that the human race is not "one with itself, and that authority was not always sympathetic with the common people" (Stapledon, *Sirius* 121).

Sirius notices that the world where he is presently residing is quite different from the other two worlds i.e., North Wales and Cambridge. All the three worlds are inhabited by miscellaneous species. He is now worried about his future. In North Wales, he was a sheep-dog and in Cambridge, he was the subject of curiosity. And, in London, he is a disciple of the human race. But his future seems hazy. He feels constricted in a town due to a lack of physical exercise and less eating.

On a day while loitering near a train station, he finds a showcase of pictures of holidaying resorts. In one of the posters, there was an image of a moorland with mist rising from it. The picture appeared to be realistic. Then, Sirius came to a resolution that he would spend his life in the moorland and not in the town. In that particular world, he can display himself with his full potential.

The relationship between Geoffrey and Sirius had become the talk of the town. Often Geoffrey was seen gossiping with the dog which others saw and declared that he had gone mad. Sirius convinces Geoffrey to sing in the church. Following a lot of reluctance, Geoffrey finally agreed to let Sirius come to the church. Geoffrey opens the vestry door and the dog sings from there. He uses the power of the eye with the people sitting there. The congregation is intensely galvanised by the dog's song. They were startled to see that a dog could compose such type of songs in which reverberations of Bach and Beethoven, Vaughan Williams were found. Every Sunday there was more crowd in the church than before.

Moved by the dog's song, Geoffrey gives a speech:
> The song gave me a view of humanity from outside humanity, from the point of view of another of God's creatures, and one that both admires and despises us, one that has fed from our hands and has also suffered at our hands. By means of echoes of the great human composers mingled with themes reminiscent of the wolf's baying and the dog's barking and howling, the singer conjured up his vision of humanity. (Stapledon, *Sirius* 130)

When war broke out in Europe, Sirius was living on the sheep farm of Cumberland to learn the ways of the shepherds of Lakeland. His experiences at Cumberland were excruciating. His master, Thwaites, was brutal as his dog who was a Border Collie ignored him at any minute. This temperament of humanity he has never been acquainted with before.

Presumably, Thwaite's hidden vexation came to the place. He was harsh and developed an unconvincing hatred towards him. He believed that the dog was an extraordinary super-sheep-dog and was secretly adjudicating him. He commands Sirius to carry heavy articles with his mouth.

He gave him to do such activities that a normal human can efficiently perform.

Days after that Sirius grew furious and snatched Thwaites' neck to death. But Sirius opined that though he has committed a crime "it was a positive act of self-assertion which had emancipated him forever from the spell of the master race" (Stapledon, *Sirius* 135). The police searched for the dog and said that if the dog was found it should be instantly destroyed. For the purpose of saving his unique canine creation, Thomas plays his trick by informing the police that the man-killing beast, Sirius has got home and now it has been killed. Later, Thomas would murder a huge Alsatian super-sheep-dog and hand over the corpse to the authorities.

Plaxy and Elizabeth were bewildered after seeing Sirius' miserable condition. He looked murky and had lost his usual shine. He seemed distressingly lean and quiet. The remembrance of the crime that he had committed horrified him. He had murdered Thwaites in self-defence for he endured him for a long time till it became impossible on his part to bear the torture.

During the holidays, Sirius strongly discussed his future with Thomas and Elizabeth. He states that he will not return to the sordid life at Cambridge. After numerous arguments concerning the ill health of Pugh, Thomas plans to reveal the truth of Sirius' powers to Pugh and propose to him to make Sirius his partner or give the entire laboratory legally to Sirius. As Sirius being a dog cannot sign any agreement or contract, Elizabeth should be given the post of resident representative and would assist in the functioning of the laboratory. Sirius would supervise the marketing business of sheep and wool. Later, the trained super-sheep dogs will be displayed for sale.

Momentarily, Sirius moved to Caer Blai to join his new position. All his belongings were transported with him including books on sheep farming, his glove that was used for writing and other materials. Pugh didn't teach Sirius anything regarding the nurturing of the sheep. It was the dog's scientific and practical knowledge that made him enhance the breeding of the sheep and the pastures. But Sirius had to acquire the knowledge of farming. He had to take a look at the prices.

Sirius writes to Thomas that he is all set for his new journey. Learning this, Thomas sends three puppies to Sirius for training. He also brings his two scientific colleagues to talk to the dog. Sirius feels it is the finest time of his life as he is using his canine powers to his full potential. Every evening in the company of Elizabeth, he listened to the broadcast music and recorded his voice in a radiogram.

In the meantime, puppies were escorted from Cambridge to Caer Blai and were trained to become super-sheep-dogs. As the war was in place, Thomas' canine creatures had got a new work to execute. The super-sheep-dogs had a pivotal role to play during the war as the Government was training normal dogs to transfer messages in the battle region. Thus, Thomas searched for a simplified procedure to produce super-sheep-dogs in large numbers.

By the autumn of 1940, Sirius had become popular as 'Pugh's man-dog' in the region of Caer Blai. He was also efficient in speaking the Welsh language. He familiarised himself with the farmers and residents of the village. The church people thought that Sirius' original master was not Pugh but the devil, Satan. Pugh has offered his soul to the devil to assist him in dealing with the shortage of labour.

Elizabeth received the shocking news of his cousin, Geoffrey's death. His church was demolished and as he was trying to help the parishioners, he was killed in the time being. Sirius was devastated upon hearing this distressing news as if someone close to his heart had left him forever. He now rightly understands the effect of war.

All the female members of the family were deeply affected by Thomas' death. But Sirius' misery was combined with a sense of liberty. The dog's canine personality was saddened over the departure of his master but his human intellect breathed relaxingly. Although he had intensely remembered his master's love and affection on the other hand, he realised that he was now his own master.

No doubt Sirius was emotionally detached from his master, Thomas but he had to devote himself to his foster mother, Elizabeth. And, Elizabeth also dedicates herself to nurturing of the dog, a unique creation of Thomas. Her attentiveness was obsessively laid upon the dog.

As years passed by, Plaxy and Sirius developed a sense of intimacy between them as if, "in spite of her fundamental joy in her love for Sirius, was increasingly troubled by a fear that she might irrevocably be losing touch with her own species, even that in this strange symbiosis with an alien creature she might be losing her very humanity itself" (Stapledon, *Sirius* 173). This terror of being detached from being a human aroused hatred in her for Sirius but she was assured that this kind of closeness is spiritual.

At times, Sirius consoles Plaxy saying:
> You are always fully human, but just because you are also more than merely human, and I am more than merely canine, just because we are both in essence intelligent and sensitive beings, we can rise far above our differences, to reach across the gulf that separates us,

and be together in this exquisite union of opposites. (Stapledon, *Sirius* 173)

The narrator says that Plaxy frequently writes letters to him stating her frustrations regarding her new sense of being. Even though she yearns for human intimacy and affection and the emotion of being a normal girl, she clings to the peculiar life that nature has designed for her.

Although Sirius treats the narrator with kindliness, but he disparages him and hates his closeness with Plaxy. The narrator imagines how an animal has mutilated the human essence that Plaxy possesses.

Stapledon has bestowed the protagonist with a noticeably sturdy postulation of mind. He tracks down the binary opposites between the self and other otherwise named as human and the nonhuman. He introduces a tripartite replica in which the first subject merges with the second to pierce into the minds of the third subject. The novel, *Star Maker*, embodies minds and the cosmos of escalating entanglement, the discernment of which demands transcendental enterprise or in the words of Richard Maurice Bucke alternately known as 'cosmic consciousness'.

In the novel *Frankenstein* by Mary Shelley, the protagonist, Victor Frankenstein is characterised by a specific infirmity of mind, relating to the creature to whom he is determined to ascribe negative features starting from its initiation. In a similar context, Stapledon is intent on assigning a lesser prejudiced outlook as the protagonist is comparatively more non-partisan than Victor.

The central figure in Stapledon's *Star Maker* is unprejudiced to the extent that as the narration develops, he lets his mind merge with the minds of others to associate himself with the cosmic mind. He strives to delve into the enigma of both life on Earth and the interstellar. He also endeavours to appreciate the mind of imaginative urge lying in the back of the universe.

The novel explores the condition of man and his relation with the extraterrestrial. The protagonist utilises his imaginative faculty and undertakes an astral experience in the sky. He traverses through the space far and near, into the bottomless pit, and stumbles across new planets and species. These species include peculiar creatures who imitate the ships. They possess numerous legs and augmented sensory parts. The stars are also a part of their community.

These beings accompany the narrator to the core of the macrocosm ultimately transforming into the collective conscious. The narrator also finds an atmosphere to survive on the remote planets. After voyaging throughout the extraterrestrial atmosphere, the narrator eventually encounters the Starmaker.

As, the narrator was musing over his originally inhabited planet, he continued his space exploration. He advanced towards the eastern direction and witnessed the Earth diminishing in its size. It appeared to be rotating underneath him. All the planetary features swayed in the western direction. It transformed from a massive half-moon to a hazy crescent contracting in its dimension. The Earth's satellite, i.e., Moon looked sharp and miniscule.

The Science fiction writer, Arthur Clarke declares to be impaired by the works of Stapledon, uniquely by *Star maker*. He writes that it is the most influential work ever drafted. He is mostly influenced by the scope of the novel. The narrator is possessed by "A keen hunger… for insight into the significance of men and of any manlike beings in the cosmos" (qtd. in Boyarkina 1).

The narrator moved swiftly through a persistent shower of meteorites. They were visible only when he passed alongside them. The meteorites gleamed with the light of the Sun and looked like bands of light similar to the headlight of a train. The narrator almost collided with a meteorite that was similar to a massive rock.

In the novel, Stapledon attempts to adapt to the cosmological strata based on the myth of the creator and the creation (Liddle 20).

Momentarily, the planet Earth was transfigured into a star. At present, the period has become unintelligible. When the narrator tried to find himself, he discussed that he was on the farther side of Mars' orbit and dashing into the passage of the asteroids. A few tiny planets happened to be so near that they simulated the stars.

The planet, Jupiter motioning at a far-off distance appeared brilliantly shining and relocated itself amid the stars. The enormous Globe gave the impression of a disc which later cropped up immensely as compared to the diminishing Sun. The clouds enveloped it in its entirety. The narrator moved in his direction. There was no time of demarcation between night and day. He discovered that within no time he would be reaching beyond the confines of Pluto. The Sun came into sight as the most gleaming star, fainting behind the narrator. Nothing was noticeable now except the extensively glittering airspace.

The narrator was uncertain about his existence. He questioned, "Was I doomed to hang thus forever out in space, a bodiless view-point" (Stapledon, *Star Maker* 18)? In his imagination, he moved back to his home on the top of the hill. But in reality, he found himself among the stars. He spotted the Sun and the stars that were hung near to him.

The stars facing the contrary pole of paradise seemed to be of an icy blue texture.
 The narrator travelled as fast as a beam of light can pass. The light failed to cope with his pace. The stars that lay behind him were visibly dark red. Those stars that were in the front had violet hues. The ruby-coloured stars lay at his back. There were other stars of topaz and sapphires. The stars that lay beside him vanished in the meantime when he moved forward in his endeavour allocating two starless pits in the sky.
The lines that explain it entirety are:
> For, if ever the cosmic ideal should be realized, even though for a moment only, then in that time the awakened Soul of All will embrace within itself all spirits whatever throughout the whole of time's wide circuit. And so, to each one of them, even to the least, it will seem that he has awakened and discovered himself to be the Soul of All, knowing all things and rejoicing in all things. And though afterwards, through the inevitable decay of the stars, the most glorious vision must be lost, suddenly or in the long-drawn-out defeat of life, yet would the awakened Soul of All have eternal being, and in each martyred spirit would have beatitude eternally, though unknown to itself in its own temporal mode. (Stapledon, *Star Maker* 286–287)

 Both the starless holes proceeded to trespass the other stars. The narrator increased his pace faster than the speed of light. The sky was a cavernous and inert well. The narrator was horrified by the bland dimness. He felt a lack of sensation like palpitation, perspiration and panting. Being too alone in the vast expanse of the sky, he yearns for his home. He forages the beings of his own species or being similar to humans to do away with his isolation.

The narrator ruminates over a few questions:

> Was man indeed, as he sometimes desired to be, the growing point of the cosmical spirit, in its temporal aspect at least? Or was he one of many million growing points? Or was mankind of no more importance in the universal view than rats in a cathedral? And again, was man's true function power, or wisdom, or love, or worship, or all of these? (Stapledon, *Star Maker* 20)

In accord with Stapledon, the spirit is inextricable from the evolution of the universe in the initial occasion of survival. The atom is depersonalised from the spirit and is the microcosm filled with exact space, time and other extraterrestrial beings. These beings blow up due to the prospect of time and space, in appropriation with the Big Bang theory. The universe is in a state of expansion but each of its parts hang on to itself as a kind of memory. The whole cosmos contains the nuances of the dissociated single spirit of the entire universe.

But dissociation adheres to the lower rank of evolution. Stapledon promotes unification in all forms such as humans integrated with the telepathic transmission and symbiotic link with the cosmic mind.

After a lot of self-questioning, he affirms that he is no more an outlying individual hankering for appreciation but an ambassador of humankind. He exclaims that his physical life must prematurely end. He must abandon his family and proceed for an interstellar exploration. He senses that his inherent potentials were assisted by superhuman creatures.

He glimpses that stars are surrounded in every direction and their hues are normal. He is also conscious that to go near a star he has to travel faster than the pace in which a streak of light passes. But this procedure is nonetheless out of the question. As physicists have proved movement quicker than the light's speed is unintelligible. Therefore, he resolves that his movement must be "in some manner a mental, not a physical phenomenon". He attempts to search for terrestrial planets by setting himself about "on a voyage of astronomical and metaphysical research" (Stapledon, *Star Maker* 21).

Arbitrarily, the narrator guides himself towards one star that is the brightest and not far enough. His momentum is so high that the celestial objects pass him like meteors. He inconsiderately dangles to the hot Sun. On the blotchy plane, he sees with his supernatural vision, a set of cosmic black Sunspots. Each looks like a ditch in which multiple planets like Earth can drop.

Adjacent to the star's limb, there are growths in the chromosphere that have the appearance of a large tree or an ancient monster. On its farther side, pale clouds of corona unfurl in the dimness. He moves around the star in search of a planet but finds only meteor showers and comets. He explores one star after another and perceives that "they were too large and tenuous and young to be Earth's luminary. Some were vague ruddy giants broader than the orbit of Jupiter; some smaller and more definite, had the brilliance of a thousand Suns, and their colour was blue" (Stapledon, *Star Maker* 22).

He observes sizeable clouds of fine particles that look like enormous constellations. These massive clouds overshadowed "the star-streams; and tracts of palely glowing gas, shining sometimes by their own light, sometimes by the reflected light of stars" (Stapledon, *Star Maker* 23). These enormous clouds are the storehouse of light that act as embryos for the upcoming stars.

He looked fixedly at the union of stars that were either couples, triumvirates or quartets. These stars seemed extravagant. The dead stars lay hither and thither in the galaxy. He made his way in search of planets and was well aware of the fact that "the birth of planets was due to the close approach of two or more stars, and that such accidents must be very uncommon" (Stapledon, *Star Maker* 23).

The narrator was directionless due to "the appalling desert of darkness and barren fire, the huge emptiness so sparsely pricked with scintillations, the colossal futility of the whole universe" (Stapledon, *Star Maker* 23). In due course, his power of locomotion failed to work and his pace began to decrease. As time passed by, he regained his locomotive power that was hindered by his longing for his native planet, Earth and his self-piteous and emotional state of mind.

In the expectation that he would be coming across a great variety of remote stars and planets, he aimed for a faraway and densely populated cluster. The heavenly lights travelled past him and seemed like the beams of a far-off ship. He reached a starless area that looked like a cleft in the Milky Way.

At the present moment, he moved across an over-populated starry galaxy. He exclaimed "on every side the sky blazed with suns, many of which appeared far brighter than Venus in the Earth's sky. I felt the exhilaration of a traveller who, after an ocean crossing, enters harbour by night and finds himself surrounded by the lights of a metropolis" (Stapledon, *Star Maker* 25). He reiterates that in this region "many close approaches must have occurred; many planetary systems must have been formed" (Stapledon, *Star Maker* 25).

He again resumes his search for young stars that are similar to the Sun's kind. He comes across a small number of young stars but none possess any planets. There are also dual and tripartite stars but their orbits are indeterminable and there are huge gaseous continents where upcoming stars are precipitating.

After a lot of examination, he discovers a system of planets. All the planets are in a molten state but bigger than the size of Jupiter. Again, he moves quickly from one star to another for aeons till he reaches a star that looks like a Sun. As he goes past the star, he sees many of them in line. The narrator perceives the system as similar to Earth.

He suddenly utters that "its atmosphere was evidently less dense than ours, for the outlines of unfamiliar continents and oceans were very plainly visible" (Stapledon, *Star Maker* 26). He names it "the Other Earth" (Stapledon, *Star Maker* 27). He visualises that there are not as many oceans as there are land areas accompanied by deserts.

As the narrator gradually dives into the tiny planet, he comes across a stretch of land that is similar to England. He refreshed his state of memory to note that the surroundings in the new planet will be unalike to the terrestrial environment. As a result, there would be a lack of sharp-minded beings. And if such types of beings sustain here then they would rather be unintelligible as "they would be huge spiders or creeping jellies" (Stapledon, *Star Maker* 27).

The narrator wheeled about randomly over the diaphanous clouds, forests, speckled grassland, prairies and desert. He chose a marine state near the temperate grasslands. When he drooped his way to the field, he was astonished by seeing the greenery of the landscape.

The vegetation resembled the one present on the planet Earth. The rotund leaves refresh the memory of the xerophytic plant but the stems cropped up bent and coarse. The vegetation had a graphic azure hue much the same as the vineyards that are embellished with copper salts. The plants had to survive the pests and insects with the chemical compound named copper sulphate.

He took off over a bright prairie dispersed with German-blue shrubbery. The sky achieved the deepness of blue. These were a small number of cirrus clouds. These clouds had a feathery texture cause of the precariousness of the airspace. This is corroborated by the idea that the narrator subsided on one summer morning. When numerous stars pierced the midnight, the landscape emanated a beauty that was supernatural and majestic.

The narrator moved swiftly without wings around the planet. He made his way through the meadows, over the expanse of broken rocks and the banks of a river. He staggered in the airspace like a drunkard. He loitered over the crops arranged in order and moved near an object which was placed alongside the tract of an arid region.

This instrument divulged itself something like a plough. It appeared to be strange but the blade made up of iron had developed rust on it. It was surprising on the part of the narrator to believe that he was multiple light-years away from England.

Exploring the region, he spotted a distinct cart path and a nasty fabric suspended from a shrub. He walked behind the shrubbery and saw cherries hanging on the trees. As he advanced in the pathway, he accidentally met an unusual being who "was not quite so like terrestrial man as he seemed at a distance; but he was a man for all that" (Stapledon, *Star Maker* 28).

The peculiar man was willowy in appearance. His legs looked like that of a bird. Over the waist, he was barely exhibiting an irregularly huge thorax with greenish bushy hair. His shoulders were quite manly but the texture of the skin was black.

The other planets seemed strange. Such as:

> ...his two very human eyes peered from under the eaves of hair. An oddly projecting, almost spout-like mouth made him look as though he were whistling. Between the eyes, and rather above them, was a pair of great equine nostrils which were constantly in motion. The bridge of the nose was represented by an elevation in the thatch, reaching from the nostrils backwards over the top of the head. (Stapledon, *Star Maker* 29)

The ears opened up into the nostrils. It is evident that evolution on the planet that seemed like Earth might have opted for a specific direction. The 'other men' as name given to the strangers, wore boots that were exceptionally small. It approximated to that of an Ostrich's or Camel's feet. There was no heel in his feet but an added stubby toe. His hands had no palms and "each was a bunch of three gristly fingers and a thumb" (Stapledon, *Star Maker* 30).

At the outset, the narrator noticed that the foreign minds of these creatures were incomprehensible. He opines that "their very sensations differed from my familiar sensations in important respects. Their thoughts and all their emotions and sentiments were strange to me" (Stapledon, *Star Maker* 30). He failed to acquire any obvious familiarity with the psyche of other men.

The relevant features of this planet must be elaborated. Most of the regions are overcrowded with cultivation and there is an advancement of Industrialisation. The mammal or quasi-mammal-like beings grazed over the grasslands. Farming of leather and food was common in the savanna regions. The quasi-mammals, although being viviparous, could not suckle. So, it is noteworthy that "the chewed cud, chemically treated in the material belly, was spat into the offspring's mouth as a jet of pre-digested fluid" (Stapledon, *Star Maker* 32).

The chief kind of locomotion on this planet is the steam train. These trains are quite large and resemble the porches of houses. These trains functioned from the railways that were present due to long-distance journeys in all the parts of deserts. As compared to the advancement in the railway system, water transport was underdeveloped. For the conveyance of mail and armour for war rockets were hired.

The metropolis was enchanting. The streets were circumscribed and overcrowded. The women looked unusual as they were "breastless and high-nostrilled like the men, were to be distinguished by their more tubular lips, whose biological function it was to project for the infant" (Stapledon, *Star Maker* 32).

During the summer, all men and women loitered on the street undressed to their waist. But they always put on their gloves. They had nostrils and a damaged mouth. This planet is known as the 'other Earth' who have the traits of Homo Sapiens but is nevertheless different from them. The mannerisms and characteristics of the other men are similar to that of the humans.

In human civilisation, there have been, "dark ages and ages of brilliance, phases of advancement and of retreat, cultures predominantly material, and others in the main intellectual, aesthetic or spiritual. There were Eastern races and Western races. There were empires, republics, dictatorships" (Stapledon, *Star Maker* 34).

There have been countless similarities and differences between the Homo Sapiens and other men. Some of them comprise: the animal nature of other men is at the lowest level similar to that of the Homo Sapiens. When required they acknowledge with annoyance and hatred. But their sensory organs are benumbed by colours. While the auditory equipment is equally responsive as that of Homo Sapiens.

The other men were able to smell and taste not only with the help of their mouths but also, they use their damp dark hands and feet. Consequently, they gained "tastes of metals and woods, of sour and sweet earths, of the many rocks, and of the innumerable shy or bold flavours of planets crushed beneath the bare running feet, made up a whole world unknown to terrestrial man" (Stapledon, *Star Maker* 34).

The sexual organs were endowed with gustatory organs. Taste has a pivotal role in imagination and ideas. Based on their olfactory and gustatory parts, they either liked or disliked a person. As "differences of race, which in our world are chiefly conceived in terms of bodily appearance, were for other men almost entirely differences of taste and smell" (Stapledon, *Star Maker* 35). Each of the races considered their taste and smell unique to others.

In all of their countries, a specific taste was regarded as an official mark of the ethnic groups. The country with which the narrator was most acquainted proclaims that a variety of salinity that was beyond the reach of man acts as their racial taste. In developed countries, newborn babies were constrained to condone the flavour of humans and eliminate perfumes and deodorants.

With the advent of industrialisation, a newly developed taste and smell had come into place. This has occurred due to the overcrowded and unhealthy atmosphere that has resulted in mutation. The principal means of manufacturing such as factories and landmines are managed for private gain. The owners obligated their workers to work till starvation. The production of goods was mostly based on maximum production rather than the realization of the essential needs of the population.

In the case of media like television and radio, 'the other men' were more advanced. The pariahs took with them a receiving instrument. As they had no tones of their own:

> ...the place of music, moreover, was taken by taste- and smell- themes, which were translated into patterns of ethereal undulation, transmitted by all the great national stations, and restored to their original form in the pocket receivers and taste-batteries of the population. These instruments afforded intricate stimuli to the taste organs and scent organs of the hand. Such was the power of this kind of entertainment that both men and women were nearly always seen with one hand in a pocket. A special wave length had been allotted to the soothing of infants. (Stapledon, *Star Maker* 39)

During the final years of the narrator on the new planet, 'Other Earth', a human could stop working and retire to his bed and utilise his remaining time to get a radio broadcast. The person's sustenance and functioning of the body were made possible by doctors of the Broadcasting company who attended to him regularly. The regular physical exercise was replaced by an electric massage.

At some time in the future, the medical practitioners would not exist. There shall be a large structure of mechanised production of food and circulation of liquid pabulum through the use of pipes pointing at the mouths of the resting beings. The medical examination shall be supplanted by a mechanical endocrine system so that their physiological growth can be maintained with the mechanised regulation of the person's blood by drawing chemicals from the drug pipes.

In the upcoming generations, infants might be born ectogenetically. The World Director of Broadcasting shall keep a record of the physical and mental details of the perfect listening breed. These infants will then be provided education by exceptional radio programmes to get them ready for a radio life in adulthood. And during the last years of life, if medical theory fails to bypass infirmity and death then the individual can assure a pain-free end with the press of a button.

The astronomers of the other Earth regard the galaxy differently than the astronomers of the Earth. The other men perceive that "the great star-system was much less flattened than we observe it to be" (Stapledon, *Star Maker* 57). They consider it a kind of bun. But the Earth's astronomical agents claim that "it is like a circular biscuit five times as wide as it is thick" (Stapledon, *Star Maker* 57).

Moreover, the other Earth's astrophysicists are convinced by the fact that the galaxy contains gaseous elements that have not been precipitated into stars. But the astrophysicists of Earth regard the galaxy as to be almost entirely stellar. After a lot of comparison, the narrator opines that "the whole cosmos of galaxies known to them differed from the whole cosmos of galaxies known to us" (Stapledon, *Star Maker* 58).

In the company of Bvaltu, while the narrator was going through the star maps designed in outlandish fashion, they saw a distorted figure of a human standing on the opposite side. She was frog-faced and had a heart similar to that of a pigeon's heart. Although this creature appeared to them a zombie she is regarded as attractive on the other Earth.

She was sharp and witty. As the extremely bright lamps of heaven dazzled them, they moved farther in the direction. They were in a bodiless condition and as a result, it didn't matter if they collided with any heavenly object. They conversed either in Bvaltu's language or the narrator's native language. They accelerated their incorporeal flight and acquired pleasure in sweeping back and forth around the starry space. They dived into a crowded cluster and glided through it similar to a car following the city lights.

The dark cloud of particles engulfed them. As they traversed the airspace, they saw a star instantly blasting into a 'nova'. They accelerated their pace and reached the confines of the galaxy. They visualised that "the hinder hemisphere of sky was now crowded with faint lights" (Stapledon, *Star Maker* 61). Ahead of them "there were a few isolated patches of scintillation, a few detached fragments of the galaxy, or planetary sub-galaxies" (Stapledon, *Star Maker* 61).

They stood astonished and motionless seeing the entire universe before them inhabiting trillions of stars and worlds. It was also startling to be aware of the fact that "each tiny fleck in the black sky was itself another such 'universe', and that millions more of them were invisible only because of their extreme remoteness" (Stapledon, *Star Maker* 61).

The narrator thought that they should return to the other Earth to gain more knowledge in the field of astronomy. But the search for the other Earth was fruitless for them as they apprehended that they were lost in the vast cosmos. The band of nebula matter sparkled from every direction but their form and shape were perplexing.

After a long expedition through the starry space, they arrived at a planet. In some planets, they resided for a few months while in others they loitered for years as per the local calendar. It was evident that the technique of incorporeal flight was futile as it provided only liberty of space. And as planets are not easy to discover the procedure of bodily flight will give rise to no results.

Rather, psychical attraction proved to be effective which implies "a telepathic projection of the mind directly into some alien world, remote perhaps in time and space, but mentally 'in tune' with the explorer's own mind at the time of the venture" (Stapledon, *Star Maker* 63).

This practice relied on the visionary reach of the mental state. As they explored the other parts of the world, it gave them a perception of the world by expanding their visionary faculty for a more distant probing into the galaxy. This type of snowball technique is of variegated importance as it increases their powers.

Although their exploration was initiated in a lonely manner, they encountered other astrophysicists on their way. As "each group gradually acquired such far-reaching imaginative power that sooner or late it was sure to make contact with others" (Stapledon, *Star Maker* 65).

The narrator suggests that there are numerous witty

worlds. Out of which, the planet Earth is considered the most intelligent. As it is populated by Homo Sapiens who think that "though perhaps he is not the sole intelligence in the cosmos, he is at least unique, and that worlds suited to intelligent life of any kind must be extremely rare" (Stapledon, *Star Maker* 69). The narrator visited other planets that were "inhabited by races almost identical with Homo Sapiens, or rather with the creature that Homo Sapiens was in the earliest phase of his existence" (Stapledon, *Star Maker* 70).

The worlds with which the narrator came in contrast were populated by races that are either biologically alike or unalike to man. In every world the "two nether limbs were used for locomotion, the two upper limbs for manipulation" (Stapledon, *Star Maker* 70). The size of these quasi-humans couldn't be measured as they either were larger than gorillas or tinier than monkeys. Some men had wings that allowed them to fly in the floating airspace. There are men who "had developed from a slug-like ancestor along a line which was not vertebrate but still less mammalian" (Stapledon, *Star Maker* 71). These men had both rigid and flexible limbs.

On another tiny earth-like planet there was a group of quasi-humans who were partially terrestrial as they had no organs. Therefore, a man "hopped on one sturdy, splay footed leg, balancing himself with a kangaroo tail. A single arm protruded from his chest, but branched into three forearms and prehensile fingers. Above his mouth was a single nostril, above that an ear, and on the top of his head a flexible three-pronged proboscis bearing three eyes" (Stapledon, *Star Maker* 71).

In these worlds, man did not resemble a centaur who were his ancestors. In the sub-human phases of evolution, the environmental pressure constricted the parallel chunk of the centaur's parts of the body. And due to this the thighs and the rear legs came closer till they were converted into a muscular and bonny pair. So, it is evident that "man and his nearer ancestors were bipeds with very large rumps", whose internal parts display the centaur ancestry. (Stapledon, *Star Maker* 71).

A further variety of quasi-humans that have a pivotal role in the historical development of the Milky Way shall be stated here. Although Man differs immensely in form invariably Man has "developed from a sort of five-pronged marine animal rather like a star-fish" (Stapledon, *Star Maker* 72). This animal would promptly train a single prong for discerning, and four other prongs for locomotion. Further, the lungs digestive and nervous systems would evolve.

The limb would later nurture a brain. The pulpy spines would lately evolve into "an erect, intelligent biped, equipped with eyes, nostrils, ears, taste organs, and sometimes organs of electric perception" (Stapledon, *Star Maker* 72). They had thick hairs on their bodies to get protection from the severe cold of the Arctic region. The faces of these creatures named as 'Human echinoderms', were different to that of humans as they possess "large single nostrils, used for breathing and smelling and also speaking, formed another circlet below the eyes" (Stapledon, *Star Maker* 72).

These worlds of Echinoderms were destroyed due to the celestial collision. A new race started to emerge that supplanted the previous species and took over their economic and political developments.

On the huge planets, a brilliant piscatory race approximates human intelligence. There were numerous submarine creatures of all sizes ranging from tiny marine fish to a large whale. The oceans were sun-soaked that furnished a massive surge for the growth of habitats. While, in the aquatic prairies, the Sun rays were diminished to darkness that enabled the sightless sea monsters to spring up.

A creature of the combination of octopus, crustacean and fish possessed human intelligence. It was arrayed with tentacles, vigilant eyes and an ingenious brain. This creature built its nest in the fissures of the coral. This creature was produced when "few of the stars had yet condensed from the 'giant' to the solar type, when very few planetary births had yet occurred, a double star and a single star in a congested cluster did actually approach one another, and spawn a planet brood" (Stapledon, *Star Maker* 91).

This resulted in the formation of a single species that seemed like a "paddle-footed crab or marine spider" through the process of a symbiotic association between two foreign entities. (Stapledon, *Star Maker* 92). It had a mental capacity similar to that of a human but with a certain kind of disposition and capability.

In due course, the two species i.e., the fish called ichthyoids and crustaceans known as arachnoids became rivals as the fish was a vegan while the crustaceans were carnivorous. Consequently, not one of them could condone the other's presence. Each tried to slaughter the other one. As "both were sufficiently human to be aware of one another as rival aristocrats in a sub-human world, but neither was human enough to realise that for each race the way of life lay in cooperation with the other" (Stapledon, *Star Maker* 92).

The ichthyoids motion at a great speed while the arachnoids are adroit to access the dry areas. With the passage of age, both species influenced each other to unite with each other. A kind of biological interlink also takes place. There is an interchange of endocrine commodities. This procedure enables the crustacean-like creature to remain entirely aquatic. As in this manner it has ceaseless linkage with the host, it can live under the water for a long period of time.

In the case of mental transformation, the arachnoids are more sociable than the ichthyoids. Till puberty, they inhabit as a single entity and after this, they seek partners from the other species. This symbiosis "consisted invariably of a male of one species and a female of the other; and the male, whichever his species, behaved with parental devotion to the young of his symbiotic partner" (Stapledon, *Star Maker* 93).

The partners of the ichthyoid category are proficient in theory, literature and religion of the submarine arena while the arachnoid category is inept in trade, plastic arts and experimentation.

In due course of their escapade, they come in contact with other worlds populated by brilliant creatures. These creatures possess an advanced persona which is a pronouncement of not one individual but a group of individuals. These creatures are a combination of intellect and body.

A huge planet nearer to the Sun or one who owns a satellite will be wiped out by oceanic tides. The surface areas will be swamped. In this type of scenario, flying is advisable. But due to lack of strength, a tiny creature can fly. A creature with a larger brain cannot be upraised.

Life is divided based on tides. As "during the nocturnal tides the bird-clouds all slept on the waves. During the day time tides they indulged in aerial sports and religious exercises. But twice a day when the land was dry, they cultivated the drenched ooze, or carried out in their cities of concrete cells at the operations of industry and culture" (Stapledon, *Star Maker* 102).

The mental faculty of these tiny avians is contingent on the electromagnetic sphere. Specifically, on radio frequency to nurture unity in the nervous system. The only animate beings in this world on account of intellect is a flock of avians. If any of the avians move apart from the group, they lose mental communication and metamorphose into split minds of low variety.

He indulges in numerous industrial operations or the process of navigation of ships on the lakes or canals of the levelled worlds. The stars are calculated and explored with the use of a spectroscope and telescope.

In this world of insectoid, "each individual swarm had its own nest, its Lilliputian city, an area of about an acre, in which the ground was honeycombed to a depth of two feet with chambers and passages" (Stapledon, *Star Maker* 106). The surrounding regions are occupied with the raising of moss-like plants used for food by the swarms.

The swarms grew in size and colonies were established based on the radio system of the preceding swarm. But there was a lack of individual minds in all the generations. While the flocks that possess individual minds were becoming extinct as it was immortal. "The units succeeded one another; the group self-persisted. Its memory reached back past countless generations of units, fading as it receded, and finally losing itself in that archaic time when the 'human' was emerging from the 'sub-human'" (Stapledon, *Star Maker* 106). As a result, the cultured swarms have hazy memories regarding their historical ages.

The organisms of higher type seem like herbs as "their skin was green, or streaked with green, and they bore here or there according to their species, great masses of foliage" (Stapledon, *Star Maker* 110). These creatures were called as Plant-animals. They are endowed with "vegetable eyes and ears, vegetable organs of taste, scent and touch" (Stapledon, *Star Maker* 110).

For locomotion, "some of them simply withdrew their primitive roots from the ground and crept hither and thither with a kind of caterpillar action" (Stapledon, *Star Maker* 110). Some creatures fly in the air by spreading their foliage. They act as predators with their "muscular boughs as strong as pythons for constriction, or talons, horns, and formidable serrated pinners" (Stapledon, *Star Maker* 111).

Due to the lack of gravitational pull and direct heat rays of the Sun, the atmospheric molecules incessantly escape into the cosmos. This in turn leads to the shortage of water and air in most of the world which affects the passage of life from the sub-human level to the human level.
In few other worlds, one can witness:

> ...a biological mechanism appeared by which the remaining atmosphere was imprisoned within a powerful electromagnetic field generated by the world's living population. In others the need for atmosphere was done away with altogether; photosynthesis and the whole metabolism of life were carried on through liquids alone. The last dwindling gases were captured in solution, stored in huge tracts of spongy growths among the crowded roots, and covered with an impervious membrane. (Stapledon, *Star Maker* 111)

Since time immemorial, interstellar and interplanetary exploration began in the galaxy. The planets were isolated from each other. The life inside the planets could only communicate telepathically. At first, they introduced the rocket flight in the vast expanse of space and were successful in colonizing the nearest planets.

Later "with the advent of interstellar travel the many distinct themes of the world biographies gradually became merged in an all-embracing drama" (Stapledon, *Star Maker* 134). Formerly, voyages between the planets were accomplished by "rocket-vessels propelled by normal fuels" (Stapledon, *Star Maker* 135). The previous endeavours were affected by the danger of the clash of meteorites.

The most structured rocket-vessel crashed at any time. The operation of unearthing the sub-atomic energy came to light. Then the ships and crew members were guarded with an extensive covering of power which rerouted or demolished the faraway meteors and extraterrestrial emissions.

The interstellar travels also were attainable after the initiation of sub-atomic energy. Numerous natural calamities took place that resulted in the disappearance of the world. The real interstellar travel at first started by distancing a planet from the orbit by a sequence of seasonable rocket inducements and then protruding it into celestial spaces at a momentum exceeding the standard stellar and planetary momentum.

The stars lie at long distances due to which the interspace between them is measured in light years. He states "Had the voyaging worlds travelled only at speeds comparable with those of the stars themselves, even the shortest of interstellar voyages would have lasted for many millions of years" (Stapledon, *Star Maker* 136).

In earlier times, the voyage from one star to another was tenuous. But later when other worlds were occupied by alien races, interstellar voyages became quite easily accessible. Huge exploration containers were built in space from unnatural matter. This was feasible by extrapolating the rocket phenomenon and with growing momentum till the momentum achieved partly the light's speed.

The space invaders had consumed half of the matter of the artificial sun. They lessened their amount of light and heat till they discovered a new system of planets. They traversed the other leftover worlds and found a hospitable location to adapt to it. They come in disagreement with the natives for depleting their planetary resources.

The natives belong to a lower rank in the category of Homo Sapiens. They arrive at disputes with the superman who possesses sub-atomic power and extreme intelligence. Telepathic communication between worlds was quite popular by then. The galaxy rose from its infancy to lead a solitary existence. With this type of communication, "the Earth is now shrinking to the dimensions of a country, so, in this critical period of the life of our galaxy, the whole galaxy was shrinking to the dimensions of a world" (Stapledon, *Star Maker* 141).

A couple of worlds of high level have witnessed the situations telepathically. They perceive the borders of the kingdom make progress near them. They had the amplitude to conquer their opponent. They planned to remodel their social strata and modernise their minds to secure military success.

On a distant island, away from the galactic empire there existed a symbiotic race consisting of Arachnoids and Ichthyoids. These creatures come under the category of ancient civilization. They have acquired human intelligence before the other men. They have also secured commendable progress in many fields. Both the race Ichthyoids and

Arachnoids maintain telepathic communication. It is clear that "their little island universe, their outlying cluster of stars, had come wholly under their control" (Stapledon, *Star Maker* 147).

This system contains numerous planetary systems. It also accommodates a world where the ancient Arachnoids paid a visit telepathically. When these worlds arrived at their dead end, where the humans inhabit, they moved towards a condition of utopia. The symbiotics tried to hide themselves from the primitives, "lest they should lose their independence of mind" (Stapledon, *Star Maker* 147).

CHAPTER VI

Conclusion

"Why does it take three Jinxians to paint a skyscraper? ... It takes one to hold the paint sprayer, and two to shake the skyscraper up and down." (Larry Niven, *Ringworld*)

The above lines are quoted from the novel *Ringworld* by Larry Niven. It presents Louis Wu who is a terrestrial being, cracking jokes with his companion, a 'Pierson's puppeteer' originating from another planet named 'Hearth'. The characteristic of a Jinxian is a type of distant life that has an association with the human world. The puppeteer possesses a dual head with three legs making his appearance horrific and alienish.

Taking this stance into account when one contemplates the philosophy of Humanism, it is revealed that it has advanced a long way starting from the period of the Renaissance to the contemporary times during which the concept of man has been deconstructed. The flaws of the basic nature of man have also been noted. The deconstruction of man has led to the genesis of a new field of study known as Critical Posthumanism.

Based on the old orders of subjectivity and power, the

nonhumans are regarded as others. They are marginalised and are subject to numerous controversies. These dualisms are shattered by the theory of Critical Posthumanism. As Stephen Herbrechter asserts, "the posthuman body makes the body omnipresent but increasingly hybridized, mediated and consumptional form, which corresponds to a fragmentation and dynamization of the body after the end of the myth of unity and identity between body and body image, or the body as a given, presupposed as either abject or sacred, untouchable physical-biological entity" (99).

Similarly, Rosi Braidotti, in her book *The Posthuman* extends her view on the nonhuman others, "these are the sexualized, racialized and naturalized others, who are reduced to less than the human status of disposable bodies. We are all humans, but some of us are just more mortal than others" (15). This belief has been made incumbent on humans by the culture. In the words of Braidotti, the purpose is to, "detox our world from false assumptions. The so-called 'others' need to be taken as powerful and alternative subject positions rather than as markers of exclusion and marginality" (19).

Here, Braidotti asserts her theory of Critical posthumanism. In this, the world makes indistinct the frontiers of other species and humans living on earth with the help of the Human Genome Project, intervention of biotechnology in plants and animals, and stem cell engineering among others. All in all, Braidotti designs what these mediated beings can perform.

In the novels of the three writers, A.E. Van Vogt, Don Delillo and Olaf Stapledon, the theory of Critical Posthumanism expands ethical concern to the beings that are dissimilar to humans and specifically to those species with whom humans' conjugate. Chapter II of the book entitled, "Relocating the Contemporary Human: A Paradigm Shift from Humanism to Critical Posthumanism" serves as a kernel. It builds the theoretical framework of Critical Posthumanism by focusing on specific aspects such as aliens, interstellar travel, body freezing, and telepathy among others. It puts forth an evaluation of Transhumanism and Humanism focusing on rationality and logic. It rejects the exceptionalism and instrumentalism of man in the natural world.

In chapter III which is titled "Enhancing the Human: Vulnerable Bodies and Posthuman Vision in A.E Van Vogt's Novels," there is an explicit muddling of bodies by dint of paranormal transmission with peculiar creatures, telepathic conversations, genetic interchange among other things. The cognizance of the fact that humans possess an animate body and therefore are unguarded for intermingling with nonhumans or machines. It meticulously presents an organised inspection of the grounded convictions in the field of life sciences where recently developed theories based on the evolution of man disseminate.

For instance, In the novel, *Slan*, Kier Gray is visualised as ruling the world in the distant future. The slans possess tendrils on their head that helps them to analyse the mind of other beings through the process of telepathy. In *The World of Null A*, Gilber Gosseyn escapes to a utopian universe in the outskirts of the solar system where galactic creatures who have supercilious state of mind reside. He is examined by a huge machine controlled by Artificial Intelligence. Later, he observes that he has additional bodies getting activated after he dies. On a similar note, Steve Hanardy, in the novel *Supermind*, reveals himself as something more than human due to his partly animalistic and partly humanistic appearance. He looks fleshy like the animals but has a rational mind. He travels to a meteorite so as to meet Professor Ungarn.

All the three novels are an endeavour to explode the sovereign rational mind of man as the core of the cosmos. The novels suggest a 'non-anthropocentric' interpretation of life in the course of which humans are symbiotically linked to several other forms of life and technologies.

Chapter IV specified as "Intertwining Human Subjectivities: Hybridising the Idea of Man in the Novels of Don Delillo," attempts a comprehensive inspection of humans as lay bare to revolutionary exchanges because of technological advancement and volatile climatic conditions. It showcases how the universe is subject to modification and how humans mobilise and personify those modifications. The brand-new automations namely, virtual reality and robotics have given way to reinventing the conception of man.

To illustrate, the novel *Zero K* concerns the illness of the wife of Ross Lockart, a billionaire. She is suffering from Multiple Sclerosis and aspires to attain immortality through the process of Cryopreservation. This procedure entails the preserving of bodies at a particular temperature so as to bring it back to a mortally fit condition. Similarly, Jack Gladney, in the novel, *White Noise* desires to rise above death. In the other novel of Don Delillo, *Point Omega*, the protagonist, Richard Elster escapes to an empty desert where he later encounters suprahuman creatures. He attempts to search for meaning in the unexplained universe. Lastly, all the three novels initiate an interdependence between humans and nonhumans based on the hope of a paradisal mixed-species community where they can inhabit peacefully.

Chapter V of the book titled, "Apocalypse of the Human: Human Mutation and the Practice of Critical

Posthumanism in the Novels of Olaf Stapledon," delineates the humans embracing the consequences of a mechanical civilisation. Humans are made to discern beyond their age-old impediments and embrace the possibilities of merging or becoming nonhuman others.

The novel, *Sirius*, presents an extraordinary sheep-dog. This Sheep-dog's brain is biologically engineered that allows him to behave like humans. The dog is also brought up with a human baby named Plaxy that nurtures the demeanour and temperament of the dog making it something more of a human. In the novel, *Odd John*, John Wainwright, a mutated person or considered as belonging to the species of Homo Superior has intellect that matches to that of a genius. He invents numerous instruments at such a minor age. The novel, *Star Maker* traverses the situation of man and his association with the extraterrestrial being. The protagonist undertakes an astral flight.

All the three novels delineate a new transformation which is not focused on a technological implementation of humans but rather more of an intensifying suspension or dissolution of distinctness. This dissolution will no longer create differences between a biological animal and the mechanical circuits in which the creature is entangled in a way blurring up the frontiers of humans and nonhumans. As Melzer reiterates, "blurring of boundaries, the growing inability to draw clear distinctions between self and other" (Melzer 73). So, this does not entirely erase the principles of liberal humanism rather proffers a readjusted or altered shape of humanity.

These relations are in the form of a rhizome which gives birth to an indivisible creature on multiple levels. Here, the human is a hybrid in many ways. The hybridity at the first level is a mixed creature viz, organic and inorganic, human and nonhuman among others. The second level of hybridity denotes the method in which the human is a mechanical being that conjures up the significance of being human. Theorists such as Callus and Herbrechter note that it may give a reaffirmation of the concept of man.

The Posthuman being is both theoretical and speculative. It showcases humans who use technology to acquire abilities. The artist Neil Harbisson gets rid of his colour blindness by installing an antenna inside his skull. This allows him "to perceive visible and invisible colours via audible vibrations in his skull including infrareds and ultraviolets as well as receive colours from space, images, videos, music or phone calls directly into his head via internet connection" (Harbisson 1).

The artist, Harbisson is officially recognised as a cyborg in the year 2004 in England. He has set up two establishments, one is the Cyborg Foundation and the other is the Transpecies Society. Both organisations were co-founded with Moon Ribas, a cyborg dancer in the years 2010 and 2017 respectively. This organisation of Cyborg Foundation proposes to nurture the rights of cyborgs. The Transpecies Society raises the voice of non-human beings and encourages the development of advanced organs and senses in the community. These beings with technological augmentation stretch the restrictions of human awareness and question their position of humans as entirely homogenous.

In the manner that cyberspace has strikingly modulated the expense of information transference, Artificial Intelligence has toned down the tariff of perception. Large firms offer experiences amplified by Artificial Intelligence. This in turn presses the business leaders to adopt technology, and gain an understanding of harnessing its possibilities for the establishment of businesses. Therefore, it is now not impossible to discern that by 2030, AI will change the course of production in the manufacturing and financial sectors.

During the Industrial Revolution, humans were displaced by allocating their hard work to machines. The machines are nowadays ready to perform cognitive exercises namely, identification of language in speech as well as writing. In the twenty-first century, AI is reinstating its position to be worthier than humans. This compels humans to allocate their intellect to automation.

Artificial Intelligence and Human Intelligence taken together possess the ability to transcend each other. While AI is quick and rational but isn't instinctual and emotional that defines the quality of humans. Present-day computers are considered as intelligent as they own the capacity to resolve based on the data they assimilate. Focusing on the philosophy of Alan Turing, Artificial Intelligence emulates how individuals perceive and make decisions. This allows AI to single out information that is relevant to the field. While performing this act, AI doesn't get mortally tired.

In the year 1997, the chess player, Garry Kasparov was defeated in a game with a supercomputer program of the IBM known as Deep Blue. It made him reconsider that the game can be accessed in a different manner, not like an isolated attempt but a shared one. Later with the unanticipated success, he decides to work together with Artificial Intelligence.

A similar kind of game of chess was organised by an online gaming site known as playchess.com in the year 2005. Many champions partnered with their supercomputers in the chess tournament by coordinating and giving proper direction to the computers.

In the present times, food is being produced in factories with the help of Artificial Intelligence. These industries are laid out all over the world and create a lot of revenue. Due to the large population and demand for food on a large scale, AI is necessary in agriculture for the examination of soil, controlling the metrics of harvest health and implementation of the irrigation process.

Recognition of images is the first step towards machine learning. This allows one to acquire physical profundity. It assists in tracing various crops by examining the substances that are used in them. Artificial Intelligence can help in saving the workforce. Farmers can devote their time to inspecting the crops in place of carrying out manual jobs.

The Chatbot, a program set to simulate the language of humans, is installed in rural areas. These programs contain Natural Language Processing to assist the farmers in understanding the regional language of a farmer while connecting them to a skilled farmer. Artificial Intelligence also promotes visual surveillance of crops for saving the crops being destroyed by weeds.

The harvest is also being analysed with the help of drones. These drones reach the corners where the bare eye cannot reach due to the thick wintery fog. The spraying of fertilizer on crops has been made easy with the use of drones somehow keeping watch on the health of the farmers. These sorts of automated procedures have changed the scene of the Agricultural sector in every aspect.

Human Intelligence in general abides by a cycle namely, perception, understanding, action and processing of information. Humans initially sense the world encompassing them and then decide what can be done by measuring all the existing alternatives. However, AI programs perform similar things by processing data in the form of algorithms.

The navigation of UAVs or automated aerial vehicles is comparatively plain sailing. The radars expand the world model based on which the UAV is working and convert it into real-time by designating which heights are devoid of any obstacles. The GPS assists the UAV to move in the safest direction and avoid any no-fly area.

Automated or driverless cars work in the amalgamation of sensors known as LIDAR or Light Detection and Ranging, radars and axonometric computer vision. These cars keep track of all the adjacent vehicles and hurdles. It also estimates the best possible intersection in traffic. While humans in the case of manual cars perform this with their cognition.

In the case of exploration of space, mission vehicles are deployed. The recent Chandrayaan-3 is quite conceivable in this case. The AI has a principal part in perfecting the algorithms and later formulating the development of the Pragyan rover, the Vikram lander and the recent Chandrayaan-3. The safe landing of Chandrayaan-3 on the Moon's Southern pole is no doubt made a success by Artificial Intelligence.

The AI has lent a helping hand to the work team of ISRO to predict the topography and recognise any possible hazards during the landing of Chandrayaan-3. The information and pictures were examined from the orbiter of Chandrayaan-2 with the help of AI to estimate the accurate landing zone. The precision landing is made possible with AI-fused altimeters, velocimeters and accelerometers among others. These devices help in estimating the conditions of the moon and adjusting with concurrent lunar vehicles.

A similar kind of innovation was launched in the

year 2016 by Elon Musk known as Neuralink. These are supple threads that can be embedded in the brain by a sewing machine that seems like a robot. This endeavour will comprehend the signals in the brain of a paralysed patient and transfer the data to a computer so that the patient can meddle with it. With the approval of the FDA, the foremost clinical trial was made on humans. The goal of Musk is to gain a symbiosis between humans and AI so that humans are not excluded in the age where AI is advancing.

The humans are to be trained so as to comprehend the systematic functioning of Artificial Intelligence so that better results can be derived from it. The amplifying and combining prospective that one visualises seems to be in sharp contradiction to the inflexible divinations of what the Artificial Intelligence has sketched out to do for the society. Alternatively, one thinks that more efficiency and automation of analytical practice is a reward. The contemporary technology comes with a havoc during the period of administration and phases of evolution. It displays its actual worth much time later.

The pre-eminence lies in the exploration of how Artificial Intelligence acts in conjugation with humans. It also focuses on how the humans anticipate and perform to consolidate new automations judiciously into the system so that the system or any firm functions effectively. Initially the combination of humans and more than human jointly act which is cited as the advent of a new kind of diverseness. The attitude of this current diversity carries with it innovations in tasks that are being performed. In bygone days, the machine is reviewed as a fellow worker in any organisation. It solves problem efficiently but is conjectured with utter negativity and lack of trust.

This assumption of machine or automation with

suspicion is now rejected. The alignment of humans with machine is the chief endeavour that has been introduced so as to attain better productivity. Artificial Intelligence scuffles to adjust with the man's foreknowledge, circumstantial wisdom and sensibleness. But it has tried to replace man in numerous fields that involves structured information. Consequently, man has to team up with machines and Artificial Intelligence so as to escalate the values of many firms. The machine can assist man by automatising the monotonous works. It can analyse information and supply essential information with regard to the complex data.

In the contemporary times, the world is cladded with a crisis that questions the value and worldview of man. There is an incessant transformation in the climatic conditions, wars, cyberattacks, pandemics and the resulting poverty situations. These conditions have put man's survival at stake. During these times, there is a constant rise in the use of AI or Artificial Intelligence and machine learning. These technologies are implemented in numerous domains such as in education and health sectors. This has in turn expanded the abilities of man and placed him in the light of new adventures.

Thus, Critical Posthumanism is not regarded as an exclusive rather a miscellaneous and wide-ranged field of study. It explores the connotations of remaining human in an arena where humans have lost their position of a dominant being. It questions the anthropocentric attitude and prepares alternate ways for comprehending the world.

It addresses the limitations of man's intelligence in comparison with Artificial Intelligence and machine learning. It also focuses on the ethical insinuations of communicating with other artificial beings. The influence of technology on man and his surrounding is also reflected in it. Man's potential after his enhancement through technology is given much insistence.

The procedures of nanotechnology and genetic engineering have changed the course of the world. Critical Posthumanism does not signify a future visioning utopia or dystopia. It is more of a critical thinking about the present and the near future. It takes under its purview not a complete rejection of man but a continuation of man assisted by enhancement and transformation. It provides scope to rethink and reconsider the idea and capability of man in a technologically-driven universe.

BIBLIOGRAPHY

Primary Sources
- Vogt, Van A.E, *Slan*. Orb Books; First Edition, 1998.
- _____ *Supermind*. Sidgwick & Jackson Ltd,1978.
- _____ *The World of Null A*. Orb Books, 2002.
- Delillo, Don. *Point Omega*. Picador, 2011.
- _____ *White Noise*. Picador, 2011.
- _____ *Zero K*. Scribner, 3 May 2016.
- Stapledon, Olaf. *Sirius*. Gateway, 2011.
- _____ *Odd John*. Albatross Publishers, 2021.
- _____ *Star Maker*. Dover Publications Inc. 2008.

Secondary Sources
- Allender, Paul. "Derrida and Humanism: some implications for post-humanist political and educational practice." *Power and Education*, Vol. 5, No. 3, 2013, pp. 11.
- Aristotle. *Nicomachean Ethics*. Penguin UK, 2004, pp. 10.
- Armesto, Felipe Fernandez. *So You Think You Are Human? A Brief History of Humankind*.
- Oxford: Oxford University Press, 2004, pp. 1.
- Arnold, Matthew. "Dover Beach and Other Poems." Dover Publications Inc, 2000, pp. 5.
- Asimov, Issac. *Pebble in the Sky*. New York: Tom Doherty Associates, 1978, pp. 34-39.
- Badmington, Neil. *Alien Chic. Posthuman and the Other Within*.

London and NewYork: Routledge, 2004, pp. 30.
- Badmington, Neil. *Theorizing Posthumanism*. Palgrave, 2000, pp. 4-27.
- Badmington, Neil. "Pod Almighty!; or, Humanism, Posthumanism, and the Strange Case of Invasion of the Body Snatchers." *Semantic Scholar, Textual Practice*, Vol. 15, no. 1, 2001, pp. 5–22.
- Baker, Herschell. *The Image of Man*. New York: Routledge, 1961, pp. 63.
- Barad, Karen. "Agential Realism: How Material-Discursive Practices Matter", *Quantum Physics and the Entanglement of Matter and Meaning*, Durham: Duke University Press, 2007, pp. 136.
- Baudrillard, Jean. *Fatal Strategies*. MIT Press; New edition. pp. 37-63. (1 April 2008)
- _____ *Simulacra and Simulation*. University of Michigan Press. pp. 1-17.
- Beechler, Michael. *Border Patrols, Aliens: The Anthropology of Science Fiction*, edited by
- George E. Slusser and Eric S. Rabkin, Southern Illinois University Press: Carbondale and Edwardsville, 1987, pp. 32.
- Behrooz, N., and P. Hossein. "The Ridiculous Sublime in Don DeLillo's White Noise and Cosmopolis." *GEMA Online Journal of Language Studies*, vol.16, No. 1, pp. 183–197.
- Best, Kenneth. "Know Thyself! The Philosophy of Self-knowledge." *UConn Today*, University of Connecticut, 2018, https://today.uconn.edu/2018/08/know-thyself-philosophy-self-knowledge.
- Boyarkina, Iren. "The destiny of life and mind in the universe in the works by Arthus Clarke and Olaf Stapledon." *Central and Eastern European Online Library*. Vol. 3 No. 49, pp. 1.
- Boxall, Peter. *The Value of the Novel*. London: Bloomsbury, 2015, pp. 253.
- Braidotti, Rosi. *The Posthuman*. Polity Press, 2013, pp. 15, 19.
- Bullock, M. "Watching Eyes, Seeing Dreams, Knowing Lives."

- edited by Nigel Rothfels, *Representing Animals*, Bloomington: Indiana University Press, 2002, pp. 98-118.
- Burrell, P.S. "Man the Measure of all things: Socrates versus Protagoras(I)". *JSTOR*, Cambridge University Press, Vol. 7, No. 26, 1932, pp. 1.
- Cazamian, Louis, and Emile Legouis. *A History of English Literature*. Macmillan Publishers, 1927, pp. 24.
- Chappell, Brian. "Death and Metafiction: On the Ingenious Architecture of Point Omega." *Orbit: Writing around Pynchon*. Vol- 4, No. 2, 2016, pp. 45.
- Crowell, Donneva. "White Noise: The Rhetorics of Media, Technology and Authority." *JSTOR*, Texas Tech University, 1991, pp. 45.
- Collini, Stefan. *What are Universities For?* London, Penguin Books, 2012, pp. 49.
- Dacey, Austin, and Lewis Vaughn. *The Case for Humanism: An Introduction*. Rowman & Littlefield Publishers, 2003, pp. 7, 12.
- Dahiya, Bhim S. *A New History of English Literature*. Delhi: Doaba Publications, 2005, pp. 29, 31.
- Davies, Tony. *Humanism*. London: Routledge, 1997, pp. 24-51.
- Delillo, Don. "In the Ruins of the Future." *The Guardian*, 2017, pp. 12.
- Derrida, Jaques, and Wills, D. "The Animal That Therefore I Am (More to Follow." *Critical Inquiry*, vol. 28, no. 2, 2002, pp. 396, DOI: https://doi.org/10.1086/449046.
- Descartes, Rene. *Discourse on the Method*. SMK Books, 2018, pp. 73.
- DoCarmo, Stephen N. "Subjects, Objects, and the Postmodern Differend in Don DeLillo's White Noise." *Lit: Literature Interpretation Theory*, vol. 11.1, 2000, pp. 1-33.
- Dunphy, John. *The Humanist. Medium*. 1983, pp. 13.
- Duvall, John. "The (Super)Marketplace of Images: Television as Unmediated Mediation in DeLillo's White Noise." *White Noise: Text and Criticism*, New York: Penguin, 1998, pp. 432-455.

- Edwords, Frederick. "What is Humanism?" *The Secular Web* 1989, Internet Infidels, 2010, http://www.infidels.org/library/modern/fred_edwords/humanism.html
- Ferenczi, S. *Introjection and Transference.* First Contributions to PsychoAnalysis. London: Karnac Books, pp. 35-109.
- Ferrando, Francesca. *Philosophical Posthumanism: Theory in the New Humanities.* Bloomsbury Academic, 2019, pp. 191, 243.
- Foster, Thomas. *The Souls of Cyberfolk: Posthumanism as Vernacular Theory,* Minneapolis, MN: University of Minnesota Press, 2005, pp. 27.
- Foucault, Michel. *The Order of Things: An Archaeology of the Human Sciences.* Translated by Tavistock, Routledge, 2002, pp. 23, 400, 422.
- Fromm, Harold. *From Obsolescence to Transcendence, The Ecocriticism Reader: landmarks in literary ecology.* edited by Cheryll Glotfelty and Harold Fromm, The University of Georgia Press, 1996, pp. 37.
- Gandhi, Leela. *Postcolonial Theory.* New Delhi: Oxford, 1998, pp. 16, 53.
- Gibson, William. *Neuromancer.* New York: Ace, 1984.
- Gloria, Steinem. *American Humanist Association.* Library of Congress, 2002, pp. 29-73.
- Graham, E. L. *Representations of the Post Human: Monsters, Aliens, and Others in Popular Culture.* Manchester: Manchester University Press, 2002, pp. 9.
- Gove, Philop Babcock. *Webster's Third New International Dictionary.* Merriam Webster, U.S., 2008, pp. 99.
- Halberstam, Judith, and Ira Livingstone, editors. "Introduction: Posthuman Bodies." *Posthuman*
- *Bodies,* Indiana University Press, 1995, pp. 8.
- Hayles, N. Katherine. *How We Became Posthuman: Virtual Bodies in Cybernetics, Literature, and Informatics.* Chicago, IL: University of Chicago Press, 1999, pp. 2-291.
- Haraway, Donna. "A Cyborg Manifesto." *Socialist Review* US, 1985, pp. 7-152.

- Haraway, Donna. *Simians, Cyborgs and Women: The Reinvention of Nature.* New: Routledge, 1991, pp. 149, 152.
- Harbisson, Neil. "Colourblindness and antenna." https://www.cyborgarts.com/neil-harbisson. *The New York Times*, 2013, pp. 1.
- Herbrechter, Stefan. *Posthumanism: A Critical Analysis.* Bloomsbury, 2013, pp. 99.
- Holland, M. k. "This Is the point." *American Book Review*, Vol. 34 No. 4, June 2013, pp. 10, 146.
- Hollinger, V. "Posthumanism and Cyborg Theory." *The Routledge Companion to Science Fiction.* Edited by M. Bould, A. Butler, A. Roberts & S. Vint, Oxford: Routledge, 2009, pp. 267-287.
- Iyengar, K.R. Srinivas. *Rabindranath Tagore: A Critical Introduction.* New Delhi: Strling, 1987, pp. 112.
- Jastrow, Robert. "Post-Human Intelligence: Natural History." vol. 86, no. 6, 1977, pp. 12-18.
- Johnson, Anthony P. *Karl Marx: Epitome. SSRN*, Nova South, 2010, pp. 348.
- Jones, Gwyneth, *North Wind.* Tor Books: 1st US Ed. Edition, 1996, pp. 275.
- Kakutani, Michiko. "Make War. Make Talk. Make It All Unreal." NY Times, 2010, https://www.nytimes.com/2010/02/02/books/02book.html.
- Kant, Immanuel. *Groundwork for the Metaphysics of Morals.* Translated by Allen W. Wood, London: Yale University Press, 2002, pp. 46.
- Keen, Sam. *Faces of the Enemy: The Psychology of Enmity.* New York: Harper & Row, 1988, pp. 16.
- Kirby, V. *Quantum Anthropologies: Life at large.* Durham: Duke University Press, 2011, pp. 233.
- Laist, Randy. *Technology and Postmodern Subjectivity in Don Delillo's Novels,* Peter Lang Inc, electronic edition, 2009, pp. 2, 180.
- Lamont, Corliss. *The Philosophy of Humanism.* New York: Routledge, 1950, pp. 21.

- Larry, Niven. *Ringworld*. Gollancz, 1970, pp.11.
- LeClair, Tom. "Closing the Loop: White Noise." *White Noise: Text and Criticism*. Edited by Mark Osteen, Penguin, 1998, pp. 387-411.
- Lifton, Robert Jay. *The Nazi Doctors: Medical Killing and the Psychology of Genocide*. New York: Basic Books, 1986, pp. 561.
- Lyotard, Jean-Francois. *The Inhuman: Reflections on Time*. Translated by Geoffrey Bennington and Rachel Bowlby, Stanford, CA: Stanford University Press, 1991, pp. 2.
- _____ *A Postmodern Fable*. University of Minnesota Press, 1999, pp. 12.
- _____ *The Postmodern Condition: A Report on Knowledge*. University of Minnesota Press, 1984, pp. 20.
- Latour, Bruno. *We Have Never Been Modern*, translated by Harvester Wheatsheaf, Harvester Wheatsheaf, 1993, pp. 50.
- Legouis, Emile, and Louis Cazamian. *A History of English Literature*. Littlehampton Book Services Ltd, 1964, pp. 212.
- LeClair, Tom. "Closing the Loop: White Noise." *White Noise: Text and Criticism*. Edited by Mark Osteen, Penguin, 1998, pp. 387-411.
- Liddle, A. *An Introduction to Modern Cosmology*. London: Wiley, 2003, pp. 20.
- Lifton, Robert Jay. *The Nazi Doctors: Medical Killing and the Psychology of Genocide*. New York: Basic Books, 1986.
- Livingstone, Rodney, and Gregor Benton, translators. *Karl Marx, Early Writings*. London: Hammondsworth, 1975, pp. 348.
- Maffey, Ross, and Yugin Teo. "Changing Channels of Technology: Disaster and Immortality in Don DeLillo's White Noise, Cosmopolis and Zero K." *C21 Literature: Journal of 21st-century Writings*, Vol. 6, Issue. 2, pp. 1–23.
- Maltby, Paul. "The Romantic Metaphysics of Don DeLillo." *White Noise: Text and Criticism*, edited by Mark Osteen, Penguin, 1998, pp. 498-516.
- Marshall, Alan. "From this point on It's all about loss:

Attachment to loss in the novels of Don Delillo, from Underworld to Falling Man." *Journal of American Studies*, Vol, 47, Issue 3, 2013, pp- 134, 621-636.
- Martins, Susana S. "White Noise and Everyday Technologies." *American Studies*, vol. 46, no. 1, 2005, pp. 87-113.
- Melzer, Patricia. *Alien Constructions. Science Fiction and Feminist Thought*. Austin: University of Texas Press, 2006, pp. 69, 73.
- Mirandola, Picco Della. *On the Dignity of Man*. Chicago, IL: University of Chicago Press, 1948, pp. 5.
- Moses, Valdez Michael. "Lust Removed from Nature." *New Essays on White Noise*, edited by Frank Lentricchia, Cambridge University Press, 1991, pp. 63, 75.
- Morton, Timothy. *The Ecological Thought*. Cambridge, Harvard University Press, 2010, pp. 22, 88.
- Morton, Timothy. "Tensions in the Mesh: Thoughts on The Ecological Thought." *Environmental Criticism for the Twenty-First Century*, Harvard University Press, 2010, pp. 163.
- Myers, F. *Human Personality and its Survival of Bodily Death*. London: Longmans, Green, 1903.
- Narwane, V.S. *Modern Indian Thought*. Bombay: Shinde, 1989, pp. 113.
- Nayar, Pramod K. *Posthumanism*. Polity Press, 2014, pp. 20-47.
- Pepperell, Robert. *The Posthuman Condition: Consciousness Beyond the Brain*. Intellect books, 2003, pp. 33.
- Pagan, Nicholas Osborne. "A.E. Van Vogt's Slan: Intimations of Superior Theory of Mind."
- *Theory of Mind and Science Fiction*, University of Malaya, 2014, pp. 45-54.
- Parvaneh, Farid. "Don Delillo's Point Omega; Ecstasy and Inertia in a Hyperreal World: A Baudrillardian Reading." *Semantic Scholar*, Department of English Language and Literature, Islamic Azad University, 2015, pp. 67, 172.
- Raizada, Harish. "Humanism in the Novels of Rabindranath

- Tagore." *Perspectives on Rabindranath Tagore*, edited by T.R. Sharma, Ghaziabad: Vimal, 1986, pp. 78.
- Rice, Philip, and Patricia Waugh. "Section One: The Subject." *Modern Literary Theory: A Reader*, 2nd ed., London: Edward Arnold, 1992, pp. 119.
- Roden, David. *Posthuman Life: Philosophy at the Edge of the Human*. Routledge: Taylor & Francis Group. pp. 18.
- Sartre, Jean Paul. *Existentialism Is a Humanism*. Yale Univ Press, 2007, pp. 2-4.
- Shelat, Jay. "Convergence: The Meeting of Technology and Art in Don Delillo's Cosmopolis and Zero K." *Scholarworks*, Georgia State University, 2017, pp. 66.
- Shewry, and Ken Hiltner, New York: Routledge, 2011, pp. 19-30.
- Shippey, Tom. "Literary Gatekeepers and the Fabril Tradition." *Hard Reading: learning from science fiction*, Liverpool University Press, 2016, pp. 42.
- Singer, Peter. *Animal Liberation: A New Ethics for Our Treatment of Animals*. New York: Random House, 1975, pp. 8.
- _____ "Animal Rights Debate between Peter Singer and Richard Posner." *UMKC School of Law*, 2001, https://famous-trials.com/animalrights/2601-animal-rights-debate-peter-singer-vs-richard-posner.
- Singh, Kunjo. *Humanism and Nationalism in Tagore's Novels*. New Delhi: Atlantic, 2002, pp. 143.
- Singh, Wazir. *Humanism of Guru Nanak: A Philosophic Enquiry*. Delhi: Ess Ess Publications, 1977, pp. 177.
- Sophocles. *Antigone*. Prestwick House Inc, 2005, pp. 11.
- Stapledon, Olaf. *Last and First Men*. London: Victor Gollancz, 1999, pp. 286-287.
- Sturm, Jules. "Weighing Posthumanism: Fatness and Contested Humanity." *Amsterdam School for Cultural Analysis*, University of Amsterdam, 2016, pp. 72.
- Tabbi, J. "Postmodern Sublime: Technology and American Writing from Mailer to Cyberpunk." Ithaca: Cornell

University Press, 1996, pp. 10.
- Varela, Francisco J. "Autonomy and Autopoiesis." University of California San Diego, 1981, pp 2, http://mechanism.ucsd.edu/teaching/w22/Phil147/Varela%20-%201981%20-%20Autonomy%20and%20Autopoiesis.pdf.
- Vermeulen, P. "Posthuman Affect." *European Journal of English Studies*, 2014, vol. 18, no. 2, pp. 124.
- Vint, Sherryl. "Animal Studies in an Era of Biopower." *Science Fiction Studies*, vol. 37, no. 3, 2010, pp. 444.
- Vint, Sheryl. *Bodies of Tomorrow: Technology, Subjectivity, Science Fiction*. Toronto: University of Toronto Press, 2007, pp. 7, 19.
- Vivekananda, Swami. *The Complete Works of Swami Vivekananda*. Vol. 1, Kolkata: Advaita Ashrama, 2001, pp. 391-392.
- Warwick, K. I, *Cyborg*. University of Illinois Press, Urbana et al, 2004.
- Wernick, Andrew. *Auguste Comte and The Religion of Humanity: The Post-theistic Program of French Social Theory*. Cambridge University Press, 2005, pp. 256.
- Wegenstein, Bernadette. *Body*. edited by W.J.T. Mitchell and Mark B.N. Hansen, *Critical Terms for Media Studies*, University of Chicago Press, pp. 19-34.
- Wolfe, Cary. *What is Posthumanism?* University of Minnesota Press, 2010, pp. 13-25.
- Wolheim, Donald A. *The Universe Makers: Science Fiction Today*. London: Victoria Gollanca Ltd, 1972, pp. 31.

Black Eagle Books

www.blackeaglebooks.org
info@blackeaglebooks.org

Black Eagle Books, an independent publisher, was founded as a nonprofit organization in April, 2019. It is our mission to connect and engage the Indian diaspora and the world at large with the best of works of world literature published on a collaborative platform, with special emphasis on foregrounding Contemporary Classics and New Writing.

www.ingramcontent.com/pod-product-compliance
Lightning Source LLC
Chambersburg PA
CBHW060550080526
44585CB00013B/514